CHRIST'S JUNGLE

CHRIST'S JUNGLE

HOMER DOWDY

VISION™
HOUSE
PUBLISHING, INC.
Gresham, Oregon

CHRIST'S JUNGLE
© 1995 by Homer Dowdy

Published by Vision House Publishing, Inc.
1217 NE Burnside, Suite 403
Gresham, Oregon 97030

Edited by Steve Halliday

Printed in the United States of America

International Standard Book Number: 1-885305-17-6

95 96 97 98 99 00 01 02 03 04 - 10 9 8 7 6 5 4 3 2 1

To Elka

Prone to sin like all of us,
he nevertheless gave himself to God,
and through him the Amazon jungle was
blessed with heaven's salvation.

Preface

I had to write this book. For years after *Christ's Witchdoctor* was published (1964), readers kept asking me, "How's Elka doing?" "Are the Wai Wai still going on for God?" They insisted on an update.

I had kept up with this Christian Indian tribe of the Amazon jungle, even visiting them briefly in 1978. But not until I seriously began to dig into the developments of thirty years after the end of the last chapter did I discover that a mere epilogue would not do. I came across more than enough in their thrilling story to fill a second book—the one on the following pages.

As in the first book, I have sought to present a people's walk from fear to faith just as they experienced it—with the uncertainties from day to day, the hopes and frustrations, the suspense that the people went through. I dared approach it this way because of the uncanny ability of the Wai Wai to relate the ins and outs of their personal and community histories. Perhaps easily explainable, they've had a written language for less than fifty years—traditionally, they've relied on oral history. In interviews with more than forty individuals (some lasting all day and well into the night), Kirifaka, Forosha, Yoshwi, Kurunaw, and many others told me the details—the sequence of details, where this one sat, what that one said—in hundreds of happenings. In a striking number of cases these accounts dovetailed one with another to flesh out a scene or to verify another's version of an incredible occurrence. A trip on the trail or through the rapids or a gathering in the umana, the village communal workhouse, came alive in their spirited re-creation of events. And in some instances, I was able to walk the same trails and shoot the same rapids and in others to sit on a tiny stool in a house and for a little while be a part of a family.

Though the Wai Wai are independent people, running their own affairs, and their church bears many marks of maturity, the missionary is important to their spiritual and intellectual growth. Irene Benson (Ayrin to the Wai Wai) has been with the tribe since 1966, serving in many roles, but always as a teacher. She helped me immeasurably through her skillful translation from Wai Wai to English, and the reverse, through her wise understanding of the Wai Wai culture and through her serving as a gracious hostess even deep in the jungle. She hiked a long jungle trail and helped navigate a hard two-day canoe trip up a Brazilian river—just so I would have a means of communication with my Wai Wai companions as we journeyed to Kurunaw's village on the Jatapuzinho River.

Bob and Florine Hawkins (Bahm and Ferochi) first settled among the Wai Wai in 1950, learning their language, their folkways, the needs of bodies, minds, and spirits. Bob completed the translation of the New Testament in 1984, and is now fine-tuning the Old, and Florine's hymns are among those sung by the Indian believers. Both were very helpful to me by sharing their memories and insights and correcting errors of fact, particularly in the use of Wai Wai words and phrases.

No one has been more loved by the people than Florence Riedle (Achi, "Big Sister") who at her retirement in 1986 completed forty-three years of service in the jungle. For days, Flo answered my questions, provided important shadings of meaning, suggested provocative areas to research on my trips to the Mapuera and Jatapuzinho Rivers.

Though they departed the Essequibo for Surinam in 1961 to evangelize the Trio Indians, Claude and Barbara Leavitt did not stop ministering to the Wai Wai. Claude had a number of teaching visits, and led a four-hundred-mile tramp through the jungle, out of which came the first Wai Wai contact with the fierce and dangerous Atrowari tribe.

Seldom recognized but essential to any missionary endeavor are the folk who work in agency administration, be it on the field or at home headquarters. John Miesel, vice-president of UFM International in Bala-Cynwyd, Pennsylvania, was most kind and generous in his aid. In Boa Vista, in the far north of Brazil, Pat and June Foster and numerous co-workers helped in many ways. Bill Lubkemann and Tim Ault of Mission Aviation Fellowship flew me over the trackless forest and with their great professionalism always found the tiny clearing in the jungle alongside the Mapuera River. Bill also pinpointed the map coordinates for every village, past and present, in the narrative.

I must recognize Dr. Henry R. Brandt, who encouraged me when I needed it and introduced me to John Van Diest, Vision House's publisher, a man with a heart for missions and an author's friend. And there is Mrs. M. A. Mijnders, a Dutch lady who for years, when awakening in the middle of the night, got out of bed and down on her knees to pray for Elka and the Wai Wai. She also has been extremely practical in her concern for the welfare of these jungle believers. Jack Gillikin rescued me several times when my word processor developed a rebellious mind of its own. My wife, Nancy, has stood by me, as always, patiently reheating lunch, assuming the role of temporary widow, and critically reading my manuscript. And not least, a couple now living in retirement in England, Claude and Barbara Wavre, may be the real inspiration behind this book. While we were neighbors in the small town of Nyon, Switzerland, during the 1980s they exhorted time after time that *Christ's Witchdoctor* had a sequel waiting to be written.

Many years ago this story might have turned out quite differently. Joe Hill, whom you'll come across in the book, told me of a missionary and a linguist who together paddled up

Brazil's Rio Negro in 1928, hoping to make contact with the Atrowari tribe, though mindful of the fact that "nobody comes out alive from Atrowari territory." They happened across a lone man, an itinerant seller of Bibles whose motor boat had stalled on the Atrowari border. Later, canoes filled with Atrowari bore down on the three, but seeing one was the colporteur, the Atrowari did them no violence. He had once befriended a sick man among the tribe and forever since they had been his friends. Perhaps a gospel work might have started then among these people, but it did not, and in the years following the Atrowari became known, for good reason, as a killer tribe. Why they were not reached with the life-changing gospel at that time is an explanation lost to us, and perhaps just as well, for now we are left to concentrate on what presently can be done to make Christ known in the Amazon forest.

Are the Wai Wai continuing in their faith? Happily, yes, though like churches in Flint and Portland and Annapolis, there are lukewarm Christians among the fervent, troubles among the triumphs, battles of the spirit against the world, the flesh, and the Devil. But, thank God, there are hopeful signs as well as disappointments. The North American church, indeed, all of the "civilized" world can learn much from the experiences of the Wai Wai—in cultural assimilation, the pull of materialism, the adoption of technology, the making of life-molding choices, the hurdles inherent in indigenous leadership, a reliance on God's Spirit.

Elka "retired," his health broken, his days often seared by intense pain; seemingly, everything was done for him that modern medicine could do. In late summer of 1994 he died. Other old leaders are still around and active—Kirifaka, Yakuta, and, in Guyana, Mawasha. But today there is a new generation of leadership—Forosha, Kurunaw, Fawtaw, and Kuhku, who were children during my first stay among the tribe in 1961. It is on these young stalwarts that the future of this Christian community rests. My hope is that after reading their story you will join in an unending prayer chain for the Wai Wai Christians deep in the Amazon's rain forest.

The People

Note on pronunciation of names:
Wai Wai is pronounced like the letter "Y," as though spelled "Y-Y." Most names are accented on the final syllable, el-KAH (Elka).

Achi — Missionary Florence Riedle dispelled sickness by prayer and a shiny thorn.

Atrowari — A wild tribe of killers caught in the sights of Wai Wai spiritual weaponry.

Ayrin — Missionary Irene Benson taught the Wai Wai to make their papers talk back to them.

Bahm — Missionary Robert Hawkins whose task was to cause God's Paper to speak Wai Wai.

Camarâo (Brigadier) — a small man who was a big help.

Charamcha — Everybody's right-hand man.

Comprido — The Long One, this much-feared chief led the Atrowari in violence.

Deaks (Henry) — Kanashen's first government officer who liked streets to be straight.

Elka — Once a witchdoctor, he became the first Wai Wai Christian and the chief for many years.

Emehta — A trained health worker who didn't mind being last.

Fanahruwi — Son of Kirifaka and a young man with many talents.

Faryayaka — Leader of the stone-age Karafou tribe.

Fawtaw — A serious Katwena youth who grew into a visionary with steady legs.

Fehya — Kirifaka's tiny wife who always accommodated one more.

Fekuku — Katwena leader who "got ears" for God; his fate became a pivot for Katwena faith.

Ferochi — Missionary Florine Hawkins aided her husband's translation and wrote hymns.

Forosha — He fought becoming chief but succeeded where his father failed.

Hill (Joe and Tamara) — Missionary couple who helped unravel the mysterious Atrowari tongue.

Jacobs — Guyanese teacher whose lessons took only too well with Wai Wai parents.

Katwena — A Brazil tribe that migrated for a new life in British Guiana.

Kirifaka — A lover of children, devoted family man and an original church elder.

Kron — Missionary Claude Leavitt often proved himself "more Wai Wai than the Wai Wai."

Kumana — An articulate spokesman for God up through his final sermon.

Kurunaw — Elka's eldest son, a leading churchman, missionary and village chief.

Kuhku — She looked like a chief's wife, which she became when Forosha was installed.

Kuruyeme — A Shedeu (or perhaps Katwena) who tried to leave his sorcery behind.

Mamichiwa — He couldn't add, but was expert on the jungle trail.

Mawasha — Tall, taciturn, utterly sincere, one of four original church elders, a Guyana chief.

Mistoken — Neill Hawkins, Bahm's brother and a pioneer among missionaries to Brazil Indians.

Prara — Shikin's brother; a rare Atrowari believer who prevailed against great odds.

Shayukuma — He put his hand to witchcraft and into an alligator's hole.

Shedeu — A crude, rude tribe transformed into jungle saints.

Sheshwa — For fear of jails, he ran in the middle of the night.

Shikin — With Prara, an Atrowari orphan; he stood up to Seetin's self-styled servant.

Shirfa — He brought stone-age people to Mapueran culture.

Tamokrana — He successfully led his family but not his fellow tribesmen.

Viana — An Atrowari chief; behind his smile were greed and cold-blooded cruelty.

Wai Wai — They traded fear for faith and scoured the jungle for other fearful tribes.

Yakuta — Elka's brother, a brave emissary to a hostile tribe, one of four original church elders.

Yarka — Known for his errant sons.

Yoshwi — Though blind in one eye, she had great insight.

1

The South American rain forest is for many a place of terror, for others an oasis in a parched world. For a comparative few it is home. On a glassy stretch of the Essequibo River, just over the mountains from numerous headwater streams of the great Amazon, villages of the Wai Wai Indians pierce here and there the tall, leafy green curtain that hedges in the forest traveler. Today's voyagers, attentive only to their eagerness, bear straight down the river toward the first of those villages, ignoring the impudent call of a crow and the chatter of monkeys in the treetops. The company fills as many canoes as can be counted on the fingers. As they push on, the thump, thump of their paddles hitting the sides of the dugouts skips through the midday stillness. Their leader has said they are nearing their destination. So they send out their signal. People bent on mischief travel the river stealthily, tie up some distance away and approach a village with noiseless steps through the jungle, arrows in their bows. More peaceful souls slap the sides of their canoes to announce their coming.

The signal was heard.
"They're here! They're here!"
A throng had just started swarming out of the palm-leaf

church at the edge of the village of Kanashen. No one needed to be told that people—a lot of people—had reached the bend in the river.

"Whoever in the world might they be?" asked one young woman warily. Despite her anxiety, she broke into a run, along with the others, from old to very young.

"It's our chief's younger brother—that's who," answered someone alongside. The dispersing congregation quickly gathered again, this time into a file of brown bodies that slithered fast like a snake past village houses, toward the port at the river.

"He said he'd come back with people," called out a man, but over the jubilant cries of anticipation he was scarcely heard.

"The Katwena. Can it be they've come to get ears?"

The Katwena had come—a restless, ruffled tribe brought from the Brazilian forest by Yakuta, the brother of Chief Elka and an elder of the Wai Wai church.

"We've come, my brother!" called Yakuta.

For some among the arrivals now busily beaching their canoes, that they had come was a daunting fact. To all but a few, the eagerness to conclude their journey had in the last stretch of river given way to uncertainty over the reception they might receive. Men yelled to dredge up courage, children cried, women sat stoically hiding their fears as best they could. Yakuta jumped from his canoe, tossing aside his paddle. He looked to the top of the steep clay bank where Elka stood, the chief a rock of serene composure amid roiling currents of excitement.

"It was God, *Nyo-Nyo,* my older brother, who brought us home."

The chief's smile and wave of his hand were lost in the confusion that engulfed the mingling of villagers and visitors. The boldest of the newcomers had stepped from their dugouts and waded ashore. Others debarked more cautiously, slowly clambering over clay pots and baskets, past hands of bananas, clusters of palm fruit and barking dogs, trying to put off the encounter as long as possible. A few toted children, a woman carefully hoisted a pet parrot on a stick and another cuddled a puppy at her breast.

"Oh, you came," said Elka to one, then another of the Katwena men as they mounted the bank to assemble in front of this Wai Wai leader about whom they had heard so much. Amiable villagers repeated the chief's greeting. One of the newcomers, showing far more confidence than the others, reached out to touch Elka's arm.

"God was good to us on the trail," he said. He felt free to speak because he had been to this village before. In fact, with three of his fellow tribesmen he had spent an entire year among the Wai Wai.

"These people are hungry," Elka said, raising his voice above the hubbub around him. Responding to his quiet signal, a few men and several women broke from the crowd and hurried back to the village.

Their friends among the Wai Wai warmly greeted the four returning men, and all noisily welcomed the entire party, half of which had now climbed to the top of the high bank. The more timid still hovered in the canoes or on the spit of sand at the river's edge. Some among these—and not only women and children—looked as though they'd prefer to hide. Two or three did attempt concealment behind clumps of small bushes. The appearance, however, of a white face among the brown—then another and yet another—at the edge of the high bank lured them out of seclusion. The more traveled among the Katwena had told tales of men and women with white skins, but only a daring few had actually beheld this wonder.

So much for the Katwena perspective. The Wai Wai wondered, what would a horde of descending Katwena be like? This question had been asked again and again among the Wai Wai. Now here in their midst were people who talked much as they themselves talked, and looked like them: Bronze flesh, long, thick inky-black hair—the men's greased and sporting downy white feathers—their faces

high-cheeked, smooth and, especially those of the men, decorated with red and black paint. They were alike, too, for the
bobs in their ear lobes and their bare, callused feet. But they
were not alike in dress.

Wai Wai men wore short pants, and this day being
Sunday, a few of the nattier ones short-sleeved shirts. Their
women wore plain skirts and blouses except for a few who
held on to the once-common bead apron. Other than the
naked toddlers, the young dressed quite like their elders. In
contrast, the Katwena men were clothed in the briefest of
red-stained loincloths and the women in diminutive aprons,
theirs made of a variety of seed stitched together.

There would scarcely have been more excitement at the
port had a big cat sprung from the forest to prey upon the
village. Wai Wai boys of all ages ran up and down the steps
cut into the clay bank, shouting at the newcomers, at their
dogs, at each other. Some emptied the canoes of their pots
and baskets and hauled up bows and arrows taller than
themselves. *Hnnnnn.* These weapons looked like Wai Wai
bows and arrows. Perhaps *their* forests were like the forests
of the Essequibo.

Wai Wai men asked Katwena men if the river had been
high or low, just where it was that a canoe had sunk, if game
had been plentiful on the path over the high mountains. Wai
Wai women reached out for Katwena babies, and though the
mothers were agreeable to giving them over, none of the
youngsters went willingly to unfamiliar arms. For the most
part, the Katwena women stood together in a frightened,
cowed huddle, content to leave intertribal dealings to their
men. From behind them, the children peeked out. As with all
children, their curiosity slowly conquered fear. They gazed
steadily at the white faces, but edged away when they saw
they were seen.

"What will they do with us?" one old Katwena asked
another apprehensively.

"Maybe they'll kill us," her neighbor replied.

"*Kofi!* How scary!"

A few of the Katwena women got up courage to feel the material of Wai Wai blouses and skirts. Whatever in the world was it like to wrap yourself in a cocoon? The men in general attached themselves to Yakuta, pushing, elbowing one another, seeming to seek protection through proximity to this one man they knew.

The chief saw it all and with a glint in his eye nodded through the crowd to his brother, as if to say, "We'll have many opportunities to exercise our patience."

Aloud, he called for order out of the commotion. Others took up the cry, and after many false starts, reasonable quiet finally replaced the racket.

"We did not expect so many of you, but we are glad you came," Elka said, beginning a welcoming speech, his voice cordial, his expression sincere, revealing him to be a man of good spirit. Some among the Wai Wai recalled that he spoke similarly when they had first arrived out of the forest in a past year. "We knew of you. We cared about you. I sent my brother to find you, and God led him to you. Now you will live with us and we will teach you about our Father in the Sky. We will tell you about Chisusu, Jesus, God's Son, and how He cared about you enough to die for your badness. First, though, my brother and his helpers and all of you Katwena are hungry. We will go eat, then we will decide where you will hang your hammocks for tonight."

The crowd moved away from the river and past the village houses to the big, round umana, the community workhouse. Mawasha, a church elder who lived in the shadow of the umana, had with the help of others assembled several piles of meat and fish, a towering stack of cassava bread and countless pots of starchy drink. There was enough for everyone, though some families who contributed to the impromptu feast would run short in the next several days as they replenished their supplies from their fields and the river and forest.

Once again at the river, Elka, assisted by Yakuta, assigned the Katwena to temporary housing.

"Where do you want to be, Little Body?" the chief asked a young man who stood protectively over his little wife and their young child.

"I want to sleep in the shadow of the one who brought us."

Others gave the same answer. Over the several weeks that Yakuta had been in their villages on the other side of the mountains and with them on the trail to this side, the Katwena had learned to trust him.

"You, we are not afraid of," one said to their friend.

"My village is farther downstream," Yakuta explained.

"Then we will go farther. We want to live near you."

"My brother's village is my village, too," said Elka. "We welcome you to it. But there are more of you than we can take care of."

The Katwena numbered more than seventy; Elka looked at his fingers and toes and shook his head. He was able only to say there were a lot, a great lot. He might have said that though slow in numbers the Wai Wai had learned things that more isolated Indians did not know—that people were divided into countries such as Brazil and the Guianas and America, that guns could kill and gasoline engines saved work, that one day the God of heaven came to earth and lived among men. But all this in due time. Now, he continued:

"For a while, some will have to sleep in the umana here. Old unused houses can be put to use again. One day, we will help you build houses like our houses and cut fields like our fields. We will do this because we are God's children."

"So that's what you are!" a Katwena man said, his head shaking in wonder at this revelation.

Elka looked every bit a chief. Not yet old, not nearly so young and gangling as when he took over old Muyuwa's duties several years before, but now mature, deliberative, cool-headed, he was known as a wise, fair and far-seeing leader. Once he had been a witchdoctor. His people sought him out to expel the fever of a child or to plead that he "go to the sky." By this esoteric flight, his spirit was enabled to search the creeks and bywaters for the best places to fish or to lure his special pets, the wild pigs of the forest, to within range of a hunter's arrow. Old Muyuwa had been a witchdoctor, too. Unlike the youthful Elka, he was not always careful that his ministrations be for people's good.

"Old Muyuwa sent his spirit into the jaguar," one man once complained. "It stole into my brother's village across the mountains and bit off the head of his little son."

"Old Muyuwa performed *farawa* against our village," another said, speaking of the avenger's ceremony. By *farawa*, the culprit who by casting a spell had caused someone to die was himself mysteriously struck down within six days. Muyuwa's accuser, as soon as he had spoken, clamped a hand over his mouth. Who could know? The tell-tale bird perhaps heard his talk, and if it did this little wren would fly straight to the vindictive old sorcerer and sing in his ear. There would then follow dreadful days and nights of waiting for Muyuwa to settle on an appropriate punishment for one who had been so foolish as to speak ill of him.

Happily, Elka had learned his sorcery from a kind old uncle who admonished him to only help his people. Elka knew the spirits to be evil; they extracted a heavy toll among the Wai Wai—loss of crops, a sinking in the rapids, sickness, death. He would work hard to appease them, to win for his people a respite now and then from their destructive ways. At one time he thought he might enjoy double powers, those of Kworokyam, the embodiment of all the spirits of the forest, and also of the God of heaven.

Some people had come one day from outside the jungle to learn the Wai Wai language and ways in order to teach the Indians about God, particularly to translate into their tongue the book God had given man about Himself. Not knowing that the young, intelligent, accommodating Elka was a witchdoctor, they selected him as the likeliest person to help them accomplish their goal. For a long time Elka continued

to go to the sky to ask the spirit of the hummingbird to possess him so he could work his supernatural powers. At the
same time, he had started to pray, to ask Chisusu, Jesus, to
work a miracle among the sick as He had done years before
in the book Elka was getting to know.

"A war went on in the pit of my stomach," Elka once said,
looking back. "I didn't know who would win out—
Kworokyam or God." He began to fail at witchcraft, and in
praying, too, and this troubled him. Eventually it became
clear. He couldn't go on serving two masters. Neither
seemed pleased to receive his divided devotion. Finally, one
day the truth of some words in God's Paper that he had
helped translate struck him between the eyes. "Greater is he
that is in you, than he that is in the world."

It was God who would possess him hereafter. He
announced to the people who recently had made him their
chief that they should no longer come to him and ask him to
go to the sky. If they wanted him to pray for them, he was
readily available to do that. Few came seeking prayer, for
Elka stood alone in his new faith. Then one day he gave
over his sorcerer's charms, and everyone was certain he
would die, as all witchdoctors who forfeited their charms
had died. But Elka lived, and gradually the light that was
within him began to dawn in the lives of those who closely
watched him.

The tali-tali locust sang twice, perhaps three times, each
time ushering in the annual dry season, and before it sang
once more nearly every Wai Wai living on the Essequibo
River had become a companion of Jesus. Even old, mean,
spiteful Muyuwa became a believer—and a changed person—before he died.

The Wai Wai had once lived in constant fear: Fear
of other people and the threat of old vendettas being rekin-
dled, yes, but fear mostly of the spirits that were pledged
to every man's harm and destruction. Now fortified by
the greatest of spirits, God's own, dwelling in the very
pits of their stomachs, they became concerned about the

people they once fought and feared.

"They live in fear like once we lived in fear," Elka said to his people in church, in the umana, and in their fields or on the river. "We must go in search of them and tell them that God is stronger than the spirits they loathe."

Mawasha had led a party to find the Mawayena, Kirifaka to teach the Trio and Tunayena, Elka himself to witness to the Waica. Some of these people, and those of other tribes, left their isolated homes in the vast rain forest and returned with the itinerant Wai Wai to live alongside their new friends and learn of God and in essence become Wai Wai.

Yakuta's contact with the Katwena was the latest missionary thrust.

For years the people at Kanashen had heard of the Katwena. A man from that tribe had come across the mountains many years before and cast his lot with those on the Essequibo. At one time several of the Wai Wai men had gone across to level a stretch of forest for an airstrip for the Brazilian government. There they were close to the Katwena, but had no chance to follow the Cafuini River to the creek up which one of several Katwena villages stood. The Katwena had heard of the Wai Wai. Other Indians had told them about the people across the mountains, that they were Indians, too, but that they made scratches on bark so thin that it was called paper and later made the paper talk back to them.

"People of the forest can do that?" The Katwena were impressed.

Their informants, Trio Indians from beyond the source of their streams, described the Wai Wai way of life. The Wai Wai cut and planted big fields, which made food plentiful; they had big knives and sharp axes by which they did their work. The Katwena shook their heads. Their own fields were small and scraggly, their houses crude, and their canoes flimsy and unreliable. Their tools were few and poorly made. To them, anything more seemed unattainable. What they had heard—could it be true? Some thought it might, so when Yakuta and his small party one day walked into their village, saying they were Wai Wai, the Katwena received them hospitably.

"I want to tell you about God," Yakuta said.

"We don't know God," came the reply.

"Today is a different day," Yakuta said. The Katwena gathered around him and his companions and, though eager to be genial hosts, were nevertheless puzzled. Hadn't the sun come up in its usual path over the trees this morning?

"Today is Sunday," Yakuta said. "It is a day that belongs to God."

"God, is that the name you give to your father?" demanded a young man. He was robust, not particularly tall, a warm, affectionate fellow, an earnest one whose eyes seemed to bore deep under any surface they lit upon. It was he who had been quick to tell the newcomers that the Katwena knew nothing about God.

Fekuku, this young prober, expanded his question:

"Does your father live in the sky?"

They went inside the main house in the village. It was dark and smoky, the door the only opening. It contained a score of hammocks made haphazardly from jungle rope, shelves of sticks around the edges that held a dozen snarling, yapping dogs, and a smoldering fire over which the carcass of an alligator roasted on a spit. On one side of the twisted trunk that supported the house's conical roof, a dozen or so men perched on tiny wooden stools or squatted on their haunches. About the same number of women sat opposite on the dirt floor, their legs stretched out in front of them; some twined thread by a dangling spindle, others picked lice from a friend's head. A few children crowded into the doorway, too frightened to come into a house with strangers, yet too curious to stay out of sight.

"Now," said one whom Yakuta had learned was the village chief, "tell us why you have come."

That day and every day for a number of weeks Yakuta spoke of the ground and who had made it, of the water in the creek, the animals in the forest, the Katwena, the Trio, and the Wai Wai.

"God made everything," he said. "God loved everything and everyone He made. Though we were bad and did not obey Him, He cared about us, cared enough to send His Son to the earth to die for us."

He would at times sit on a tiny stool and lower his head. As he talked, obviously not to them, the Katwena looked all around.

"He says God is here. He talks to him. I don't see Him. Older brother, do you see Him?"

"I think I am beginning to get ears," the young Fekuku volunteered.

Others, however, wondered if they would ever understand.

One morning Ufuru, the chief, gathered the people of The Place of the Armadillo, his village, to a close-in field. What they had heard was good, he said, but they needed to hear more, and their visitors would in a few days return home.

"The one who speaks of God has urged some of us to go with him," said Fekuku. "I for one think we should go."

"I will go and take my wife," one named Marakri volunteered.

"I don't have a wife, but I am one to be going with the Wai Wai men," offered a fellow who, according to custom, should have been married long ago but found bachelorhood more attractive. He half-hid a cryptic smile. Fekuku looked at him skeptically. "Chownyon, you rascal," were perhaps the words that sketchily formed on his lips, "you may talk about Wai Wai men, but everyone knows it's the Wai Wai women you have on your mind."

Several said they might like to travel over the mountains to Yakuta's village.

When asked about it, Yakuta said he would take only men who had wives. That left out Chownyon.

"The day we arrive I'll take one of the Wai Wai girls for

my wife," the free-lancer promised, pleased with himself for this nimble thinking.

"No," said Yakuta. "We give our young women only to those who are companions of Jesus."

Not to be thwarted, Chownyon quickly claimed a girl of his own village, and twenty-five years later they still would be married.

"Maybe we all should go," someone suggested.

"No, we will not all go—not this time," ruled Ufuru, the chief. "I myself am old and walk the trail only when I must. You younger fellows, four of you, will go with him. Stay long enough to get good ears. Then come back and tell us what you have learned. If it is worthy, we will all go. But for now, the rest of us will stay here. We have fields to tend."

Those who stayed continued to sing the songs Yakuta had taught them. They were songs that spoke of God as creator, of Jesus the good one who longed for them, of David and Paul and Peter and other men with odd-sounding names who lived long ago and were God's children even then. One Katwena man called Kamfeferu had memorized the lessons that Yakuta taught. He repeated them for his fellow villagers and took his borrowed message to other settlements of the Katwena. One day a small group of Katwena who lived far downstream dropped in at Armadillo. Learning that emissaries had been sent over the mountains to get ears about God, Fawtaw, a serious youth, was fascinated by the talk bombarding them.

"Son," Kamfeferu said for the tenth time, "someone came, an Indian, but he spoke like no Indian we'd ever heard. The Trio visit us, too, but they come only to trade for our dogs. This man told us of a whole new way of living."

"What kind of new things?" Fawtaw asked.

"Jesus lives in the sky," Kamfeferu said. "This man said Jesus once came from the sky and for a time lived on earth. He died loving us, to pay for all our badness."

The next day Fawtaw could not remember the name of the one who came from heaven to earth. It was necessary for

Kamfeferu to tell his story again.

The visiting kinsmen decided to extend their stay. Fawtaw's family said they would not leave until Fekuku returned and they heard directly from his lips what he'd learned about God.

But it was many cycles of the moon yet before the four were due back.

"Come when the year turns daylight," Chief Ufuru had instructed them, indicating they should return early in the dry season.

Fawtaw and the others finally wearied of waiting.

"The Wai Wai have deceived us," he said the day he packed an owchi, a carrying pack made of jungle leaves, preparing to go home. "They took Fekuku over the mountains only to kill him. I am leaving now."

At Kanashen, the large Wai Wai village on the Essequibo, the four Katwena families who had come to verify Yakuta's teaching lived in a single house, eight adults and five children. On Sundays and Wednesdays they accompanied the Wai Wai to their services in the church, and at other times Yakuta took them hunting, and several among the Wai Wai joined them in a variety of activities. One day while hunting with the Katwena, Yakuta said they should take time to pray.

"Yes, we should pray," Fekuku agreed.

"Do you know how to pray?"

"Yes, I know the right words." Katwena then prayed a simple prayer.

"You do know how to pray," said Yakuta.

Fekuku had begun to know Jesus. So had Marakri, probably not as much as Fekuku. Fekuku's ears were more developed. He was learning to read and write. Chownyon, the newlywed, was slower. Fotaya, the fourth man, was slower still.

Fekuku bore two burdens while at Kanashen. His wife ridiculed his embryonic faith. She became a chronic complainer. And their little son had been sickly from birth. He had difficulty breathing, and frequently Fekuku walked with him nights, hour after hour. These hardships, however, failed to deter the young Katwena in steadily journeying toward faith. As it came time for them to go back over the mountains to their own people, Fekuku was torn between his desire to stay and learn more and to return and teach his relatives what he had already absorbed.

At the year's end, the emissaries were back in Armadillo. Ufuru, the chief, seemed pleased that the four he'd sent away had done so well. Everyone was amazed that Fekuku had learned to scratch words on paper and then cause the paper to talk back to him. They examined closely the book he had brought.

"God's Paper," he called it. "It talks our language."

It was a thin volume, containing only a small sample of all that God had written to man. The white people among the Wai Wai had the complete record in their language, Fekuku said. Some day the Wai Wai would have more than this little book authored by a follower of Jesus named Mark. Yet, this one account of Jesus's time on earth was enough to teach them how to become God's children.

Fekuku and Marakri spent most of their time sharing their learning with their fellow villagers and traveling to other sites in the jungle where the Katwena lived. Word was dispatched to Fawtaw's family, "Don't leave home; Fekuku and Marakri are coming to see you."

The two went to Fawtaw's village. Hearing they had come, some from the neighboring Shedeu tribe dropped in. For generations the Katwena and Shedeu had alternately fought bloody battles and intermarried. Since the last exchange of fatal clubbings some years back, peace had prevailed, though precariously. After Fekuku and Marakri retraced their steps to Armadillo and the short rains subsided, both Katwena and Shedeu followed them to Ufuru's village.

"Why does Fekuku value that little book of his so highly?" one after another of the newcomers wanted to know.

"He says it is God's writing," came the answer from one who'd heard the explanation many times.

"It speaks of Jesus, God's Son. He came to earth once and will come again," another volunteered.

"Go with us over the mountains to the home of the Wai Wai," Fekuku urged the visitors. "A man called Bahm lives there, a man who comes from a far-off land. He can tell you how to become friends of Jesus."

Ufuru said he guessed all of Armadillo should go. There were people in this forest who threatened to kill them. Among the Wai Wai they'd enjoy safety. Besides, the teaching the four had received there held an attraction for him.

Those who lived at Armadillo made ready to go across the mountains to Kanashen. So did many of their Katwena visitors. The Shedeu thought long and heavily about what Chownyon and Marakri and Fekuku had taught them in these past days, but leaving familiar territory for unknown surroundings and people was too risky. From time to time a few slipped away down river until no Shedeu remained at Armadillo.

The Katwena knew changes would come as they left the old place for the new. The Wai Wai, they were informed, had renounced strong drink. They no longer indulged in wild spirit dancing and promiscuous revels. And there was the Katwena witchcraft to consider. The Wai Wai's Elka, who himself had been a powerful witch doctor, had abandoned Kworokyam for God, and none among the Wai Wai went to the sky any longer or cast spells. What should the Katwena do? Three of their men were sorcerers—two brothers and a cousin, Yawari, the most forceful, and his two apprentices, Kamfeferu, the one who had memorized Yakuta's lessons, and Chownyon, who married quickly in order to spend the year with the Wai Wai.

"We will leave our charms behind," the three announced after making their decision.

In his buoyant, convincing way, Fekuku had been the prime stimulator for all at Armadillo to leave for Kanashen.

Some were persuaded to go only because they feared being left behind. But for the most part, the Katwena departed their village filled with hope for a new life, though few would deny an apprehension because now, lacking the sorcerer's tools, they had no remedy should any get sick on the trail.

The plan was for their group to meet up with another contingent of Katwena at the primitive airstrip on the Cafuini. For some reason, the other group failed to show, and to everyone's surprise, Yakuta and a party of Wai Wai arrived one day from the opposite direction. For some time they waited, then decided to move on to Kanashen. They made temporary bark canoes to travel in, and started on what turned out to be a slow, exhausting journey.

An old man developed a sore on his arm. It soon made him quite ill. A canoe sank in some rapids one day—the people were not used to so big a river. Yet, there were favorable circumstances, too. On the trail over the high mountains, which took five full days to travel, they made use of "turkey-tail" structures prior travelers had crafted from poles and palm leaves as overnight shelters. At one abandoned village they found a field that still produced cassava and bananas and at the headwaters of the Essequibo the canoes were still there that Yakuta had used in paddling upstream. The trip down that river to Kanashen would be quick and easy.

Early on the day they were to arrive, they beached on a large rock to apply face paint and fresh feathers. The four families for whom this second arrival would be a sort of homecoming pressed to get on with the trip. The others were in no hurry, now that the encounter with new people was almost at hand. But depart on this last leg they did, and pushed to finish the journey. As they approached the bend just before the village, they tapped the sides of their canoes. Knowing their venture into the unknown was about to happen, the children began to cry, a few women clutched at their throats, and the men beat out their nervous staccato all the harder—and to it added high-pitched whoops and hollers.

The old man who had become ill from the sore on his arm died shortly after the Katwena settled in, some at Kanashen, some at Yaka Yaka, the village of Elka and his brother, Yakuta, just minutes downstream from Kanashen. Because the man was old and counted for little, none of his fellow Katwena paid much heed to his passing. Besides, they were preoccupied with getting on with their new lives.

The young Fawtaw, a handsome, intelligent, inquisitive youth, soon cast off his fear of the Wai Wai and gladly let the boys of the village show him around from house to house. Three brothers took him under their wing. The brothers stopped now and then and said they should pray. Once when they did, Fawtaw tapped one on the shoulder.

"Who are you talking to?" he asked.

"God is a spirit," came the explanation.

"A spirit? *Hnnnnn* . . ." Fawtaw knew about spirits. Back over the mountains he'd heard his father talk to the spirits. "So, God doesn't have a body?"

"No, but you can see His Son, Jesus," Forosha, the younger brother, said. "Come over to the church. There's a picture of Jesus there."

On the way to the church, one of the boys said to Fawtaw that if he wanted to get acquainted with God he should say, "Come live in my stomach."

That was precisely what Fekuku had told them at Armadillo after his year's stay among the Wai Wai. Over the next several days Fawtaw tested other things Fekuku and Marakri had taught them, and found their teaching matched what the Wai Wai now said. This caused the young Katwena to want Jesus to live in him.

Marakri, who had heard it all before, was getting good ears, too. But perhaps none understood about God as well as Fekuku. One day he approached the missionary the Wai Wai called Ayrin, who was Irene Benson, the most recent

American to come and live at Kanashen.

"Elder Sister, do you have Jesus in the pit of your stomach?"

"Yes, Little Brother."

"Long ago, were you put into the water?"

She knew he meant baptism, which since their arrival the Katwena had seen performed. She said yes, she'd been put into the water.

"Elder Sister, I am thinking much about Jesus. I want Him to live in the pit of my stomach, and I want to be put into the water."

Even Fekuku's wife had stopped her complaining, and if her spiritual hearing had not improved much, at least she was no longer interfering with her husband's.

Fekuku rounded up the Katwena each Sunday and Wednesday and marched all seventy-two, from oldest to babies in arms, in loincloths and bead aprons, feathers and fresh paint—*throom, throom, throom*—down to the very front rows of the church. He saw to it that every adult attended the classes Ayrin conducted to teach them how to read. Because the white women at Kanashen were the first that most of the Katwena had seen, men as well as women were at the start timid and reserved, but when Ayrin lured their voices into a mysterious box and then made it spit out their own words at them, in voices they recognized as their very own, they almost tore the box apart. Ayrin, they charged incoherently, had stolen their spirits. She worked patiently to make amends, and after a while one, then another began making their papers talk back to them.

Occasionally Fekuku expressed impatience at the rate of Katwena learning. He had confessed his badness and asked Jesus to invade his stomach and clean out all his corruption. Why shouldn't every other Katwena have done the same? But if he sometimes became angry when demanding a prompt answer, he quickly got over it, asked forgiveness, and re-established good relations all around. He made people laugh and infected them with optimism. More than a few among the Wai Wai likened him to their leader, Elka. Now that Fekuku had become a companion of Jesus, the Wai Wai chief was giving serious consideration to appointing him as one of his assistants. Elka usually provided this governing voice for every tribe that joined them.

From the day of their arrival, the Katwena were impressed by the spirit they found among the Wai Wai. They could not help but notice that the Wai Wai often had to scrimp to feed them, but did not grumble. They marveled among themselves that most of the men were kind to their wives—they often helped carry the heavy loads of firewood or cassava tubers from the field, something the usual Indian man never did for any woman. Both mothers and fathers appeared to love their children, and in the time the Katwena had been at the Essequibo they'd not seen a single newborn baby clubbed to death. The Wai Wai men did not entice the Katwena women into their hammocks, and even if a Katwena forgot and left an ax lying out in front of the house, the Wai Wai did not steal it. The Katwena were affected by the way the many families worked together—to clear a new field or to help build the new school that was arising in Kanashen. Everyone, Wai Wai and Katwena together, had cut and planted new fields for the sole benefit of the Katwena.

Perhaps most of all, they were moved by the devotion their hosts gave to God, how they held nothing back when, bowing their heads and closing their eyes, they talked to him, how God talked to them out of the thin volume scratched by Mark so many years ago.

"This is the way you are, huh?" one said to his new Wai Wai friend. "*Hnnnnn . . .*"

It was becoming easy for the Katwena to want to be what the Wai Wai were.

Then fell the blow that threatened to smash their new world.

Since the arrival of the seventy-two from over the mountains, the moon had gone through almost three full cycles. Many of the Katwena now had houses of their own, set in a small clearing a little distance from Yaka Yaka, the village of Chief Elka and Yakuta. They had also been lent some fields, two days down river, to tide them over until their own should start to produce.

It was to one of these fields that Fekuku one day led a number of his people for the purpose of treating their cassava plants against the destructive leaf-cutter ants. Their task finished, they did some hunting and fishing, then Fekuku took to his hammock early; he was sick, suffering from fever and diarrhea and a pain in his stomach, a surprising development in that he was a young, vigorous man who seemed never to be ill. The next day, Sunday, he felt fine and conducted a worship service for the little group. They stayed at the field the following day, and when Fekuku awoke Tuesday he was sick again, this time bleeding from within.

They should quickly take him to Kanashen, said Marakri. Achi was there and could stick him. Like the Wai Wai, the Katwena had come to look on Florence Riedle, the missionary nurse they called Achi, or Big Sister, as an invincible foe of all bodily ills—as long as she could stick them with the shiny thorn she called her medicine needle or could coax tiny white pebbles of bitter chalk down their throats. So it was to Achi they started; after paddling hard all day they begrudged the fall of darkness that made them once again sling their hammocks on shore.

The next day Fekuku continued to fail. He lay in the bottom of one of the canoes, his head cradled in the arms of his wife. In the middle of a rapids, while the men waded warily in the river to pull their craft past the rocks and the women remained seated and tried to control the excited children, Fekuku quietly died.

A Wai Wai field lay at the head of the rapids and it was there that the Katwena buried this one who, more than the old chief, had in recent days been their leader. They headed home with a lighter canoe but with weighted spirits, some in the sad funeral procession wondering if they'd also buried their hope for a new life. Back at their village, someone set fire to Fekuku's house. Burning a dead man's home to chase away evil spirits had long been the Katwena way. The talk among the shock-ridden people turned to their leaving the Wai Wai, to return over the high mountains to their old home, to their old ways again.

In a day or two, Fekuku's infant son, the boy who had been affectionately tended by his father through many long nights of difficult breathing, became hot and writhed from diarrhea.

"The spirit of the boy's father is standing over him," Fekuku's wife said, swaying slightly in her hammock, certain of what she saw before her. She herself was similarly ill, and Achi had been called from Kanashen to care for the child.

"Kworokyam wants to take my son."

"No!" countered Achi. "God won't let the spirits have this child."

She had been summoned in the night, and until dawn treated and walked the baby, several times getting him quiet, then handing him over to his mother. Each time the boy screamed loud enough to wake the village. Each time Achi took him back and soothed him in her arms.

"Satan is here," Achi said to no one in particular. "I can feel his presence. But God"—she cast her plea beyond the palm-leaf room—"in this tug-of-war your strength is greater."

Inside of two days the little boy pulled through, but his mother fared worse and thicker grew the oppressive spirit that seemed to envelop all in the house. A man dropped by who was convinced a curse had caused Fekuku to die.

"The Wai Wai were kind to us," he said. "They were, until they caught us off guard and then killed our leader."

He offered to perform *farawa,* the revenge rite that would

punish the person who caused Fekuku's death.

"Don't do it," Bahm, senior missionary Robert Hawkins, urged.

Though he spoke graciously and in sympathy for their troubled minds, Elka ordered, "There will be no *farawa*."

The one who volunteered was obeying his old Katwena instinct. He had discovered that Yawari, once their most effective witchdoctor, had after all carried his charms with him as he journeyed over the mountains. All that was needed was the consent of the widow to dig up one of Fekuku's bones.

His widow was, however, too sick to even hear the man's proposition. Her tragic loss and the fever had caused her to care about nothing.

In time, she, too, got well. Talk of revenge killing gradually faded, but not the sentiment for turning their backs on the God they were beginning to know. They discussed walking out on Him by striding back over the mountains and their plans for leaving were well advanced. They suddenly grew even more firm the day old Ufuru died.

The chief's was the third death among the Katwena since they arrived at the Essequibo.

"We came here as living ones," Marakri said. "Instead of living, now we are dying."

"Let us be ones who are going back to the life we know," another said, and several sucked in their breaths, giving assent.

Some set off for Achi's house to say goodbye. A few crowded into one of the Katwena houses to pack owchis for the trip. As they did, they looked through the doorway and saw Elka approaching.

2

Elka paused in the doorway. He warmly greeted those in the house, and at their invitation stepped inside. For some time he spoke with Chownyon and his new wife and the few other persons about inconsequential things. Then, as if he were making ready to leave, Elka said:

"I'll be missing you. I'll be missing you a lot."

Chownyon slinked behind his wife and hung his head. When no one else spoke, he finally said:

"We don't know why Fekuku died."

"All men must die," Elka said.

"He became a companion of Jesus."

"At some time, they, too, die."

"We were not dying ones in our village across the mountains. We were not dying ones on the trail. We came here, and now we are dying."

"God protected you until now, when you could get ears about Him. Maybe your brother had heard enough, and Jesus wanted to take him. I can't tell you why as a young man he died."

A woman grabbed a stack of cassava bread and threw it into an owchi.

"Don't be ones to leave us," Elka pleaded. "Stay here and

get more ears about God."

"*Hnnnnn . . .*" said Chownyon, and others picked up his quizzical hum.

"Don't be quick ones to go," Elka entreated. "That is all I have to say to you now."

He crossed to the door and looked out at the position of the sun. He had other Katwena households to visit before the day ebbed away.

Upstream at Kanashen, Achi checked the medicines in the box mounted on the wall of her clinic. This center for treating the cuts and burns and pains and fevers and aching teeth of the people was lodged in a closed-off section beneath her house, which stood on legs as tall as a Wai Wai man. She heard a whispered dialogue outside and stepped to the open doorway.

"You came?" she said in greeting three men, none of whom seemed eager to be the first to enter the clinic.

"I came," replied Marakri, and because neither of the others said a word, he stepped through the doorway. Since Fekuku's death, and particularly old Ufuru's, Marakri had by tacit approval filled the void in leadership among the Katwena.

"Which of you is sick?" asked the nurse. "Or do you come to take me to someone who cannot leave his hammock?"

All three shook their heads.

"We are well," Marakri said.

"God loves us even when our bodies are not well," Achi said. "Our bodies are mere houses like the ones we live in. Your house may rot and some day fall down, but you go on. The house that is your body will some day die but the real person inside will live forever."

"I know that—a little," Marakri said.

"That is why you should not move over the mountains now," Achi advised. Marakri was surprised. He had not yet said he was leaving. Could Achi have picked up on their plans?

"We came to say . . . goodbye," he stammered.

"I'll be missing you. Bahm and Ferochi will be missing you. Ayrin and Elka and Yakuta will be missing you—a lot."

"*Hnnnnn . . .*" This was all his reply.

"When you were in the jungle and no one else was concerned about you, God was. He brought you here. He wants you to stay. He wants to tell you more about Himself. Here you can receive the teaching from God's Paper. It is the one true thing in this world."

Again she said she would be missing the Katwena if they left. Marakri said they would not go today. With the coming of the dawn, would they go then? He did not know.

By now, Elka had visited all the Katwena homes, and several of the people had been to the clinic to see Achi. Others had told Ayrin and Bahm of their uncertainty about leaving. Yakuta spent many hours trying to persuade the Katwena not to turn their backs on God.

As some of them pointed out in their talk that evening (and two or three following), they generally had had enough to eat—not abundantly, but enough—before coming across the mountains. Their lives had not been easy, but except for the times when the spirits became really angry, they managed to limp from one day to the next. They asked, was there more to life than this? Death was a mystery to be feared more than life; the future something never thought of because it never came—every day was always today or yesterday. What could be more simple? It had been no great rapids to navigate to look on the God of heaven as Creator and Savior; before, they'd had no organized system of belief. They had never focused on a Supreme Being; their vision was clouded by a confusing, subjective spirit world. In order to become a companion of Jesus, they did not have to renounce a false salvation. They knew no salvation. The Katwena, like other Indians of the forest, were intimately acquainted with the spirit world. Becoming children of God meant acknowledging God's Spirit to be greater than the evil spirits, that it was powerful enough to overcome the badness of their world and give them hope.

Yes, they could return to the stream up from the Cafuini with their new and better knives and axes and, having learned techniques from the Wai Wai, could now cut and plant fields that would produce more plenteously. And when these tools wore out or were lost, they could visit the Wai Wai and replenish their stock. Some of the men now wore pants and a few of the women dresses, and those who didn't at least expressed their modesty in loincloths and aprons. They had paper on which to make their scratches, and while waiting for crops to grow could at their leisure make those scratches and then indulge in the fun of causing the paper to talk back to them.

There was hardly anything learned or acquired during their stay on the Essequibo that would be denied them there up from the Cafuini. Except the teaching. If they were to change their minds and stay with the Wai Wai, the teaching about God would be the sole reason.

Yet, if a companion of Jesus died, as Fekuku died, would it be safe for them to continue on with God?

One day during this collective dilemma, Marakri called all the Katwena to a meeting. None but a Katwena was to be there. A single question demanded decision, firm and final: Are we ones to be leaving, or ones to be staying here?

They gathered in one of the houses. There was considerable agitation until Marakri got control. He directed that they speak one at a time, but whoever in the world could stick to that?

"I am missing the strong drink we used to have on the other side of the mountains," said a man who let it be known he was in favor of leaving.

"The Wai Wai are really walking with God," another countered. "They don't bother our women, and when the call for work went out, they all cut and planted our fields."

"Achi said she would be missing us."

"She talked with me from when the sun was in the middle until it dropped behind her house. If she had said, 'Oh, you made up your minds. All right, go,' I would be one for leaving now. Instead, she said, 'Stay here and hear the rest of God's teaching. Become God's child and be put into the water. Learn the teaching until you can teach each other. Then if you want to go, go. I won't hold on to you forever.' "

"One who showed me where the tapir lives came by my house. He said God's Paper is true. 'You should become a child of God.' "

"Yakuta said if I want to see Fekuku again, I must be like our leader was and ask Jesus to live in the pit of my stomach."

"Achi showed me a picture of Jesus. She said how much He loves us. She promised to tell other people in the world of our sadness and to ask them to talk to God about us."

Everyone spoke who wanted to. By the time they did, the decision required no call of the roll. They would stay until their understanding of God's ways was more complete. Then, any who wanted to could leave.

Fawtaw, too young to speak out before his elders, was overjoyed at the outcome. With some hesitation and a little trepidation, he had asked Jesus to enter his stomach. Now there would be opportunity to find out if Jesus actually came.

Kamfeferu at one time had parroted Yakuta's teaching about God. Perhaps half of what he said he had understood—a little. Now, in his own words he was starting to talk about God and His creation and how the Katwena could become friends of God. Chownyon spoke to his wife most evenings about his growing understanding of God's Paper. Over and over he would repeat the essence of his new faith; like other Katwena women, she found it hard to comprehend any idea not clothed in physical properties, and perhaps with this she was content. Like them, she was strong of will and stout of body and was clever in making use of these endowments. Katwena women fairly dominated all but the strongest husbands. A man might depart tradition, but at the family fire, to which he resorted for daily sustenance, his woman, if she chose, could keep old embers glowing.

In another household, Yawari finally relinquished his basket of witchcraft charms.

A most unlikely newcomer to become a believer was a man with a name to match the deeds of his life. Okoye had lived among the Tunayena, the Water People. This dwindling tribe, like the Katwena, spoke a language almost identical to that of the Wai Wai. Years before some of the group had joined with the Trio, who lived off toward the sunrise, and others came to Kanashen. Okoye was one who had gone to neither place. People thought it just as well that he stay hidden in the forest. His name meant snake.

One of the Wai Wai elders, Kirifaka, perhaps the first after Elka to become a companion of Jesus, went to search for the remaining Tunayena about the time Yakuta made his first contact with the Katwena. He invited the ten persons he found to return to Kanashen with him. They begged off. Not now, they said. Maybe when the year next turned daylight. Kirifaka returned home without new people, but persistent as was his nature, he went back to the Tunayena at the start of the dry season. To his horror, he discovered that Okoye had just killed all in the village but four women. Okoye, he learned, had wanted a certain woman for his wife. The men of her family looked on him as a wanderer and so refused him. He killed them, and as Kirifaka entered the clearing, Okoye ran to the woods with his woman and her sister. Kirifaka brought their badly-shaken mother and grandmother to Kanashen.

Now Okoye himself had come, along with the two younger women. Not everyone shunned him because he was a dangerous, evil man. From various ones he heard the news about God, His standard of goodness, and Jesus as the means to be good. Okoye became a believer.

"I was a bad one," he said in front of the congregation one Sunday. "I killed many people. How many?"

He spread the fingers of one hand.

"I was one who got very angry. People were afraid of me. I talked bad. I heard about Jesus and then I didn't want my badness. Now I am God's child. Now I am a different one."

Slowly he raised fingers on his other hand.

Okoye built his house next to his mother-in-law's. In rage he had killed her husband and sons. Now they lived side by side in the harmony of God's peace.

Other Katwena, their food nearly exhausted, arrived from over the mountains, not nearly so many as in the first party, and these soon assimilated with their fellow tribesmen.

Teetee had two wives. He devoted much of his energies to pleasing them and to providing for his children. In the short time he had been married, it appeared his effort to care for the needs of his family would be overrun by the family's rate of growth. Always, one wife or the other had just given birth, or the evidence pointed to another child on the way. Teetee, however, reserved for himself one gratification. He was determined to learn to read so that one day he could make God's Paper talk back to him.

Every morning before daylight he left his house to walk to Ayrin's for a lesson.

"Why don't you wait for the dawn?" one of his wives would call after him.

"No," he would answer, turning half around and waving the primer that was his textbook. "I want to learn *now*."

He memorized the little book before he learned to read it. When he did master a page, he would go to Mawasha's house and ask him to read the page to him. Teetee listened carefully; he wanted proof that the marks on the paper really said what he had made them to say. From Mawasha's he'd cross to Kirifaka's for a second opinion. This he did with every page. By the last page, he had built up considerable confidence in his own ability.

At a baptism of new Wai Wai believers, two Katwena also were put into the water. Marakri and the youthful Fawtaw then asked to accompany Kumana, a happy, hard-working man, a man of much spiritual depth, who planned to cross over the mountains to visit the Shedeu people and seek to bring them to Kanashen.

"The Katwena and Shedeu have warred in the past," the volunteers were reminded. They didn't need anyone to point out the possible danger to themselves, but it mattered little. They had caught something of the Wai Wai passion to share Christ with those who were ignorant of Him.

From time to time, a table had been placed at the front of the church to receive the missionary offerings of the people.

"What will Kumana need for his trip to the Shedeu?" Chief Elka asked the Sunday morning after the table was once more installed. "Food to be used on the trail—cassava bread and farina. Beads and knives to give as gifts to the Shedeu. Arrows for men to hunt with. Canoe paddles to replace those lost in the rapids."

Over the next few weeks the table was covered with these and other goods. Women staggered to church under heavy loads of farina, each representing days of hot, hard work in their fields and over the roaring fires in their kitchen shelters. Both men and women stripped off colorful bead necklaces and bracelets and unwound the strings of white beads from their arms and legs, leaving them devoid of the material marks of maturity. The pile of arrows and bows and paddles expanded. It became a question of where all the items would ride when the six commissioned men left the port for upriver.

The Shedeu appeared cut from Katwena cloth. With inferior tools they scratched a meager living from paltry fields. They maintained a watchful eye and a listening ear against approach of other Indians, the only people they knew. They had heard there were people far down the river who were quite unlike themselves, who were not jungle people—"whoever might they be?"—but had no contact with them. Their minds dwelt constantly on the spirits that beset them all around. A man placed curses on those he didn't like and tried to ward off the curses sent his way. Many more newborns were killed at birth than picked off the ground and saved. Men shot arrows at the full moon and, failing to hit it, turned to the humbling of women as consolation. The strong drink to which the Shedeu were addicted often threw them, much as a wrestler throws his opponent to the ground. Drunkenness went hand-in-hand with long spirit-worship dances; these devolved into orgies which habitually ended in fights and sometimes clubbings. In fear and superstition and in a hard life all around, the Shedeu were not unlike the Katwena and the Wai Wai before they became children of God.

A generation back, the Shedeu had every bit matched their arch enemies, the Katwena, in killing—frequently by witchcraft and hardly less often by warring raids. The Shedeu lived on a creek flowing to the Trombetas River, and though this site was far from the Katwena settlements off the Cafuini, each tribe had too often traveled to the other's villages to exchange a wild swinging of cudgels. Every killing, of course, raised the expectation of reprisal, either by clubbing or a well-aimed arrow or by *farawa*.

Regardless of who had struck the last blow, seldom did a tribesman or even a young boy get a good night's sleep. In the night, dogs barked and everyone in the crowded house awoke, each man grabbing for his bow and arrows. Then for some time they would sit in their hammocks, waiting for the attackers. Often, men would leave the house for a hidden post near the path from the river, to guard against unwelcome visitors. This could happen night after night, and often did.

Women were carried away as the spoils of war. In one such Shedeu triumph, a boy was born to a ravished Katwena woman. Though his father may have been a Katwena, he was raised as a Shedeu and when grown to a young man— the smiling one, folk called him—he visited his mother's people in the village of Armadillo. While there, the four Katwena families who had been sent over the mountains to get ears about God came back to report and Kuruyeme heard them speak of a way of life that centered on love and peace. He liked what he heard, but was among those Shedeu who refused to travel across the mountains to Kanashen. With his tribesmen, he went back home, to think about, rather than to experience, the new life the Katwena were going to seek.

Even as the Katwena traveled, Kuruyeme recounted to his neighbors what he heard Fekuku and his companions teach—the story of the Creator God and His Son, how both Father and Son longed for the companionship of the people of the jungle. But his telling was incomplete. He said he needed to hear more of it himself.

The Shedeu lived in nine scattered villages, each about a day's walk apart. By this time, Kuruyeme's mother had four other sons, all grown and with families of their own. This clan dominated one village. Their chief had died, so for the time they got along without one. Kuruyeme since boyhood had worked as a witchdoctor, and with the position came authority. So it was not surprising that he persuaded his brothers to have their wives bake extra bread, then for the whole village to carry it and their few possessions on a peaceful visit to one of the last remaining Katwena villages. It lay two days away over the trail. The trip would be a diversion and they'd have their first contact with these particular Katwena in many years.

Unknown to Kuruyeme's village or to anyone outside each settlement's own little, separate group, the other eight Shedeu villages, none in contact with any other, all journeyed at the same time on their individual paths to this one Katwena village.

The residents of all nine Shedeu villages met there, all having turned their backs on their hardscrabble fields and bringing food to last many days, which they had never done for a trip of only an overnight or two. Each villager was amazed to meet those from the other villages.

Why had all nine come without plan or provocation? What strange power had propelled not two or three but nine villages to visit the same place at the same time?

They had no answers to their questions, but inside of three days Kumana and his small troop of Wai Wai missionaries, having pushed over the mountains and down the streams, arrived in this same village. Kumana's intention had been to stop here a while before proceeding to the Shedeu region.

Not one person present had seen Kumana before, but because he was of the storied Wai Wai and an obviously good person, all believed him to be one who merited not only their attention but obedience. They listened carefully as he taught them from God's Paper.

Kumana wasn't born a Wai Wai. Part of his ancestry lay in the Hishkaryena far down on the Nhamunda River, and part in a branch of the Shedeu which once inhabited the banks of the Mapuera, but which for the most part had long since moved to Kanashen and been assimilated into the Wai Wai. Kumana made no distinction among tribes or splinters of tribes. Like others among the Wai Wai, he would not rest until all the forest people had heard of Jesus.

"The teacher about God urges us to go with him over the mountains," one of the brothers said to Kuruyeme after a few days of the teaching.

"I want to go," Kuruyeme replied.

"Will you take your charms?"

"No. I have thrown them away."

"Your stones, your pets?"

"All of them."

"But, my brother, a witchdoctor without his charms—"

"I am not afraid." Kuruyeme smiled, as he usually did. Today, his cheer provided the confidence his family needed. "We are going to seek a new life. I say leave the old things behind."

The Shedeu were ready to go. They had food to carry, their knives, such as they were, their hammocks and—very important to all—their dogs. No one had to return home for anything. The few Katwena in the village started on the trek, but turned back. Still, the number of travelers was large; if none sank in the rapids, calculated young Fawtaw who with

Marakri had accompanied Kumana, there would be more
Shedeu arriving on the Essequibo than Katwena on the day
his people came.

No one drowned in the many rapids they passed through,
but their hastily built bark canoes fared poorly, some breaking up and sinking. They jammed the women and children
into Kumana's huge dugout, which he had reclaimed from
its shelter at one point along their route. Many of the men
walked much of the distance, at times on high, heavily
wooded ground, at other times through marshes where they
frequently disturbed sleeping alligators and encountered a
couple of fearsome anacondas. Like the Katwena who had
made the overland leg of the trip before them, they slept in
old turkey-trail huts on the mountain path. On the Essequibo
they loudly slapped their paddles on the canoes as they
approached the first Wai Wai village.

How would seventy Katwena react to the arrival of an
even greater number of Shedeu? Though there was intermar-
riage between the tribes, the prime link had been warfare,
and the fathers of the present-day Shedeu had struck the latest blow in this long, bloody history. Probably all of the
killers on both sides were now dead, not one having lived to
old age. How and by whom had their lives been cut short?
Who could tell what all took place in the dark spaces under
the canopy of the vast forest?

For their part, the Katwena gave no sign of repaying or
even remembering old grudges. They joined the more spiri-
tually ripe Wai Wai to teach the Shedeu the elements of
God's Paper.

"Don't be afraid," one Katwena was overheard saying to
the Shedeu who sat in the cooling shade of a big mango tree
near Achi's clinic. "We love you people now because God
has taught us how to love."

As changes had come into the lives of the Katwena, so
they now came for the Shedeu. One woman about to give
birth asked Ayrin if she might lift her baby up. She'd kind of

like to save this one. Others had been bashed to death right where the delivery had dropped them on the ground.

Another woman confessed she had killed her newborns—as many as the fingers on both hands, plus a thumb. She said she'd had enough of this practice.

On the trail over the mountains it was a mother who died and her newborn child lived—barely. Several of the Shedeu women took the baby, carried and nursed him. On arrival at Kanashen they lost interest in the boy, kept him out of sight, thinking it only a matter of time before he would die, releasing them from their burden. One day Kirifaka chanced to see him. This hollow-eyed, shriveled, bony little body, seemingly only a few wheezes from death, brought tears to Kirfaka's eyes. This innocent child must not be allowed to die.

Kirifaka, one of the original elders of the Wai Wai church, loved children intensely, possibly because he had been an orphan child. Fehya, his wife, was a tiny woman, the top of her head reaching only to the armpit of her husband. They were very much in love and had been from the time they broke the marriage mold of parental arrangement, the Wai Wai way, by eloping. Left to himself, Kirifaka never would have violated tribal custom to gain his idol. Fehya, however, acted for them both, audaciously coaxing him to an upriver village, and there in the communal house she hung her hammock beneath his, an act that sealed unspoken vows and put them beyond the power of any matchmaker.

The couple now had six children, the youngest a tiny bundle riding in the bark sling that hung from the mother's shoulder. After seeing the almost-dead Shedeu baby, Kirifaka went home and told his wife that they must take this child in.

"He's a little person," he said. "If we do not help him he will die."

"The people who have just come must know he will die," she countered.

"They know it. But they don't yet have Jesus living in them."

"What about the father?"

"He can do nothing. He doesn't have a wife."

"If the boy is sick, he will probably die. I don't want a baby to die in my arms."

She reminded her husband that their youngest still sucked at her breasts. Did he want her to put their own infant daughter aside to care for this unwanted waif?

"I will help you," Kirifaka pledged.

"Then I will take him," Fehya said. She had held out for such a promise. Her native compassion would not in the end have allowed her to refuse the Shedeu baby, but her nimble and sometimes slightly mischievous mind closed the deal, like her marriage, on terms of her own.

They took in the baby, who was almost the same age as their own infant. The two were handled like twins. She nursed one child while Kirifaka held the other, then they traded. The Shedeu baby came back from the brink of death. They named him Rasaru . . . Lazarus.

No one worked harder than Kirifaka and Fehya to help the Shedeu settle in and to teach both the Katwena and them about God. The same could be said of the other elders: Mawasha, Yakuta, Kumana, and, of course, Chief Elka. Mawasha went over the mountains to sweep the forest for any remaining Shedeu, as others had done for isolated, nomadic Katwena. Elka and Yakuta made trips to tribes in which there was a Christian witness, their aim to forge bonds of fellowship. Kirifaka assumed responsibility for the Kanashen school.

Yet, in the midst of all this endeavor, a new challenge thrust its way into the lives of the Wai Wai, a challenge so large and so fraught with danger that for some time it ruled their thoughts by day and their dreams by night and kindled their prayers with new urgency. The tribal leaders, the missionaries, everyone—excepting scarcely any among the total population—were caught up in it.

News had come of a fierce tribe some distance south over

the mountains. These were wild men, Indians who not only killed Indians, but who with their steel-tipped arrows shot any person with white skin who blundered into their homeland, dark-toned men wearing black robes and white collars, women and children at home in bordering settlements—indiscriminately and with no apparent motive.

Were they the Karafouyena, the giant People of the Bow, who, back three or four generations, were an arch-enemy of the Wai Wai? Muyuwa, the old chief and witchdoctor before Elka, had spoken of the Karafou. They had been lost to the Wai Wai. Perhaps after the last mortal blows rendered them by Muyuwa's grandfather and his tribesmen, they roamed the forest like a wounded panther. If they were the same, Elka had long made known his desire to bring them to the teaching about God. If they were another people, it made no difference. He would add them to his list to be visited and, with the help of God, to be taught.

News also had come through Bahm's brother that the government of Brazil was asking for missionaries to undertake the schooling and agricultural training of Indians in the vast Amazon forest. Presumably, this service would not guarantee freedom from danger.

Had the time arrived for the missionaries and Indian leaders to lift the vision of God's children to an even broader horizon? Might the Wai Wai be called on to minister to a tribe having little in common, perhaps even in language, with anything they had known?

To answer this summons, they surely would confront a savagely brutal clan. Whoever these people might be, their murderous rampages were not old history, not something done by their now-dead fathers and grandfathers, nor by a solitary butcher like Snake—but were deeds done yesterday by mysterious men who apparently lived for the purpose of killing again tomorrow.

3

"Go down this path and you'll find angry killers who've never caught hold of Jesus."

One of the Wai Wai brothers who had befriended Fawtaw, the teen-age Katwena, lifted his chin and pointed his lips in the direction of the fierce tribe whose reputation had saturated village talk in recent days. He and his hunting partner halted in their pursuit of monkeys and birds and anything else that chanced to move in their little square of the forest. They peered down a trail branching off from where they stood, their bows slack, their long, wood-tipped arrows cupped loosely in their hands.

"Down there?" asked Fawtaw, his eyes wide, his breathing momentarily stilled.

"Oh, a long, long way," his friend said. And to head off this inquisitive Katwena from investigating a route that might or might not end precisely at the destination attributed to it, he added, "Better to paddle upstream and then walk the trail over the mountains."

"How far is a long way?"

"How far? Bahm says you must go two hundred miles."

The terminology puzzled Fawtaw.

"How far is . . . is what you said?"

"Miles . . . well, you walk and walk and Bahm calls it a
mile. Two hundred miles you walk and walk and walk much
more. It's . . . well, it would take a full cycle of the moon,
maybe two, to go that far. If you didn't sink in the rapids on
the way."

"*Hnnnnn . . .*" said Fawtaw, exhaling slowly. He was
thinking of people who killed easily and so probably died
easily, and, unlike himself, had not gotten ears about God.
At that moment the roots of his faith dug deeper into his
soul and there came over him a consuming desire to find
these people and tell them that Jesus loved them.

For a long time the Wai Wai had heard vaguely of a tribe
called the Atrowari. Bahm's brother, Neill Hawkins, had
once asked permission of the Brazil government to set up
mission stations among the tribes north of the Amazon
River.

"Any tribe but the Atrowari," the government replied.

The Atrowari, Neill Hawkins was informed, were in open
warfare with Brazilian settlers. He began work among the
Waica, and later among several other groups, and once flew
low in a light plane over the area where the Atrowari lived.
He saw eight villages, each centered in one large, round
thatched house. From the moment he spotted them, his ever-
percolating mind plotted ways to reach them. Hearing him
talk, the Wai Wai reasoned Atrowari could simply be the
Brazilian name for the Karafou. Along with Mistoken—their
name for Mister Hawkins—they hoped one day to meet up
with the Atrowari, possibly their former foe, this time peacefully.

The government repeated its refusal.

The impasse started the Wai Wai praying for the Atrowari.
Though that was several years back and pointed prayers
later waned, the Wai Wai never completely forgot about the
Atrowari. Then recently came word that these wild men had
lashed out with new killings. Concern on the Essequibo
intensified. The fresh stimulus came through Claude Leavitt,
Kron to the Wai Wai when he worked among them before

leaving to carry the gospel to the Trio Indians in a neighboring country. By the little noisy box he called his radio, he heard a man say the Atrowari killed four officers the government had sent to win their favor. Over the years, Kron related, they had slain a hundred Brazilians. To explain that number to the Shedeu, Yakuta counted off the fingers and toes of five men.

According to reports reaching Kanashen, there remained today less than half the number of Atrowari who fifty years earlier had lived on the Alalau River. That they had been exterminated less by disease than by the white man's wanton slaughter made more plausible the contention of some that the Atrowari killed to avenge as much as out of unprovoked viciousness. Yet, how could it be explained that one day they swooped down on an unguarded outpost village and wiped it from the banks of the Rio Negro?

With decades of hostility walling the Atrowari off from the world, how could the Wai Wai expect to make a breach? On some of their trips over the divide they had tried to find this tribe, but never located even Anaua Mountain, which aerial reconnaissance said was the first essential landmark.

"It's going to be hard and take long to reach these people," one of the Wai Wai women said. Her statement was prophetic.

"How can we tell them about Jesus when they're so far away that we don't know how to get to them?" pondered Elka.

His question met response not in Kanashen but in Georgetown. Bahm, called Bob Hawkins by all but the Wai Wai, had recently moved to the coastal city to oversee three mission stations and to concentrate on translating the New Testament into Wai Wai. A knock on his door one day disturbed his concentration; it also prepared the way for evangelizing the Atrowari.

His caller introduced himself as a civil servant in the Queen's employ. Mr. Thompson would soon retire and for his many years of duty his reward of choice was authorization to walk through the jungle south to Manaus. It would be a gesture of friendship between his country and Brazil, and at the same time he might add to his cherished collection of tropical plants.

"Why are you coming to me?" asked Bob Hawkins.

"I need Indians as guides."

"And for them, you'll need an interpreter."

"Precisely. Do you know of one?"

Bob did. Claude Leavitt would be just the man. With the Wai Wai he had tramped the jungle trails, most always out-lasting them in strength and spirit. If in fun they wrestled, he generally threw them. He came close to matching their shots with the bow. None was better than he in guiding a canoe through dangerous rapids. He teased them and accepted their teasing; once he cut the hammock cords of a sleepyhead to tumble him out of bed. He understood their small talk, their jokes, their arcane idioms, their quest for light in the dark areas of tribal life. The Wai Wai found it difficult to say his name, so they called him Kron, just as Bahm was their natural pronunciation of Bob and Ayrin for Irene. Forget trying to say Florine, who was Bob's wife, and Florence, the nurse; early on they became Ferochi and Feero, though to many the nurse became simply Achi, Big Sister.

"Mr. Leavitt appears to be just the man for the task," Mr. Thompson said with appreciation. So the contact was made and arrangements completed for Kron to return temporarily to Kanashen.

"One more thing, Mr. Thompson," Bob said. "You must know that your route to Manaus will take you right through the homeland of the Atrowari, a very hostile group of Indians."

No, he wasn't aware of that fact. Although a lover of nature, he was not on familiar terms with any Indians and did not wish at this stage of life to encounter those who could threaten the tranquillity of his retirement. He diverted his planned route by some thirty miles to skirt the danger area.

Emehta couldn't say how many men would momentarily shove off from the high clay bank at Kanashen and head upstream on the first leg of the long, long trip to the storied Amazon. There were more than you totaled on your hands and feet when you counted Kron, Mr. Thompson and his cook from the city, and Yakuta, who with six chosen men would break from the party at one point and go off on their own to search out the Atrowari.

It was the likelihood of at last making contact with the Atrowari that convinced the Wai Wai to make this difficult journey. For most of the way they would have to hack through jungle. They well might run out of food or some might fall sick or an unfortunate one be bitten by a snake or be stalked by a big cat and pounced on when falling behind the group for only a moment. Yakuta and his men—who would separate when nearing Atrowari territory—faced possible death at the hands of humans. For these reasons the selection of the party had been made with prayer and the utmost deliberation of church leaders.

"Yaymochi—is he a strong one?" Elka asked the other elders. "Can he walk day after day without falling down? Is he one who won't get sad easily?"

"Aawa is not long into his armbands. Should an older one go in his place?"

"He is one who has been put into the water. He says he is ready to die."

"Emehta, yes. When men get sick, he can stick them. Achi has trained him well."

From the more than a score of men selected, Yakuta chose the few who would accompany him to the Atrowari. He was satisfied he had a good team.

On the morning set for departure, nearly the entire populations of Kanashen and Yaka Yaka and the few minor settlements converged on the river port. Canoes were packed only to be unpacked and repacked. Women pressed thin palettes of cassava bread into the already loaded arms of voyagers making their way to the river. Both men and women tore decorative beads from their arms and legs as additions to the offerings they had left on the missionary table at the front of the church. A man carrying an ax bounded down the river bank, intent on contributing it, and in so doing stumbled and came within a hair stroke of chopping off another's toe. An old man handed down a canoe paddle he just that morning had finished carving. A young woman offered several canes of sugar she had cut in a nearby field. Children jumped and shouted, having the most fun ever in their young lives. A mother bathed a child in the river, then to dry him off she and the father swung the infant by his arms between them.

Confusion ruled the waterfront; how ever in the world could anybody be certain this trip would get underway?

Kron, however, took charge. He pointed to where a two-way radio should be placed. He signaled for Mr. Thompson to take his seat in one of the canoes. Yakuta already sat in another, the calmest person at the river. Bows and arrows and a couple of shotguns were stowed, some last-minute items wedged in where it seemed there was room for nothing more. Elka stepped down to the small, sandy strip at the water's edge, prayed for the travelers, and embraced Kron. Then with a hush having overtaken the crowd on the bank and tears here and there replacing excited laughter, the crew shoved off and in a little while quietly disappeared beyond the bend.

The following day was Sunday, and in church Elka reminded the people that they, too, had a part in this first venture to the Atrowari.

"The wives and children of the men we sent will need our help," he said. "Their fields must be planted. Men must bring them meat from the forest and fish from the river. You women—when you visit with these without their husbands, don't be carrying on as sad ones."

All who remained at home should talk to their Father in the Sky every day for the absent ones and for the Atrowari.

"We will set one day apart and on that day we'll stay away from our fields and from the forest and river and will pray from daybreak until the sun reaches the middle."

And then in a practical vein he said, "Let us ask God that our men will meet up first with only one person among the Atrowari."

Indians knew that coming across just one individual initially would improve chances for a friendly—and perhaps life-saving—contact.

Life continued without letup in the Wai Wai villages. When they were not in their fields or the forest or on the river, men spent their time weaving hammocks and baskets or turning the straight, stiff cane they grew into arrows as tall as any man in the tribe. Once these tasks were done (or if they could be put off to another day), they rested in their hammocks, a father perhaps nuzzling a young child in his arms. The women incessantly worked the cassava, cutting, grating, squeezing, kneading, baking it; or if instead of the round, flat bread they made, they stood the whole morning over a hot fire, turning and stirring the meal until it toasted as loose, yellow kernels. It was women's work also to spin cotton thread and to transform tiny seeds and beads into useful or decorative items, to sweep the ground with palm fronds and keep the fires burning, tote wood from the forest and harvests from the family field—all this frequently accomplished with a suckling youngster riding high in a bark sling hung from the mother's shoulder. Children's chores emulated those of their parents, the girls' centering on care of younger siblings and the boys' on learning the skills of a woodsman.

Though with the arrival of the Katwena and the Shedeu each village had grown considerably, still a sense of community prevailed, and this carried both positive and negative qualities. Little occurred in this society that was not immediately known under every roof, and if the facts were not always clear, *ha tu*—they say—filled in the missing details. The natural neighborliness also brought mutuality. Nothing was more welcome than an *onahariheh!*—the communal meal.

Hunters from Yaka Yaka delivered a good portion of their game to Elka the chief, and those from Kanashen to Mawasha or Kirifaka, who shared leadership there. Large catches of fish were similarly distributed. These men then called for a village feast, and everyone answered the cry, "*Onahariheh!*"

Evenings were special times for families. Mother, father, all the children, and granny went always at dusk to bathe in the river. Everyone carried water back to the house for use tomorrow. Refreshed and cool, the family sat on tiny stools or on the ground before their doorways. As the sky darkened, they liked to look up and pick out the stars and constellations they knew by name—Big Star, the Legless One, Tapir's Jawbone. Often in the light of a brilliant moon they sang the hymns Ferochi had written or they just talked over the day's happenings.

If any reminder were needed that the Wai Wai village was a compact community, it came after people had taken to their hammocks. The low mumble of voices filtered through the palm slats that walled the houses, merging into a single, soft buzz. Later, tumbling loudly through the walls, piercing the soothing hum, were the hawking, spitting, and snoring from every direction, raucous sounds that could keep a less-than-heavy sleeper awake half the night. And if he became inured to human din, there was the domesticated animal utterings to contend with. Even in the blackest of night, a rooster on the far side of the village would crow. It would be answered first by a brother in mid-village. Then would come the flapping of wings on a perch just outside one's door, followed by a piercing screech from one's own bird, and by this time fifty roosters were singing in unison—or discord. From its shelf in a house anywhere in the village, a dog might bark at any hour; instant chain reaction drew empathizing barks from every house.

When he first arrived from over the mountains, a jittery Katwena or Shedeu on hearing the dogs would bolt upright and instinctively reach overhead and draw his weapons from the ceiling thatch. It was a sign of his having traded innate fear for the balm of peace when that same man, after some months in a Wai Wai village, would awaken merely to stretch from his hammock to renew his warming night fire, lay back, perhaps play a wistful melody on his bamboo flute, then placidly drop off to sleep again.

The wake-up call sounded before dawn. An old fellow who either had been appointed or volunteered—no one could remember which—carried out this unwanted chore by sauntering among the houses of Kanashen, half-muting his voice as he called, "*Rahhhheeee. Whooooahhhh.*" He made his rounds only once, but that was enough. Soon the rhythmic thump of paddles on canoe sides could be heard; a crew had assembled at the port and was heading out to cut a new field or to burn the trees where they had fallen in a previous cutting.

For those remaining in the village, the penetrating moan of a cow horn drew a number of the faithful to an early morning prayer meeting in the church. On Sundays, of course, almost everyone attended the service, and most returned for a similar gathering on Wednesday mornings. Friday mornings the women held their own meeting. The recent arrival of Bahm's newly translated John kindled new enthusiasm in the reading of God's Paper whenever they gathered. This second Gospel was added to Mark, and the people were glad to be closer to the day when they would have all of God's words in their own tongue.

The prayers were often for everyday things. One morning Elka prayed, "Father in the Sky. This is old Elka. You are good, *Ahfah*. You are the one who fed five thousand people on fish and bread. That's a lot of people, more than we've ever seen. There are only a few of us here today, but we want fish. You are the only one who can give us our food . . . "

From that service a canoe-load of men went up a nearby creek, cut a particular vine, beat it, threw the lacerated fibers into a pool of still water—and waited. Soon fish after fish surfaced, deprived of oxygen by the vine's spreading toxin.

Skilled bowmen then shot them with arrows, and others used clubs as a handier way to kill them.

The party brought home enough for an *onahariheh!* Elka's prayer had been answered, with abundance.

Once the Wai Wai, like other Indians in the great Amazon forest, had no Providence to aid them—at least, none that they were aware of. Only a spirit world that was dedicated to their misery and destruction. Appeasement was the word to live by. If only the witchdoctor could persuade the spirits to turn their backs for a little while, to give respite from recrimination, just until the day dawned or they navigated the rapids or finished walking the trail to the village!

In those bygone days they planted fields—small ones then, compared to those later on—but because they thought their efforts would scarcely avail, they did little to nurture a crop. If they lacked motivation, it was because mere subsistence required next to none. One of these days, they believed, they'd all be dead. Hadn't a related tribe, the Taruma, all died when their skins broke out with splotchy bumps and their heads got hot? To make them forget their fears and despair for a time, they drank strong drink until their glutted bellies revolted—but these revels always ended in fighting and more sickness and the return to a fright-filled existence.

Breaking into the isolated, fatalist world of the Wai Wai, Bob Hawkins and his brother Neill offered the first alternative the Wai Wai had known. The brothers were transported up the Essequibo in 1948 by Wapishana, a savanna tribe living on the edge of civilization in southern British Guiana. Immediately the pair began to learn the Wai Wai language. Accompanied by Elka, then a youth in his mid-teens, and others, Bahm went further south, over the high mountains, to contact Wai Wai and any other Indians he could find on the rivers and creeks that emptied into the Mapuera of Brazil. Many of those he met left their sagging houses and scrubby fields to move over the mountains in order to give Bahm's teaching a hearing. Eventually, Bahm settled in with his family at the high clay bank of the Essequibo, drawing a number of the Wai Wai to form the village of Kanashen. They were joined by the Claude Leavitt family—Claude quickly becoming Kron, "more Wai Wai than some of the Wai Wai"—and Florence Riedle, a nurse to the sick and a sister to everyone.

His people recognized leadership in Elka before the missionaries came. Always he had shown himself to be quick-witted, resourceful, and compassionate. As a small boy he shielded his new-born brother from the murderous arm of his step-father, an evil-tempered man who had vowed to kill this boy, as he had killed other of his children before. Until lifted from the banana-leaf pallets where they were born, Wai Wai babies could be killed with impunity. Thus Elka, only seven at the time, performed a feat as heroic as the rescue of a drowning person. Yakuta and Elka became close companions, though when the younger brother reached adolescence he freely used his handsome build and charisma to seduce women, at times seeming to be driven by a desire to defy Elka's stand for purity.

Sober, taciturn Mawasha, almost a head taller than the other men, said with his kind eyes and gentle manner what he sometimes failed to put into words. Even he had once thought of killing his first-born, a girl in place of the boy he had wanted, a boy with whom he could hunt and who when he himself fell sick would bring him meat and tend his field until he was well again. Yet, when the time came, he couldn't carry through his intent; he was beginning to make God's Paper talk back to him, and he'd learned enough of its content to know that killing his child was wrong.

Kirifaka, very much the social being, had had more opportunities than any in the tribe to become a companion of Jesus. For some time he lived with Bahm and Ferochi and when Kron came to their village he was greatly influenced by this missionary's contagious spirit. Yet it was not until Elka defied the forces of Kworokyam that these young men actually "caught hold" of Jesus.

It was one thing for their young chief to make room for the God of heaven in the pit of his stomach; it was quite another for him as their devoted witchdoctor to rout Kworokyam, the collective total of the demon spirits. That is precisely what Elka did the day he shot two wild pigs—the pigs had been his spiritual pets and therefore Elka was forbidden to kill or eat them. But Elka did both, kill and eat, and all in the village gathered around to watch him die, the victim of his own insensitivity to the spirit world that kept them all enslaved. Elka did not die, and one by one Kirifaka, Mawasha, and Yakuta let go of their fears and the practices that had kept them from believing, and became companions of Jesus.

Another soon joining the circle was the half-blind Yoshwi, who with her one good eye had carefully watched Elka for many cycles of the moon and decided that what he said was backed by what he did. Others included Kanahmachichi, a woman who when sitting on a chair in a missionary house swung her feet because they couldn't reach the floor, even though her hair reached to her waist. Then there were Fehya, the diminutive wife of Kirifaka; Ahmuri, Elka's wife; and Mawa and Tarishi, the wives of Mawasha and Yakuta.

Within three years, almost everyone professed to having received Jesus into the pit of his stomach. Thus, it appeared a Christian society was born, as much like the church in the book of Acts as an isolated region nearly cut off from the twentieth century could produce.

But like the church in Acts, the believers on the Essequibo were not content to remain fenced in their holy enclave. They circulated throughout their known world to share the knowledge that had given them faith. The response diluted their Christian company; when new people first came it appeared on some days that pagan forces might overwhelm those of God. But in large measure, faith prevailed. Kumana and Tamokrana arrived from far down on the Mapuera and soon were counted among the stalwarts of the church. The remnants of the dying Mawayena came, followed by the Chickayena and Tunayena, some from the Hishkaryena and the Trio. A number of tribal chiefs gave up their authority in order to live under Elka's leadership, and their people, including their sorcerers, quit the realm of evil spirits to live peacefully in the kingdom of God. Tribal distinctions faded, the process quickened by language compatibility, and nearly everyone sooner or later considered himself to be a Wai Wai.

With the arrival of the Katwena, followed by the Shedeu, the teaching of basics began anew. Again, there were days when the question was asked, or at least thought, "Do we as companions of Jesus have what it will take to win these people to God?"

They were beginning to gain confidence that they really did have what it takes when the greatest challenge yet was thrust upon them. Be they Karafou by another name or a distinctly different group of people, the blood-thirsty Atrowari might well put them to the test—perhaps the ultimate test.

Yakuta and the six men he led were perhaps at this very time approaching a trial such as none of the Wai Wai had as yet encountered.

4

Ahead of them on the path through the dense forest, less than thirty paces away, a man stood, his face turned away from them. He wore nothing but a scanty vine around his middle—no loincloth, no feathers in his hair, no beads around his neck or arms or legs. His sweaty, bronzed skin glistened in a small patch of sunshine. He clutched his bow and some arrows in one hand. From what they could see, he held his other hand to his mouth as he made the sound of a fashki, a rodent about the size of a house cat that Indians liked to eat.

"*Ching, ching, ching,*" the man called. He obviously was unaware that others had come upon him and at a short distance were intently watching and listening to him.

"*Ching, ching, ching,*" he called again.

In silence, Yakuta motioned for the three men with him to sit down in the path right where they were.

"We'll sit to show him we are not fighters," he whispered.

Slowly, the man turned his head forward, seeming reluctant to believe his call had gone unanswered. He started walking on the path to where the Wai Wai men sat. As he neared, they could see his face clearly and wondered that he did not see them. Except for being naked, he could have

passed for a Wai Wai. As he came almost upon them, Yakuta
stealthily motioned to the others, stood up and threw an arm
around him. Startled, the man gasped. He broke from
Yakuta's loose hold and raised his bow, but had no time to
insert an arrow before Yakuta addressed him.

"*Kiriwanhi!*" Yakuta stood back, trying hard to look
pleasant. "We are Wai Wai. Who are you?"

"*Maaraye,*" the man said rather weakly, darting his eyes
left and right to see how many surrounded him.

"Wai Wai. We are Wai Wai," said one in the circle, seeking to reinforce Yakuta's greeting.

There clearly was no understanding; his language must
not relate to the Wai Wai's. All four in their group tried
words they knew in other tongues, including one man's
smattering of Portuguese.

"*Maaraye,*" was the only answer they got.

The four turned up the palms of their hands to show they
carried no weapons. They flashed toothy smiles. From the
basket he carried, Yakuta took out three fishhooks and
placed them in the man's free hand. The others plied him
with a deer-bone comb, a beaded bracelet, and a leaf pouch
stuffed with downy white feathers.

"Wai Wai. We are Wai Wai," they repeated, pointing to
themselves and each other. They thought he then said he was
an Atrowari. By signs and inflections and means Indians use
to communicate with others Indians who speak in strange
tongues, they asked where his house stood. Could he take
them to it?

Encircled as he was and thoroughly frightened, he shook
like a person shivering from the cold. As if four strangers
were not enough, just at this time a fifth came up the path
and joined the group. He carried a shotgun. Fearing that
reinforcements had begun to arrive—whoever in the world
could say how many intruders might there be?—the
Atrowari threw down his gifts, broke through the circle and
ran in the direction from which he had come. Right behind
him ran the Wai Wai.

He looked back and saw he could not shake them. At the point where three paths met, he halted and plopped down on the ground. So did his pursuers. Again they asked him to take them to his village. Again he refused. They then asked for something to drink. In fretful gestures, he motioned for them to stay there while he went on to the house. No, they would go with him. He shook his head vigorously and several times pointed an arrow at his heart. They understood then that if he didn't go before and announce them as friendly ones, they without doubt would be targets of Atrowari arrows.

Soon after he left they heard dogs barking, this telling them that a village was not far away. They yelled to Emehta, their fifth man who had not joined in the chase, to hurry along. Emehta had been included in the missionary team because as a medical attendant he could stick any man who got sick on the trail. It was quite evident that he thought his skills called for no front-rank duty. Perhaps in this he was bolstered by his dream of a night or so earlier. In it he was shot with an arrow. Cautiously now he plodded on, finally catching up with the others.

"I'd kind of like us to pray," he said. "Who knows if this is the day we go to heaven and meet our Father there?"

Yakuta led them. He thanked God for hearing their petition of long-standing that they come across a single individual rather than a host of armed warriors in their first encounter with the Atrowari. "You brought us one man, Father—"

Before he could add an "Amen," the armed warriors swooped down on them.

"*Wliiiiiiii!*" Their cry was shrill and menacing.

The path swarmed with running, shrieking wild men. Noisily they slapped their arrows against their bows. There were a lot of men, and each man carried a lot of arrows, each one tipped with a needle-sharp barb of steel.

It was precisely this moment for which many persons had prayed fervently over a long period of time. Preparations for encountering the Atrowari had been meticulously made. Everyone knew well the dangers inherent in such a contact. For some time the Wai Wai had recounted the blood-thirstiness of the tribe to the south, and children were often sent to their hammocks at night to dream of the tales they'd heard in the family circle around the doorway.

"The Atrowari killed fifty Brazilians all at one time," a father related to his family. "Mistoken brought in the news from outside the jungle." If Mistoken said it, surely it was true. Mistoken, Bahm's brother Neill, knew people in high places; he was told things held back from ordinary folk.

"Don't stay on," Yakuta and his team were warned again and again in discussions about their coming visit to the Atrowari. Kron had said, "At first, they'll treat you as friends, but during the night they will kill you."

The talk was enough to cause a less determined group to cancel their trip. But none in Yakuta's entourage thought of quitting. All the Wai Wai shared an urgency. The Brazilian government had announced its intention to build a road from Manaus right through Atrowari country. This, the Wai Wai knew, would produce conflict between the Indians and the builders, and because the Atrowari would have the weapons of lesser effect—even steel-tipped arrows were no match for guns and bombs—more of them than of their foes would die. While the Atrowari yet lived, the Wai Wai must tell them about Jesus. Perhaps, also, they could persuade them to move to other locations within their extensive territory and avoid the conflicts that were certain to produce death among them.

In planning this trip, they'd had the help of the government of British Guiana. Because Mr. Thompson was involved, he bearing a banner of international friendship, Georgetown asked and obtained the permission of Brazil for aerial reconnaissance and food drops to be made for the travelers. This would help immensely. A Mission Aviation Fellowship plane periodically flew into Kanashen. The MAF pilot offered to fly overhead from time to time to alert the trip leaders to landmarks along the route, which none of them had yet taken. Still, it would be the woodsman's skills that would see them through, so men were chosen carefully, especially Yakuta's team—experienced trailblazers, an able younger man, two from other tribes living with the Wai Wai, and Emehta, the medical attendant.

Husbands and fathers all—should any not return, the loss would be grievously felt.

Their first challenge was to find Anaua Mountain, one of the heights the Wai Wai knew stood toward the sunset but which had never come within sight whenever they crossed over the high trail between the headwaters of the Essequibo and the rivers of Brazil. Slashing the thick underbrush with long knives and axes, the men pushed on day after day toward this interim objective, some of them having to scramble to keep to the pace which Kron set. By Kron's radio they received directions from the plane. At set times they built smoky fires to signal where food drops should be made. On the ninth day out of Kanashen, they and the pilot rendezvoused at an old but still usable airstrip at the base of Anaua Mountain. Before they left there, Kron, Mr. Thompson, and Yakuta were air-lifted for a look at several of the Atrowari villages. Yakuta took careful note of the rivers and creeks, the density of the forest and the higher points of ground that would later help him find those same villages when—unlike now, as he glided like an eagle above the trees—he slogged slowly and laboriously and undoubtedly in danger under them.

The hike thus far had been very difficult. Less rugged ground lay ahead, but so, too, did three major rivers and numerous creeks, canoes to make or trees to fell for bridging the rivers they couldn't wade, swamps to drag through, always underbrush to cut and fallen giant tree trunks to clamber over—and as they neared the half-way mark, savage men to look out for. The party pressed on and one day arrived at the Alalau River which Kron said would lead to the Atrowari. There the men carved out two canoes. After they were finished, the seven bound for the Atrowari launched the craft in the river that pointed to where the sun found its daily resting place. The shouts of goodbye were many. Above them, they heard Thompson's clipped speech:

"Go and God go with you."

For a short distance Kron accompanied them, reluctant to send them off alone to possible death. They stopped at a huge rock jutting out into the river, and Kron prayed with the men. Then he drew Yakuta aside and spoke to him confidentially.

"I'd like to go with you," he said, his hand in a tight but fraternal grip of Yakuta's shoulder. "Thompson won't let me. He's holding me to my contract to get him to Manaus."

Yakuta returned Kron's searching gaze, realizing it might be the last time they saw each other.

"These people may kill you," Kron continued. "If they do, I want to die with you. I told Thompson that from here to Manaus anybody can find their way. Still, he said no. 'If they killed you, I'd be responsible,' he said."

"No," said Yakuta quietly. "Your place is to go on with him. If the Atrowari kill us, we'll see one another some day in heaven."

For three days the seven paddled downstream. They came across a small port where languidly bobbed a single canoe. Real people are near, they said, using their term for Indians. From his aerial survey, Yakuta remembered well this spot. They would have to walk a path to reach the village—the Atrowari located their houses a good way from the rivers, a measure known to give better control over access to a settlement. Of the one big main house here, Yakuta recalled seeing cassava bread spread to dry on the lower reaches of the roof.

"Maybe they'll give us food," he said. Since trouble could occur, two men would remain in camp across from the port and be prepared to escape hurriedly if they had to, carrying any bad news back to Kanashen.

The Trio with them had hurt his foot, so he and the youngest Wai Wai were assigned to stay behind. Bows and arrows were left with them; Emehta carried the only gun. The five crossed to the other side and began walking a wide path that appeared to be a well-traveled route. People had been on this trail quite recently; it was littered with scraps of food which forest creatures had not yet devoured. Proceeding with fearful caution, they were alert to every scratching sound, every snap of a twig. Raised on stories of the treachery of wild people, they knew that from behind any bush or tree arrows could fly, arrows that could instantly kill them. They forded creeks in which they saw fish traps quite like the ones they used at home. Late in the afternoon they happened onto a cultivated field. The house, they reasoned, must be close. Should they shoot off the gun to announce their coming? They decided against it and went on.

They found the house. Nothing around it stirred. Warily they approached it, entered it. Where had everybody gone? They searched all around the clearing. Darkness had fallen, so they retraced their steps to the Alalau, sparingly using the flashlight one of them carried.

The same five returned to the house early the next morning. Still no Atrowari. It was the day for contact by the MAF pilot. Implementing the communications plan, they spread a large white cloth on the open ground, the signal that the Wai Wai were there. Then they unfolded a yellow one, indicating they had seen the house but no people. The red cloth in their possession, which denoted they had met the Atrowari, they kept folded and out of sight. At the agreed-on time, the pilot appeared overhead. From the plane he threw down packets containing scissors, fishhooks, and knives. There was also a note saying he'd be back in eight days.

The men returned to their camp on the river and spent much of the morning looking for another likely inroad to the Atrowari. They discovered one, and as before, set up camp across the river from it. The Trio still complained of his foot, so once more he and the young Wai Wai stayed behind to guard their possessions. Yakuta led the four beside a smaller stream until at a branch they came on a landing where, by the evidence again of food scraps, a large number of people had not long ago gathered. Here when the sun rode the middle of the sky they followed the path as it turned inland. The sun had lowered somewhat when they saw the lone hunter in the path ahead and heard him trying to coax the fashki to within range of his arrow. As first he ran and they ran after him and then as he went off to inform his people that strangers lingered in the trail, they now were about to enter into the real purpose of their trip.

The time had come. The pack of fanatical Atrowari thundered at breakneck speed toward them.

The wild ones instantly enveloped the Wai Wai. How many of them? Yakuta glanced about, thought maybe twenty, probably more. A good many had inserted arrows and drew their bows. Just one man releasing his finger could turn loose a torrent that would cease only when the last Wai Wai was dead. Several of the Atrowari danced around like hyperactive children, poking and pulling at the outsiders, as if trying to discover what they were made of. They all screeched like parrots or belched the grunts of the wild pig. One grabbed at the beads Yakuta wore on his arm. Quickly Yakuta unwound the string and offered it to the man. That pleased him. He handed one of his arrows to Yakuta.

That was it! Trade might satisfy these brigands. Out of Wai Wai baskets came knives and scissors, fishhooks, combs, and beads. Turmoil still reigned, but arrows no longer threatened. Arrows had become trading stock. The Wai Wai collected more than their arms could hold. That was fine with them. Each arrow in their own hands was one less to be shot into their bellies.

While the trading continued, an old man, naked like the rest, walked toward them with some degree of dignity. He was a tall one with the legs of a crane. The Wai Wai reckoned this was the chief and the three men following him were his assistants. Fortunately, a few items remained in their baskets, and these they distributed among the leaders. The old chief sent a couple of the younger men back up the path and after some time they returned with bread and starch drink. Where, Yakuta wondered, were the women and children? He wanted to see the Atrowari house. Tentatively, he started up the path to where the village obviously was. The chief screamed at him. With eyes blazing and fists clenched, he without question was threatening Yakuta. Another step . . .

They finished eating. The Atrowari, talking loudly once more, their faces now hardened with a maniacal look, snatched at the beads and ear bobs remaining to the Wai Wai and shoved their hands into pockets to see if there were still things not yet surrendered. The Wai Wai gave up their last treasures, then made signs they would leave. That seemed to be all right. But they would not go alone. Every man present fell in with them, intending to walk them back to the river and their camp.

At one point along the path, Emehta blasted his gun at a spider monkey, his favorite food. He missed, but stirred the Atrowari to a near riot. They thought he had signaled for cohorts concealed in the jungle to attack. Calmness eventually was restored and the rest of the trek went without incident. Seeing the camp was across the river, the Atrowari insisted on crossing to it. They pantomimed that they would sleep with the Wai Wai that night.

Not so for the Wai Wai. They had vowed not to spend the night within range of the Atrowari. Bahm had warned them against it. Kron had said unless their encounter was completely friendly not to chance it. Their experiences of the day hardly qualified as friendship, and certainly not completely. But they were not to depart so easily.

Once again the Atrowari raged. They grabbed beads from the two who'd stayed in camp, the only ones still possessing them, tore shirts from several bodies, ripped off pants, emptied the Wai Wai canoes of hammocks and the owchies holding food. Was there doubt the Atrowari had accompanied the Wai Wai to the river to kill them? Death might come by arrows or a rock picked up from the river bank or, with the Wai Wai far outnumbered, by their being dragged into the water and drowned. Inwardly, the Wai Wai prayed. Outwardly, they smiled and said the friendly "*Kiriwanhi*" and one ventured what he thought was the Atrowari equivalent, "*Maaraye*."

Beads! Knives! Long knives! While guarding their captives, the Atrowari raked through every possession of the Wai Wai not once but several times, seeking the items they craved. Finally satisfied there was no more plunder to be found, they allowed the Wai Wai to pick up their hammocks and food and what remained of their clothing.

"We leave now," Yakuta said, fronting a confidence he scarcely felt. Using hands and a jerk of his head, hoping they'd understand, he added, "When the year turns light again, we will return."

The seven Wai Wai got into their two canoes and started to push off into the river. Several hands reached out to stop them. Others handled bows and arrows, and these again targeted the would-be travelers.

"Sleep here with us tonight," one of the Atrowari said in basic Portuguese, and this the Hishkaryena translated into Wai Wai.

"No," replied Yakuta. "We came as friends. We traded with you. What do you really want? We will bring it next time."

A tug of war followed, the Wai Wai trying to push into deeper water, the Atrowari holding them back. Yakuta now had the gun at his feet. He had placed a shell in the chamber. But should he shoot? Bahm had said if they got into a tight spot they should shoot the gun in the air. He might have to do that, though gun shots were not unfamiliar to the Atrowari. They knew the power of the guns of the Brazilians, and they had heard Emehta's blast today. What fear could a shot in the air hold for them?

Yakuta did not have to endure his dilemma for long. The Atrowari let them go. The seven paddled with all their might against the current. Their ordeal at last had ended. Or had it?

Emehta looked over his shoulder. Keeping pace behind them were the Atrowari canoes. In each of them stood men with arched bows. The needle-sharp tips of their arrows glinted in the setting sun.

Eight days later Eldon Larson, the MAF pilot, made several futile runs over the Atrowari villages. He saw no squares of cloth, neither white, nor yellow, nor red. But he did see that the house by which he had dropped the trade goods the week before was now burned to the ground. In his message radioed to Kanashen he did not have to spell out what this particular arson usually meant. Indians governed by fearsome spirits burned a dwelling in which someone had died. Did they burn this one clear to the ground because in it seven men had died?

Several days after that flight he flew low over the primitive airstrip below Anaua Mountain. There near the end of the runway where weeks before they had left it was a stack of food. It was intended as provisions for the latter half of Yakuta's return from the Alalau. By now, if all had gone well, the seven Wai Wai men would have reached the airstrip and taken the food and been on their way over the high mountains. The stack was untouched.

Larson felt a heaviness in his heart as he radioed his question to Kanashen:

"Where's Yakuta? Where is Yakuta?"

5

British Guiana became the independent nation of Guyana in 1966. During the land's colonial years it mattered little to the Wai Wai who claimed to govern them; Georgetown seldom punched through the formidable green curtain that shut off the upper Essequibo River from the largely black and East Indian population of the coastal region. Elka once responded to a governmental scheme to enlist the Wai Wai as voters, "They don't choose our chief; why should they want us to choose theirs?"

With independence came portents of change for the once isolated Wai Wai. The new nation of Guyana determined to assimilate all the Indians within its borders. The government formulated plans for rapidly developing the Wai Wai and the area in which they lived, its aim to integrate them into the cash economy. One day word arrived that a new airfield was to be built at Kanashen, one much larger than the present strip, one capable of landing commercial airliners. To accommodate it, more than fifty houses would have to be razed.

Landing large planes in this jungle glade would come only after many other changes had occurred. The Wai Wai, the report said, would have to clear virgin forest and then build the runway, all as government workers without pay since the project itself would be their compensation; overseers would be sent in to boss. One plan called for coastal people to be relocated to Kanashen; another to return the Indians to their pagan culture. None of this allowed for Wai Wai consultation.

Bitter winds had begun to blow in on the once-sheltered environment, exposing the people to the biting cold of the outside world.

All this was momentarily forgotten, however, when the message came crackling through the missionary radio that Yakuta and his men might all be dead.

Kron and his crew returned, flown back at the end of their journey to Manaus. They had tales to tell, good stories of successful aerial drops, the fortuitous recharging of their radio by a road-building bulldozer, the wonders of the city sights. But the best story could not be told by them. Would anyone ever hear *that* epic from the lips of the men who were living it—or had lived it, if it was, indeed, now ended? How Kron wished he could have joined Yakuta's party! If they truly had met with tragedy and he had been with them, perhaps nothing he could have done would have made a difference. But at least he would have gone down with his brothers in arms in the battle against jungle darkness, and to him that would have been consolation.

The seven Wai Wai men paddled for their lives. Once in a while Yakuta stole a backward glance, saw that at times they gained distance over their pursuers, at other times, the gap narrowed. The Atrowari archers stood or knelt in their canoes, always two or three aiming drawn bows, waiting, evidently, for the old chief's command to release them. Why did they not shoot? Did they intend to beguile their victims into slackening, thereby affording easier targets? Was it just more of their erratic behavior that had kept the Wai Wai guessing as to their intentions? Such behavior was a deadly enigma: The Atrowari were just as likely to kill as to not

kill, so at any time could come down on either side. These
thoughts were mere flashes in the minds of the fleeing men.
What seemed more likely to them was that the restraining
hand of God was keeping those fatal arrows from flying.

The sun had set and darkness was falling on the river.
Emehta looked back once more. He shouted out his discov-
ery: "They're gone!"

At some time in the last little while, the Atrowari had
given up the chase. Though the growing darkness limited
visibility, the Wai Wai could see no outline but that of rocks
on the river behind them. They hardly slowed the pace, paddling without letup until far into the night. Finally they
halted, listened intently, and satisfied that nothing rippled
the water, beached their canoes and made camp. Shaking
themselves awake before dawn, happy to find they were
alone and alive, they shoved off again, steadily working
their way toward the trail that would take them home by the
way of Anaua Mountain.

In a few days they shed their anxiety, a luxurious relief.
For days on end (and nights, too) they had danced on the
needle point of danger. Before making contact with the
Atrowari they'd moved along streams and forest paths, ever
mindful that arrows could fly at them from concealed bowmen. At night as they guardedly built their fires, they knew
their silhouettes formed easy targets. They might have given
up, turned back, and shed their vulnerability, but they did
not.

Then at last, as hopefully and prayerfully planned, they
met the Atrowari. Though brief and vexing, a first meeting
nonetheless. Now they faced only the perils of the jungle.
From time to time one or another brought up an aspect of
their contact and never failed to marvel that today they were
not only here on the trail alive and well—even the foot-sore
Trio hobbled about their night campsites almost as well as
his mates—but they also enjoyed a sense of accomplished
mission.

"I scratched some of their words on my paper," Yakuta

said. Others had written down Atrowari words, too. Their collection would have been more extensive had the Atrowari not snatched away the papers whenever they saw the Wai Wai trying to record their language.

"They became very angry when I tried to sound their words," said one.

"Only God saved us from certain death," said another.

"God and Bahm's warning not to sleep near the Atrowari," reminded the medic Emehta.

They agreed it was prudent that the two stayed behind at the river. Had there been a slaughter on the trail, the two might have escaped to bear the tidings home.

"*Gicha!*" grumped the young Wai Wai who had remained behind. "Why me? Why did I have to stay with this old fellow and his sore foot? I came to see the Atrowari."

"Little Body," said Yakuta wisely like an uncle, "you saw them as we saw them. The path to their village was not different from our paths."

The day Eldon Larson was to fly over to check on their safety, the men got out a firecracker that was supposed to attract his attention. They heard the plane approach, and at the river's edge hastily lit the fuse. But never having handled a Roman candle and quite forgetting their instructions, they pointed it flat. Skipping across a canoe, it set fire to one of their bundles and skewed away to perish quietly in the river. The plane flew on, the pilot unaware of people below him, and later he radioed his sad deduction about the burned-down house.

After observing the moon pass through its familiar phases, the little group reached the primitive airstrip below Anaua Mountain. There from palm leaves they wove simple but large baskets to carry the farina that had been stacked for them. On the trip over the high mountains the spirits of the men rose dramatically. The Trio was especially happy. The days he had yet to walk he could tick off on his fingers. Mornings now when he awoke he out-shouted the strident cries of the jays in the tree tops and often with abandon tootled on his bamboo flute. So happy was he to be nearing home that he ran on ahead of the others. But in his haste, the basket on his back got entangled with the vines along the path and he was thrown to the ground. Once more his injured food disabled him.

"Why did you have to hurt yourself again?" Yakuta asked sharply as the rest caught up to where he sprawled on the ground. "Now you'll slow us all down."

Emehta tied up his foot and stuck him for the pain. His young keeper thought he had the answer to this second play of the problem:

"Let's leave the old thing behind."

"No," said Yakuta, compassion overtaking his vexation. "Any one of us might have been hurt. He should have been more cautious, but he was excited to soon see his wife and children."

They made a large sling for the invalid and took turns carrying him on their backs. In three days they would be at the headwaters of the Essequibo and home in another day or two.

From the accounts the seven travelers gave to an ecstatic audience in Kanashen's *umana* and Yakuta's report the following Sunday in church, it was clear that two things would be required if the Atrowari were to be won for Christ. First, other contacts, probably many, were needed for the Wai Wai to prove they sought friendship. Second, before there could be any substantive communication, the Wai Wai would have to learn the Atrowari's strange language.

Formidable tasks, both, without a doubt. Yet, a bridge had been started, and though at this point it was flimsy, it stood.

Time also was a factor. The road the Brazilian government was building north out of Manaus neared the Atrowari homeland. No less than the army, it was said, would protect the road builders. Soldiers carried guns. An Atrowari arrow might kill a road worker—would then the blasts from a dozen guns kill a dozen Indians? Who but God could stop the carnage before it began?

The Wai Wai felt a missionary should accompany them on their next trip. The language skills of a Bahm or Kron could speed the process of breaking down Atrowari sounds into meaningful terms. The distance being too great for the required amounts of food to be borne on shoulders, aerial drops at designated sites would also be most helpful. Requests for missionary travel and supportive flights were forwarded to the Brazilian government. While awaiting answers, the elders called for a day of prayer.

"Remember how we used to kill our children if twins were born or if we didn't want them?" asked Elka as he launched the special day. "That is what the Atrowari are doing today because they do not know about Jesus."

He recalled, too, that in the early days when Bahm and Ferochi and Achi first taught the Wai Wai about Jesus, they laughed. How ridiculous to think that there could be a love so strong that it would cause someone to die for another's good. They just laughed and kept on in their old ways, idle and listless, caring for little beyond the drink and dance and the promiscuous frolics they fostered. Maybe the Atrowari today were like the Wai Wai then. If they were, behind their harsh talk and menacing behavior and their reckless killing they lay trapped in confusion and fear. Only Jesus could bring them release.

"These are the ones Jesus has given us to reach for Him," Elka said in a charge to his hearers.

Throughout the prayers ran a repeated request: "Let a few Atrowari walk the trail home with our men so we can begin to catch their words."

The Brazilians refused their two requests. No missionary would be allowed to travel with the Wai Wai, and no flights would be permitted.

On hearing the denial, Elka became angry. Permission was granted for Mr. Thompson's trek—why not for a missionary trip? Who were these people who made decisions affecting not only the lives of the Atrowari but their eternal fate as well?

Over time, his anger diminished and he bowed to the refusal.

"My Father in the Sky has His own way to reach the Atrowari," he said. He became convinced that he himself was a part of that way.

"I will lead the next trip," he said.

Extra carriers would go along as far as Anaua, each toting as much farina as a man could carry. For language learning, the men with Elka would get whatever words they could and try to bring back a few Atrowari to help in the process.

Once again the missionary shelf was placed at the front of the church. It soon overflowed with farina, pineapple, and sugar cane. Men and women both dropped their beads there, and the supply of knives and arrows and axes began to grow. Some even gave their hard-earned matches.

In theory they had accepted a woman's prophecy when she had said "it will be hard and take long" to evangelize the Atrowari. Now with the first rough contact behind them, it turned into experiential truth. The Katwena and Shedeu had eagerly received the offer of Wai Wai friendship. The Atrowari were not so ready.

Achi shared a verse of God's Paper that had come to her during a time of personal prayer. She reminded them that God had said through His prophet Isaiah, "This people have I formed for myself; they shall show forth my praise."

It seemed appropriate for Elka and his team to keep this declaration squarely before them as they headed upstream and over the mountains and down the trail to the Alalau. Applied to the Atrowari, it gave both purpose and promise to their perilous mission.

6

On the first day of the new year Elka and all eleven men returned safely from the Atrowari, happily bearing a good report.

Not that there hadn't been several anxious moments! Such as the time when in a playful mood the Atrowari pinned Elka's arms behind him, an antic perhaps warning that while frolicsome now, they were capable of less friendly behavior. Or when their amiable hosts sent for the chief and on his coming the air suddenly darkened. The riveted wrinkles about his scowling mouth and the venom of his eyes immediately spawned clones in men and women who an instant before sang and joked and giggled like children. Fingers that had waggishly tickled the throats of the Wai Wai now stroked taut bow-lines and posited steel-tipped arrows in them.

Fearing furtive actions, the Wai Wai stood defensively in two lines, back to back and sang "Praise God," one of their hymns, to boost their courage. They smiled at the old fellow, said *kiriwanhi* and *maaraye*, but the sullen chief ignored every friendly overture. Eventually, he turned away. Elka and his men went down the path toward the river. The Atrowari who accompanied them were again friendly and tried very hard to communicate. Then even the old chief came around. Before they reached the port he caught up with them, and now behaved as if they all were his brothers.

"Bring knives next time," he said in pidgin Portuguese, his words translated by a Wai Wai who spoke a little of that language. "Bring long knives, *maaraye*—good—not short ones. Look, you're carrying away bananas. We need knives to clear places to plant bananas. Bring lots."

He picked up sticks until his arms were full.

"This many."

The Atrowari village was surrounded by a fence of palm slats, the usual protection against a retaliatory sneak attack in an ongoing feud. Atrowari fighting Atrowari—or did they fear a raid by the Waymiri, their even more fierce cousins who shared their range of forest? Or perhaps the Atrowari were particularly sensitive at this time because they knew the road that would split their territory was creeping nearer. Up this road from Manaus would eventually come all sorts of people, some to gaze in either amusement or academic awe at their nakedness, some to roam their rivers and forests for easily-gotten wildlife, some possibly to move in and take their land for purposes never envisaged by the Indian.

On his return Elka was given news that underlined the loathing of the Atrowari for outsiders—especially civilized men. At the very time he and his eleven colleagues had approached the Atrowari from the north, from known Indian territory, twelve Brazilians, including two priests, ventured into Atrowari areas from the south, the direction in which Brazilian towns lay along the Amazon River. The Wai Wai were, for the most part, given a friendly reception. The Brazilians were all killed, except for the one who escaped to report.

Also after Elka arrived home, his determination grew for an outpost to be located at Anaua as a way station to the Atrowari, and for a village to be planted some day on the Mapuera River for reaching out to the Karafou. The Wai Wai were now convinced the two were distinctly separate tribes.

Elka's ardor for fields at Anaua and a settlement to tend them was matched by the eagerness of Bob Hawkins to start work there.

It would be hard for the Hawkinses at their age to start over, which building a new mission station from scratch would mean. But they were willing—if the Brazilian government was. The Brazilians had crimped their plans before to reach out to the Atrowari. Could they expect them to approve a permanent mission presence?

Ferochi, Bahm, Elka—all who were concerned with the Atrowari—would learn in a little while that official intransigence or personal preferences among bureaucrats did not always remain standing when one of heaven's irresistible movements swept down the path.

Colonel Camarâo was a short man, his name in English meaning shrimp. He was every centimeter a commander and was both handsome and warmly human. A neatly trimmed mustache lent him dignity, his perfectly pressed uniform of the Brazilian Air Force unmistakable authority. A quick smile and soft eyes set at ease anyone meeting up with this powerful man.

The colonel, based in Belem at the mouth of the Amazon, had as his dominion the whole north of Brazil. Once before he had been the commandant of these borderlands touching French Guiana and the former Dutch and British colonies and Venezuela. During that tenure he had gotten the Wai Wai to construct the airfield on the Cafuini River, one of a series of fields proposed for the aerial defense of Brazil. Now that he was back in Belem, after a stint in the south, he again picked up his plan to carve these landing strips out of the jungle, to keep them in usable condition and to maintain at each a fuel supply so his planes could patrol the area and his pilots would know they had safe spots to land when necessary.

Four days after resettling into his office, he flew to Boa Vista, a frontier town in the northwest. There he looked up an old friend who had been instrumental in constructing the strip on the Cafuini. Around Boa Vista, Neill Hawkins was not hard to find.

"Your Wai Wai really belong to Brazil, you know," Colonel Camarâo said to Neill in a friendly meeting at the Boa Vista post of FAB, the Brazilian Air Force. He laughed as he said, "We'll take them back some day."

"They'll be back in Brazil some day," Neill said, not completely joking.

"I'd like to bring some over as quickly as possible."

The colonel mentioned his plan to ring the Brazilian border with defensive airstrips and enlarge one specific site he had in mind.

"My government is keeping a sharp eye on border developments. Independence to the north and what may develop there give us great concern. We fear the Soviets may use a young country as a base for unfriendly operations. We need the visibility border air patrols can give."

He described FAB's reconnaissance over the area. A small savanna had been discovered and on closer examination it appeared a rude airstrip had in the past been scratched out there. To examine its potential, he had parachuted a few troops onto the field. These were later picked up, except for one man who remained as FAB presence.

"After a week provisions were flown in, but the jungle had gotten to him. He begged to be taken out. He was told he must stay. He lay down in front of the plane. We took him out."

The situation called for people who were at home in the jungle—not to do much beyond keeping the grass down; just to be there.

"That's why I'd like to have some Wai Wai move to Anaua."

"Anaua!" Neill wasn't sure he had heard him right.

"Anaua. And I think it would be best if some missionaries came along with them. I'll help set up a station and fly in food to get things started."

"But the government has blocked our settling at Anaua."

The colonel spluttered, his gentle bearing replaced with anger.

"I know them, those, those—"

He disliked that branch of his government. He despised it. They didn't understand Indians, knew nothing about national defense. If they questioned the value of mission work, he favored it. Though he might not take seriously the missionaries' message, he liked their methods with Indians. With him in command, he let Neill know, those methods would prevail.

Neill promised to write to his brother Bob. He would ask if there was any chance Kanashen could send Wai Wai and missionaries to establish a permanent settlement at Anaua.

In Guyana, Bob Hawkins, living in Georgetown at the time, kept abreast of the nation's politics as best he could. He saw only trouble ahead for missionary work among Indians. This impression—coupled with the Wai Wai push for evangelizing the Atrowari—provoked in him a strong compulsion to move to Anaua. His feeling heightened when, in flying into Kanashen for a visit, he noted the increasing pressures placed on the Wai Wai by the government. Once back in Georgetown he sat down and wrote to his brother, asking him to petition the Brazilians for permission to live at the base of Anaua Mountain.

"I know you will run into opposition," Bob wrote. He was, however, not aware of the intensity of the opposition. A national magazine had recently charged missionaries were exploiting Indians on Brazil's borders. After that publication landed on the desks of the civil servants, what chance would any missionary request have?

Except these bureaucrats did not know that their government also had in its employ and decision-making echelons a generally mild-mannered—but always determined—Colonel Shrimp.

The letters of the Hawkins brothers had crossed in the mail. Neill was flying to a mission station on the Venezuelan border when he opened his packet. He was struck that Bob's request precisely met what Camarâo was asking for; when he wrote, Bob could not have known about the colonel's request for Indians and missionaries to settle at Anaua.

Elka sent men to Anaua to cut a tract of forest and burn the fallen trees and underbrush to supply nutrients to an impoverished soil and plant cassava shrubs for future habitation. In the crew was Chownyon, the hastily married Katwena who had settled into a good family man. These days he was able to meet Elka's criterion for participation in this important missionary project—he was growing strong in his faith in God.

"If you love Jesus," the chief admonished the volunteers, "show it by the way you work. But don't be gone too long. Your wives will be missing you."

Who would leave Guyana to become permanent residents of Anaua? In discussing plans with the people, Bahm said three families would be about the right number to start the village.

No one was to go merely for an adventure, Elka ruled. Nor to get away from irritating in-laws or because the new land might be more fertile. He said they were to provide food and a staging area for trips to the Atrowari. Some day the village there would be visited by these rough, unpredictable people. The Wai Wai's only real gift to the Atrowari was their knowledge of God and His son, Jesus. Everyone at Anaua would have to be capable of bestowing this gift.

Florence Riedle returned from a furlough in March of 1970. All Kanashen hurried to the airstrip the minute they heard the plane in the sky. Once it was on the ground, the children thronged about the craft, hardly waiting for the propeller to stop spinning.

"Achi, you came!" called Elka as she stepped to the ground. The wriggling, rollicking youngsters pushed toward her, each trying to be the first to touch the friend they had sorely missed.

"I came," Achi returned the greeting. She smiled broadly. She was home.

Arriving with her in a government plane was a development officer sent by the prime minister in Georgetown. Almost ignored in the riotous welcome given the nurse, he emerged to look around at the people now thrusting out their hands to take the woman's bags and even the smallest item she carried. These Indians, some unwashed, some loud and uncouth, none of them like people he knew, made up the human element of his new jurisdiction.

They would, he instantly decided, require a lot of development. But wasn't he just the man to bring it off?

7

Yakuta was on another trip to the Atrowari. Mawasha looked
for any scattered Shedeu. Elka was away from his village.
Several families had gone a day or so upstream or down to
plant new crops. This was something Kirifaka intended to
do, but before leaving for his field he and Fehya gathered up
their children—not an easy accomplishment when there
were eight ranging from thirteen years to one month—and
shepherded them to Achi's house. She was at the time the
only missionary at Kanashen. It was something Kirifaka
wanted to do this morning, to make Achi a part of their
family devotions.

All ten climbed or were carried up, depending on their
stage of growth, the steps to the porch of her house. At first
there was a scramble for places nearest Achi—or Cha Cha,
grandmother, to the children. One of the little girls shivered
in the cool mist of the early morning; Achi got a shawl to
drape over her shoulders. Achi then excused herself for a
few minutes to go to the clinic below to bandage a man's
foot; in stepping from his hammock he had cut it on a knife.
On her return to the porch, the seating order had to be
arranged once more.

Eventually, reasonable quiet prevailed and the singing

began, each person contributing freely to the joyful noise, except the baby, who was content to add only the sucking sounds of his nursing, and four-year-old Natanu, who refused to sing. Achi thought she'd never heard a more melodious choir. For a moment she closed her eyes and breathed a prayer of thanks for this wonderful family. What was it that Kirifaka had once said to her? "God is so good to me. Look at all the children He has given me. I was an orphan, but I'm not anymore. I really love my children."

Meesu, the oldest child, was a fine girl. Always a big help to her mother, she soon would be of marriageable age and would make some young man a good wife. Fanahruwi was an extraordinarily bright boy—surely, he'd be a pacesetter some day. Perhaps he'd direct the Wai Wai in their love of music. She'd heard how at night the boy would sing in his hammock until his father would say, "Son, that's enough singing for one night," and his mother would quietly object, "Dear, he's not doing anything wrong. He's singing about Jesus. He's happy. Let him sing." And so he would.

Achi thought of these parents. Kirifaka was a persuasive preacher and an effective teacher, endowed with keen spiritual insight. Fehya was every bit as good a teacher, a frequent speaker in the women's meetings on Fridays. But it was in their home, Achi reflected, that these two best conveyed the spirit of Christ. Fanahruwi once said to his father, "*Ahfah,* I want to grow up to be a man just like you."

Kirifaka prayed constantly for his children's welfare. This morning he prayed for Achi.

"Father in the Sky, you are good. You are with us today. You are with my dear wife, Fehya. You are with Achi. You never leave us. Achi is going to be here alone for several days. Protect her. Protect her from the big cats of the forest, from snakes, from disease, and from people who do not want her to be here . . . ."

Within the hour the family launched their canoe and were on their way down river to plant their field. But in that session on Achi's porch, there had been talk about the call for some families to move over the mountains to Anaua.

"When Bahm last visited here, he spoke to me about going," Kirifaka said to Achi. "We've worked together on making God's Paper speak Wai Wai, and we could continue working at Anaua."

"What are your thoughts?" asked Achi.

"I'd kind of like to be one who will go. We have these eight children and my wife's old father to feed. But surely God can provide our food. I feel a great desire to do the translation and to go tell the Atrowari about Jesus."

His little wife, no bigger than some of the children sitting around her on the floor, nodded in agreement.

"What do you think we should do, Achi?" Kirifaka asked.

"I'd say God is telling you to go."

"*Hnnnnn . . .*" he said, and sucked in his breath. "So that's the way it is."

For many days afterward, down river in front of the leaf shelter where Fehya roasted their meat, back in their house on the edge of Kanashen, on the way to church each Wednesday and Sunday morning, the children heard their parents discuss the possible move to Brazil. They heard their father speak of Abraham, a man who lived long ago and who, when God told him to go, left his comfortable home and went to a new country, a place he had never seen. One day Kirifaka called all the children together.

"Your mother and I believe God is telling us to go over the mountains to Anaua," he said. The faces of Fanahruwi and his two older sisters brightened—the call of adventure to youth.

"It will mean leaving friends." Their faces lengthened.

"You children will have each other to play with."

Fanahruwi thought of his best friend, a boy his own age. He was sure he couldn't part from him. But, of course, he did not want to be left behind.

"It will be a privilege to serve God in a new place."

This new place—what will it be like? wondered Fanahruwi. Not even his father knew. As they went, wouldn't his father be another Abraham? He'd not been to Anaua, probably didn't really know how to find it, and once there wouldn't know until the crops grew or died whether it was a suitable place to live. But like Abraham, he was called to go, so he'd go. And wouldn't they all be like Abraham?

The two families chosen to go with them were those of a young man named Mamichiwa, with two children, and the Katwena youth Fawtaw, now married and the father of one.

Before accepting the assignment, the men and their wives had carefully considered what might lie ahead. Fawtaw talked with his family. His father said, "If you're God's child, I guess you will go."

Other relatives discouraged the move. "Why do you want to go there? Those people the Atrowari are wild ones. They will kill you. There is no food there. Why take your little girl to such a place?"

After the advice, Fawtaw decided he wanted to be God's servant. He would obey the compulsion to tell the Atrowari about Jesus, an urge that had ruled his will from the time he looked down the trail out of Kanashen and was told, "Go down this path and you'll find angry killers. They've never caught hold of Jesus."

In their resolve, he and Mamichiwa became as firm as Kirifaka.

Fehya's old father would go, too. With his full head of hair a mixture of black and white, the man was bent over, walked with a stick, and was hard of hearing, that perhaps explaining why he yelled (his voice was still strong) when he talked to people. For many years he had been called only by the English name someone tacked on him—William. Everyone knew he was devoted to his family. He couldn't bear to lose his grandchildren. As a widower in his old age he had married an elderly woman with grandchildren. She now refused to go across to Anaua and leave them. So by mutuality, they agreed to part, each to stick to his own.

As the tali-tali locust sang, piping in the dry season, the three families, accompanied by carriers and house builders, departed from a port crowded with tearful well-wishers.

"Oh, dear, you are leaving us. *Okwe*, how sad." This frequently heard lament expressed the concerns of relatives and friends for their future. It might have applied to their long journey or to the fate that awaited them in the new country.

For twelve days they walked the trail through dense woods and up and down steep grades, sometimes crossing on logs over creeks and sometimes wading through the creeks and swamps. Always they fought the stinging backlash of switching stalks and twigs and the clouds of gnats and biting flies. Constantly they shook off the carnivorous ants and blood-sucking leeches and forever tried to avoid being tripped by the mass of creepers underfoot. The children traveled better than anyone expected. The bigger ones carried the smaller ones, and the littlest rode in owchies on their fathers' backs. One place they came to, even the women rode in baskets. The route up to the ridge was very long but gradual; down the other side, it was precipitous. Handholds indenting the cliff here and there enabled the men to descend, but only with great caution and not without immense danger. They did so, but not before they let the women and children down the rock face of the mountain in baskets tied to tough, sinewy vines.

The field planted for them at Anaua was tiny. The cassava had hardly grown at all. It would be a year before they could expect bananas. Some other crops evidently had been planted, but insects had consumed them.

The field and a few leaf shelters bordered on a grassy airstrip. It ran most of the length of a natural savanna at the base of Anaua Mountain. Even higher than the escarpment they had had to climb to get to this place, old Anaua rose by degrees from the back side and from a great summit plunged almost abruptly to the edge of their clearing. The site was far from any river; only a very small stream offered a water supply. The Wai Wai were used to living on a river. A river was their highway, an important source of food, providing the water they drank and bathed in and serving as the chief playground for the children. This creek here, Kirifaka observed with near disdain, wasn't deep enough for a child to duck his head under.

The men accompanying the permanent settlers fell to work gathering indigenous materials to build better, but still temporary, houses along the airstrip, including two in anticipation of the arrival of Bahm and his family and a new missionary nurse, Sharon Hinchman. They tried standing the poles in one spot, but the poles sank in the soft, spongy ground, forcing a move further down the line. The airstrip also had a soft place and the men worked long and hard to remedy it. After a time six more men arrived from Kanashen, allowing a few of the workers to be spared from construction in order to go with Kirifaka to recut the overgrown portions of the trail to the Alalau River. It was important that this route to the Atrowari be kept open.

Before the small migration to Anaua began, Yakuta returned to Kanashen from another attempt to contact the Atrowari. He had failed. His party uncovered the hidden canoe which was to carry them down the Alalau to the Atrowari, but it had been hacked in pieces. Who did it? Had some among the Atrowari stealthily followed Elka back from the last Wai Wai visit, and not wishing the Wai Wai to return, smashed it so to be unusable? Yakuta and his men felled a tree and dug it out and heated the wood to shape it, but eight days from when they began and finally were ready to launch, their food had nearly run out. They had no assurance the Atrowari would give them provisions. Facing a journey that would outlast the full cycle of the moon, they turned back.

Then before the move to Anaua, Kirifaka planned a trip to the Alalau, but excessive rains flooded the swamps through which the path ran, so he had to postpone going. That is why he now went to recut the trail. A trail unused for a year, or sometimes even less, was no trail at all. The jungle paused for no man.

Besides building on houses and planting new fields and cutting forest trails, Kirifaka spent many hours helping

Bahm translate the book of Romans. He found it exhilarating. Less so did Fehya find tending to the feeding, clothing, nurturing, and admonishing of their eight children without the strong support of kin and neighbors who had surrounded her at Kanashen. Women in one's family helped at the times of birth—and in this area Fehya had gotten almost as much as she had given—and the extended family assumed responsibility for the behavior of the children, shared meat from the forest, worked together in the kitchen shelter, and nursed the ill. Fehya's family were all on the other side of the high mountains; here she had only her neighbors, who were in the same situation as she, and her thoughtful but very busy husband and her father.

Old William helped both his daughter and his son-in-law, and dearest to him, his grandchildren. Early in the morning he would go into the forest to find the fiber needed for twining into bow-strings. He would cut the cane and pluck the feathers of colorful birds for the fabrication of arrows. These were tasks that freed Kirifaka to do others. He minded the little ones for Fehya and told stories of his younger days to the older children. And in the field which had been greatly enlarged he planted bananas.

"These will feed my grandchildren," he proudly said.

The rainy season brought gray days with a sky that seldom shut off its dripping. Much of what these pioneers planted failed to come up. What did sprout was attacked by caterpillars. Beside this, big, voracious cockroaches, regardless of what was done against them, seemed to multiply every day. Food which Colonel Camarâo had delivered early on as promised was dwindling. The men shot a few monkeys and wild pigs, but in all the forest around came upon no deer or tapir, major meat sources for the Wai Wai. Fehya liked eggs, but had obtained none since leaving her chickens behind in Kanashen. Adding to the intensity of their isolation, the population of the tiny village shrank as the temporary helpers returned to Guyana.

Spirits lifted, however, with the singing of the tali-tali.

Three Indian families, one missionary family, and a single nurse did not make up a large congregation, yet the minuscule church at Anaua dug its roots deep into the lives of the people remaining there. As at Kanashen, they met Sunday and Wednesday mornings, and the women also on Fridays. Later, when Bahm built a house on legs, they would use the open space under it as their sanctuary.

The Anaua families now often gathered at the close of the day to chat and watch the children play and especially to look with enchantment at the riotous colors which the setting sun painted on the clouds. Usually everyone was weary from the day's heavy work and a certain amount of homesickness hung over them. On this particular evening they gathered in front of Bahm's house. Bahm sat on a simple bench, resting a foot on an overturned bucket he would in a little while take to the creek for the water Ferochi needed. His drawn face revealed his fatigue; the question he posed his discouragement: "Why haven't new families come from Kanashen?" No one had an answer, except that Elka would not permit any to leave Guyana.

Kirifaka eased the bucket from under Bahm's foot and started walking with it toward the creek. He was tired, but he thought Bahm more tired than he. He would fetch Ferochi's water. Ferochi quietly shook her head in wonder. To her and Bob, Kirifaka was like a son; as a raw young boy, he had lived with them, and during his teen years and beyond they continued to observe his ripening. What a long way he had come. What a long way the Wai Wai had come. Once no one among them would have performed a favor for another without the promise of a return favor of greater proportions. Once to be kind, to be thoughtful of others, to say something encouraging, to do good, meant that somewhere in the thought or deed was buried a selfish motive. That was then—back before any of the Wai Wai became companions of Jesus. Kirifaka was not alone in this transformation. Indeed, he had his equal in his own house. In the move from Kanashen, Ferochi's tableware had been inadvertently left in Boa Vista. Learning this, Fehya brought around the two spoons she possessed.

"Use them until yours come," she said. "We're used to eating with our fingers."

Could they be sure it was God's will that they make this place the key to ministering to the Atrowari? Did He even want them to pursue this elusive quarry? It would be easy to doubt that He did. Twice now they had been held back from even making a contact. Might not any progress toward friendship be lost when a year had passed without a visit? And here at Anaua, they had come as missionaries—but with conditions such as they were, could they hold out?

Their disheartening routine was broken one day by the unannounced visit of Colonel Camarâo, who since his last drop-in had become Brigadier Camarâo. Recognizing the tight food situation, he pledged more supplies. The brigadier's visit and generosity should have heartened the Anaua families, and this they did, but the air of good feeling dissipated the day Mamichiwa's house burned to the ground, and with it his pants and the family's limited wardrobe.

The fire should have been expected. Once before the dry leaves of the roof burned from the cooking fire inside the house; that time the family was able to snatch away the flaming leaves and save the house. But Mamichiwa didn't get around to relocating the perpetual fire away from the edge to a safe spot in the center. Mamichiwa was like that.

The next excitement came from a happy event, the first birth at Anaua—a boy born to Fawtaw and Awachee his wife just a few days before Christmas. Though their numbers were few, the folk at Anaua resolved to recreate the happy, neighborly event they had celebrated every Christmas from the time the Wai Wai first heard of the day's existence.

On Christmas Eve hunters brought meat in from the forest. That night everyone gathered at Bahm's house to sing Christmas songs. Ferochi told the old story of the first Christmas, illustrating it with pictures hung on a board. Other pictures were unrolled from a long paper strip, pictures the children had colored in their school. Each child received a small gift and the children gave their parents simple presents they had made. The next day everyone ate to the full. To work off the heavy meal, they crossed the airstrip and walked to the base of Anaua Mountain. The more energetic ones climbed up the tree-filled clefts in the stony face to the top.

Then over the next week, first one then another complained, "A cold has caught me," a logical way of speaking. It wasn't long before everyone remained in his hammock for entire days.

The rains that spring were very heavy. The low, dark clouds emptied torrents of water on the land. The little creek swelled into a small river. The rocky cliff of old Anaua seemed never to dry, even when from time to time the sun broke briefly through. To walk from one house in the village to another was to slog through shin-deep mud.

One night was especially stormy. The rain poured down as if all preceding rains were mere mists. Trillions of water pellets hitting billions of broad leaves in the surrounding forest created their own incessant clamor. The boom of distant thunders fused as a single, background drum roll, and the crack of lightning over the savanna played an instant staccato, the theme of which was the mastery of the heavens over earth.

Kirifaka stood back from the door of his house, keeping clear of the rain, his twelve-year-old son Fanahruwi crouched beside him. Even through the wall of cascading water they caught glimpses of the mountain with each flash of lightning against the stony face. There were both fascination and fear in the eyes of father and son as the jagged, branching tendrils exploded with terrifying crashes in every part of the sky. A strike at the top of the mountain threatened eardrums and rattled Old William's cache of arrow cane on a shelf in the house. Trailing its blast and seeming to grow out of it was a series of equally terrifying thuds and thumps, gratings and whooshes.

"The mountain!" screamed Fanahruwi.

"The mountain!" echoed his mother. The mountain seemed to be breaking apart. Split seconds between the major booms were filled by the peppering sound of ricocheting rock. Fehya had sat astride her hammock. Having mentally recorded every clap of thunder, she had blocked out the lightning by burying her face in the ring of children around her. Now she sat up suddenly.

"The mountain!" she cried. "It'll spill out its insides on us all!"

She had once heard a missionary say some mountains were volcanoes and sometimes they erupted. She imagined a disgorging mountain to be the most dreadful of the earth's furies. She was sure old Anaua had become one tonight. She pressed the terrified children even closer to her.

"Not the insides," called Kirifaka, hardly daring to blink as he strove to see by the lightning flashes what was happening to the mountain. "Not the insides. The rocks on its face."

He was certain that what they heard between sharp clashes of thunder and over the pounding rain were gigantic boulders rent from the cliff and bounding down to the plain below, bumping and thudding and crazily crunching trees that grew out of the crevices and surely wiping out life of any kind at the bottom.

"We'll all be buried," Fehya moaned. The children picked up her cry.

She wanted to run. Kirifaka said no. They'd be all right if the slide stopped short of the airstrip, and if it did not, the house, slight as it might be, offered their best protection. Outside in the ensnaring mud and the dark and the driving rain, how could one dodge hurtling stones?

Abruptly the great burst of catapulting rock subsided, leaving only muffled boomlets, like a blustering whirlwind passing by and fading on the far side. No more did they hear the wrenching crack of tree trunks. Kirifaka looked out once more, and in flashes of light, waved understandingly to neighbors who also stood in their doorways. He closed the door; inside the house the faithful night fire was a friendly reminder that in spite of the loosing of some mysterious destructive force outside, in here all was well. The older children gathered around their father, the young ones still clinging to their mother. He sat on a small stool and looked up at his family with a reassuring smile.

"We can't know tonight what has happened to the mountain," he said. "But when Jesus comes the noise will be more than this."

"Did God send an angel?" Fanahruwi asked.

Did he? Kirifaka hadn't thought of that possibility.

"An angel?" Maybe an angel did walk by, or rode on a bolt of lightning, and where he touched his feet the rocks shattered.

During the night the rain spent itself, and the next morning everyone in the village stepped onto the airstrip, pointing out happily that no rocks had crossed it. They hurried to the far edge of the savanna for a closer look at the destruction. Where rock once protruded and trees had stubbornly grown from the slightest cracks, there now was only an immense black hole. Below lay a disorderly mound of boulders, mud, crushed stone, and crumpled trees.

Was it lightning or the days of driving rain that had brought down in such humiliation a chunk of the proud old mountain?

Kirifaka led his family almost to the base of the cliff. There they sang one of the Wai Wai hymns and then as they stood gaping at this phenomenon of nature, he quietly spoke.

"The mountain is still here," he said. "We still see a very big rock, though some is gone. God is like a great rock. But nothing can destroy Him. Not even a little. He's always there."

He reminded the children that mountains and rocks and trees and lightning and rain—and people like them—were all parts of God's creation, and He held it all in His hand.

The lesson was not lost on Fanahruwi.

8

An attempt at revolution against the new government of Guyana in 1969 by a handful of ranch owners on the savanna passed Kanashen by. The fallout of the failed rebellion was felt among the Wai Wai nevertheless, and after a couple of years was felt rather severely.

Some Indians on the savanna had aided the ranchers' uprising, so Georgetown was not sure of the loyalty of any of its Indians. Officials found it easy to suspect the Wai Wai, isolated in the jungle as they were, three hundred miles inland and scarcely known to anyone who hadn't visited Kanashen—and that included all but a very small handful of the bureaucracy.

Official wrath came down on Mission Aviation Fellowship, Kanashen's lifeline to the outside world. MAF had sold a couple of its aging planes to private citizens in Guyana, and months later these were used in the insurrectionist cause. *Ipso facto,* MAF was a part of the revolt; its punishment was to be thrown out of the country. Severing the lifeline hurt Kanashen.

Guyana long had had problems with its neighbors Venezuela and Surinam, the former Dutch Guiana, and to protect the sanctity of its borders would hereafter vigilantly

guard them. Because the Wai Wai lived practically on a border—the less contentious one with Brazil, but a border
notwithstanding—this sequestered, hardly understood, and
therefore suspicious tribe would come under greater
scrutiny. Besides, in the new Guyana the Wai Wai had to be
lifted from their crude savagery into the mainstream of the
republic. Except that some voices, some strident ones, called
instead for their reverting to the old days of innocence, primordial happiness, and near nakedness. Rightly show-
cased—which meant to assume the primitive bit a day or
two a week for fly-in visitors—it was the stuff from which a
tourist industry could be built.

The revolt was put down in a single day at a very few
sites near the Brazilian border. However, the fear those few
rebellious hours produced did not dissipate but reflected in a
wide program of government reaction. The missionaries
were permitted to remain at Kanashen only month by
month, and heard from "reliable sources" that ultimately
they would be replaced by government personnel.
Removing the aerial lifeline appeared to be a solid first step.

Bahm's family, Achi and Ayrin were not the only targets
of innuendo and thinly veiled threats. The officer sent by the
government to live at Kanashen accosted Elka one day:

"You're only a figurehead. You do what the missionaries
tell you. You don't obey me. You let Achi tell you what to
do. Because you are this way, I want to send her away."

After the three families moved over the mountains to
Anaua, Elka was warned: If he let others leave he would be
stripped of his chieftaincy. Was it coincidence that shortly
afterward, Elka sent word to Anaua that the families who
were ready to move would not be sent until later?

In the face of the ridicule that as a chief he was a toad, the
government recognized his position by granting him a
salary. Sometimes this took the form of gift items, among
the first an outboard motor for his canoe. Some in the tribe
resented this largesse for Elka. More, however, were upset
with the government for its delving into their once internal
affairs.

Henry Deaks, the development officer, personified the government as enemy. Early on he criticized the haphazard layout of Kanashen. As the leading village, he said, it should have a main street as straight as a Wai Wai arrow. If houses couldn't be shifted to conform, they must be torn down and rebuilt and mere inches would be the margin allowed. He started a house for himself and the wife he would bring in when it was completed, building it away from the village proper, at the end of the airstrip. For material, he had cement flown in from Georgetown.

The new Main Street was not developed because he failed to follow through. At various times and for differing reasons he threatened several men, but they learned to avoid or deflect his wrath. Most of the women, however, grew to fear him.

"Is this the way the people out there are?" a wife asked her husband.

There was one command that not many in the village found they could dodge.

"Right now!" he'd say in giving an order. He failed to take Indian time into account.

"He walks around with a smile on his face," one said in a discussion of their official.

"When he speaks he loses it," said another. "He always talks in anger."

"He is one who does not ask what we think."

"If a man thinks something different from what he thinks, he says that man is not obeying." That accusation hurt. The Wai Wai placed importance on obedience, even to inconsiderate government officials. After all, God's Paper held the government in high regard.

"Remember that long ago Bahm said some day a bad ruler might try to take us away from God? The Children of Israel had their wicked kings. We have Mr. Deaks. He wants us to drink strong drink like we used to drink and to dance to Seetin like once we did."

Deaks' prime development project was a bean field, a

cash-crop venture that would yield the Wai Wai a handsome profit. In anticipation of a benefit to be shared by all, Elka asked every man to work. A large tract was cleared for it and at one time or another most of the men planted and cultivated the field. To fulfill one particular day's quota of workmen, Elka had to take ten men off another planned job and send them to Mr. Deaks for the bean field. Deaks sent them back, saying they weren't good workers. By then it was too late in the day to accomplish their original task.

Deaks said the project required the people to work on Sundays. Elka flatly said no, they would not. Then Deaks said they were to start at daybreak on Wednesdays, not go to church first as was their custom.

"You're lazy," he said to the elders who tried to explain the importance of the Wednesday morning meeting. "You shouldn't waste time sitting in church."

They agreed to shift the Wednesday meeting to afternoon. But it did not work. After working in the hot sun until noon, they became tired and sleepy. They put up with this arrangement for some time, then finally went to Deaks.

One of the elders said, "We've decided we must give the best time of the day to God."

He frowned as he waited for the explanation.

"We can't have our meeting in the afternoon. We've tried to cooperate, but *okwe*, how sad, it is impossible. God's Paper tells us to obey authority. But if what we must do is not pleasing to God, we are to obey God, not another. We will meet first with God, then we will work."

Deaks did not like it, but yielded. "Oh, all right. I guess that's the way you are."

His giving in to Wednesday mornings did not diminish the conflicts. He accused both Achi and Bahm of having stolen money belonging to the Wai Wai. He made the women join their men in the work of the bean field. Yet at season's end, there was very little profit to distribute.

When they could bear no more of his tyranny, the Wai Wai gathered in the umana and sent for him. For two hours they talked strongly, telling him he did not keep his word, that in their judgment he was a bad man. They disbanded, then most of them met again at his house and continued their appraisal of his behavior. Several times he repeated his short answer:

"I don't know what you're talking about."

Someone came from Georgetown, talked roughly to Deaks, and at one time slapped him on the mouth. Not long afterward, the government withdrew the discredited representative and sent in a replacement.

James Calder was of a decidedly different temperament. His aim appeared to be, "Stay on the good side of everyone." His effort to socialize where his predecessor repelled people was a bit too intense for Irene Benson. She repulsed his advances, but knew a wounded animal was a dangerous animal. It was only a matter of time before he would close the mission station and she and Achi would be forced to take leave of the Wai Wai.

Elka, too, had read the signs. He would be sad but not surprised when for the first time since they had caught hold of Jesus the Wai Wai would have no missionary living among them. That Achi and Ayrin were being squeezed out, just as missionaries in other parts of Guyana had been uprooted and expelled, was no longer in doubt. Their back-up system in Georgetown gone and plane service nothing now to be counted on, they might have left for those reasons. Those, yes, but also something more.

Their presence at Kanashen, Ayrin said, was not helping the Wai Wai. The pressure on the people was severe, and increasing. She sometimes wondered if the Wai Wai might be tempted to compromise their Christian values just to please some official and thereby as a reward gain reprieve for the missionaries. Decidedly, it would be better if they left.

Their going was a shock. Though there had been ample warning, few really believed they would leave. Elka broke down and cried. Before she left, Achi completed a census that counted nearly seven hundred people living in the Wai Wai community, about half of them at Kanashen. Most of these professed to be companions of Jesus. The majority of the unconverted were Shedeu, the recent additions to the population. Yet it was not just these newcomers who, on the departure of the missionary women, stayed away from church. Some who had caught hold of Jesus also walked sad, admitted to despair, and thought maybe God, too, had gone away. A few—very few—said they should go back to the old days before God entered their lives.

Sensing his people's feeling of discouragement and fear, and sharing it somewhat himself, Elka was driven one morning to find a lonely spot in his field and there to cry out to the Lord.

"*Ahfah,* Father," he said, "our teachers have had to leave us. We counted on them to talk to you about our needs. We looked to them to explain the words in your Paper. What will we do now that they are gone?"

After a short while Elka walked back into his village and to his house, his head held high, his face beaming. Over and over he repeated the message God had confided to him:

"I talk Wai Wai. I will never have to leave you."

Elka spoke in church of the change they were going through.

"Our teachers are gone, but God still hears us," the chief said. "People may be sent away, but no one can send Jesus away. We need the prayers of others, but we can pray for ourselves, too. God talks Wai Wai! *Oklee!* Good!"

The life of the church picked up. For some, inspiration flowed from the hymns that were the legacy of Ferochi, Bahm's wife. Others experienced new dedication through a morning of prayer. Some took to the forest again to scour it for fragments of wandering, fearful Indian tribes. There were baptisms, and in the believers' meetings held before the general church sessions, a welcome was given to those who testified they had recently become companions of Jesus.

The women continued to meet on Fridays, most of them eager to hear a message from God especially for them. The children were not neglected. Particularly in homes where singing and reading of God's Paper took place regularly, often as the family gently swayed in their hammocks over the night fire before sleeping, even very young children caught hold of Jesus.

The start of a second church, at Yaka Yaka, had strained the spiritual leadership, so additional elders were appointed. These were men who could preach and teach with the ring of authority and were able to hold the attention of their hearers for a reasonably long spell. Their task also was to comfort those in sorrow and to counsel in problem situations. With them, too, lay the administering of church discipline.

Even in the presence of God at work—perhaps the devil to spite it—disciplining was no uncommon thing. Ostracism—exclusion from the believers' meeting, suspension from church leadership—served as the rod of correction. Because of the strong adhesion inherent in Wai Wai society, it worked. Sitting in the house alone while others met to sing or socialize was sure to bring repentance. It was the elders who determined when one was truly sorry and a proper period of contrition had passed. The estranged one was then invited to attend the believers' meeting and relate how God had heard his confession and washed him clean of the sin.

The elders took their heavy responsibility with great seriousness. They strove to put into practice what the little Epistle of James had taught them, that God shows no partiality in regard to a man's station in life.

Elka, the first Christian among them, the one who had sided with Jesus against Kworokyam and thereby drove witchcraft from their villages, the one whose dedicated leadership had brought countless numbers of them out of the dark forest and into the light of the gospel, the first to build a private house to protect the sanctity of his marriage, he who had taught them that God's Paper plainly condemned immoral conduct and even thought—Chief Elka was judged by the elders and pleaded guilty as charged.

He had committed adultery.

Elka stepped down as a church leader. He acknowledged the elders were right to strip him of the spiritual garments that once seemed to fit him so well. Nevertheless, it cut deeply when he heard the talk that furtively entered doorways and seeped between slats in the walls of houses.

"He told us it was bad for a man to steal another man's wife. Now he's done it himself."

It hurt, because it was true.

Still chief, Elka announced on a Sunday morning the coming week's work assignments. He directed the work captains in the planning and execution of a myriad tasks. Every day he dealt with Mr. Calder and his directives. But now he had no say in the Wai Wai church.

At one time he had expressed a desire to relinquish the chieftaincy in order to concentrate on the church. He found no one ready to take on the responsibilities, so kept both tasks. Now he was down to one job, but not the one he had wanted.

He did not give up his love of God. Having confessed his sin and reconciled with his wife, he knew he could count on the faithfulness of his Father in the Sky to help him bear the stress of leading nearly seven hundred people under the often adversarial rule of a government that seemed to know little of their past or understand their present, to say nothing of recognizing their hopes for the future.

Precariously, he walked an unyielding line. On one side lay the desires of the people, particularly their determination to reach out to the Atrowari and perhaps other tribes in Brazil. On the other were the demands of the Guyanese government, chief among them that no one move out of its jurisdiction. To act against either would mean loss for Elka, the respect of his people on the one hand, and on the other, sacking as Wai Wai chief.

When he held up some families from leaving—even Kurunaw, his oldest son—the condemnation was quick to fall. Many equated his decision with an obsession to hold on to his government salary. Once he traveled to the savanna and there met the nation's prime minister. From Forbes Burnham he received permission for all who were born in Brazil to return there if they wished. This meant, however, they would leave behind the children born in Guyana.

The government gave Elka a number of gifts. Some things he himself asked for, most often items he felt would benefit his people. He had received an outboard motor, though on the second use it broke down and lay idle for some time. He asked for a second motor, so more people could cut down on the time and effort long river trips exacted. He asked for a generator and electric light system; lights would extend the work day in the umana and materially aid evening sessions in the church. The government promised him lights. His village was given a sugar-cane press, a laborious mechanism that necessitated a building to house it in and two men to operate. Canadians donated a large stock of clothing. The tent dresses were of one size, and the men's pants extra large, but they were accepted with appreciation. Particularly for the women, this shipment changed cultural patterns for all time to come. Girls and women who had clung to bead aprons now abandoned them for the dresses.

Even while asking for things, Elka talked of some day moving back across the mountains to Brazil. For this, Calder was unhappy with him.

"Why do you talk this way?" the development officer said, no longer trying to keep Elka smiling. "If you're thinking of leaving here, you should stop being chief."

Elka looked him straight in the eye.

"I am not chief because you say I am. My people made me their chief. As long as they want me, I will be chief, whether you say so or not."

Some thought they heard Calder threaten to kill Elka.

"If our chief leads people over the mountains he will follow in the path and shoot him with his gun, they say."

"He told this to others, not to Elka, they say."

It was always *ha tu*, "they say." Tacked onto the end of a sentence, it gave license to pass along as truth one's acquired knowledge whether he knew it to be true or not. It enabled harsh feelings to be expressed while avoiding direct confrontation, something remaining from their old culture. There was a lot of *ha tu* going around these days. Most people took seriously the reported threats against Elka. They shared the presumed danger with him.

He gave their concern no second thought.

A few families wanted to leave Guyana because they were angry—with the government or with someone in their village, someone who had circulated bad talk about them. Elka said no one should leave while angry. Some who asked to go to Anaua he thought not likely to bear up under the adversities of that place, or they exhibited few of the qualities required of a missionary, and he looked on Anaua as a mission station. Some were denied an exit and did not know why. With all these people unhappy and with others chafing under the government's edicts and still others envious of Elka's motor, which was working again, and not a few who were disgruntled because they seemed to have contracted discontent as a contagious disease, it was not surprising that there was murmuring and dissension. For those who knew well a man named Mingeddi, it had to be expected that he welcomed the disquiet and perhaps intentionally added to it.

Mingeddi—gossip had it—wanted to displace Elka as chief.

A middle-aged man once called Rikaru, Mingeddi was a half-Wai Wai who was raised by a Wapishana Indian both in the jungle and on the savanna. The Wapishana traditionally looked down on the Wai Wai as untaught brutes. To theirs Mingeddi added his scorn. They, however, looked down on Mingeddi. He was, in effect, an Indian without a tribe. He seemed to fit in no place, and his mean disposition either caused it or was its natural result.

No doubt what made some people uneasy around him was

the fact that many years before he was accused of murdering five people—bludgeoning in their hammocks a woman, her daughter-in-law, and the younger woman's three small children. All for a dispute over a string of beads. Mingeddi was captured and the colonial police were called in. Twice escaping, he finally was flown out to a Georgetown jail. He was imprisoned for a year, then without hearing or trial was released. Nobody in Her Majesty's Government quite knew how to apply British law to one considered a barbarous Indian. Freeing him was the lesser of sticky wickets.

Today, Mingeddi had his following, mostly among the young. They hankered after the goods he dangled before them. A few dared ask that he take them far down the Essequibo to the Wapishana settlements where he had obtained these shiny baubles.

Mingeddi would become chief only by the government's high-handed action, which was not impossible to contemplate, but just being the malicious scoundrel that he was stirred trouble aplenty. Yet the storms brewing along the Essequibo could be traced more to conflicts among the Wai Wai leaders.

The most troubling centered around Mawasha's desire to take his family and a few others across the high mountains and re-establish a village on the Mapuera where Mawasha and Elka had lived as boys. It was good land on an excellent river, and as they discussed Mawasha's plans Elka longed to be back there himself. But now was not the time to leave Guyana. There were problems in staying, but more in going. The government's threat to hold their children hostage was not to be taken lightly. And there was the matter of obedience to authority.

"My brother," Elka said to his dearest friend. "I cannot agree to your going."

Elka was visibly growing more tense, his temper more brittle. Some traced this change to the time of his adultery. He had been reinstated to the believers' meeting, but did not, as expected, resume his eldership—meetings with Mr.

Calder, settling civil disputes, attending to more matters than piglets in a litter, all these interfered, he said. Whether the cause lay in his temporary break with the church or the charged atmosphere he breathed as chief, no one, probably not even he himself, could know for certain.

What was happening to their children at the hands of the new government teacher had driven all the Wai Wai nearly to the brink.

Before the missionaries were withdrawn, Calder brought in a Wapishana Indian, Lawrence Jacobs, to take charge of the children's education. Jacobs saw immediately what, in his view, was wrong with the system. These children were reading and writing in Wai Wai. It was true they were learning English, but they frittered away too much time on a language that not a soul in Georgetown or any civilized place spoke.

Once the missionaries had gone, he banned reading and writing in Wai Wai. Jacobs explained to the children that it was a worthless language. He said they should pity their parents for not knowing English, and be glad that when as students they became proficient in it they would be much more intelligent than the old people.

He observed that the children prayed. He taught that to be heard, their prayers had to be addressed to the Mother of God. But it soon became clear it was not his own practice; his effort shifted to lifting them from even a belief in God.

It was silly, he said, to place faith in God, to believe God's Paper, to be loyal to the church. He said their elders had been wrong to deny them the excitement of the old devil dances and the strong drink and good times that went along with them. Their mothers and fathers had done these things in their youth; why should this generation be denied such pleasure?

When a person died, he taught, that person's spirit hung closely over the village, so you'd better watch out. This frightened the children.

One afternoon, people walking by the school noticed

Jacobs out in front, tending a bonfire.

"What are you burning?" one of the passers-by asked him.

"The books the missionary left," he said with a degree of triumph.

"Ayrin's books!"

Ayrin had painstakingly written out reading primers and lesson guides and course contents for all the classes in the school. These had given stability to the teaching and were in themselves a means of learning for her corps of teachers. Word quickly spread through Kanashen that Mr. Jacobs was burning the work of her dedicated endeavor. A large crowd quickly gathered.

"Why do you burn the books?" someone asked Jacobs in faltering English.

"They contain words in the Wai Wai tongue," he said. He continued to feed the flames with new material and to stir the charred sheets at his feet.

Several objected, but dared not stop him.

"*Taa,* it's all right," assured a teacher who under Jacobs had quit his post. "Ayrin wrote her books two times. One set she carried with her when she told us goodbye."

It was not all right that Jacobs had burned the books, nor what he was teaching the children. One day many of the parents met in the umana and their discontent ran high.

"*Gicha!*" spat Elka. "He teaches the children differently. It is not what we want."

"It would be better for us to take the children away from here," offered one in attendance.

"True," they all said, and collectively sucked in their breaths in agreement.

From that day the entire population began thinking about a move out of Guyana. Even Elka believed the time had come for them to obey God rather than wicked men.

Some said they'd like to go to Anaua. This choice a few would be permitted, but not many; the ability of the land there to support them was still very much in question.

Others had an eye on the Trio villages. Those with Trio relatives would be the likely ones to go there.

What about the Cafuini, where once Wai Wai men had begun an airstrip? To this Elka said no. The main body should stick together; they'd move like the Israelites departing Egypt.

The Mapuera was a good land. That's where they would go.

From his youth Elka knew that river well. They would settle at a place above some rapids his people had called Howler Monkey Rocks. Below the white water was a long, straight stretch of river. Elka had heard of airplanes that landed on water. A water plane could land there, providing their link to the outside world. It would do until they could complete an airstrip.

At this point, no one could foretell how many cycles of the moon they'd experience before they left Guyana, or even if there might be several dawnings of the year before they would get away. For one thing, it was necessary to cut fields and plant them at the Mapuera. Elka, a thorough planner, chose a few reliable men to go before them and prepare the land.

"Tamokrana, Kumana, Kuruyeme, Wuruta, Charamcha." He called the names at church one Sunday. These with their families he was sending to the Mapuera.

Tamokrana was a valued work captain. He was part Hishkaryena and part Shedeu and once lived in the very area Elka had chosen for their new village. Kumana was a good man, one who walked close to God. He would be faithful in calling the men to prayer and in reading God's Paper to them each day before they worked. Kuruyeme, the young Shedeu, had shown spiritual maturing and leadership since coming to Guyana; he also knew how to work, and was a happy man—"the smiling one," they called him. Wuruta was dependable. Charamcha—little, wiry, steady, hardworking, enterprising Charamcha—there was no one Elka trusted more to get a job done and done right.

Before sending them off, Elka composed a letter he instructed Tamokrana to deliver to the chief of the Hishkaryena on the Nhamunda River two days or so overland from the Mapuera.

"My Brother," he wrote, "this is old Elka. I am coming to live near you. I would like your help. You know the Big Chiefs in Brazil, so please tell them we are coming some day. We are six hundred. I do not want to surprise them."

9

The pots she so carefully crafted broke. The lack of suitable clay around Anaua was as vexatious to Fehya as the infestation of cutter ants in his field was to Kirifaka. Sometimes a bowl just suddenly fell apart, spilling the drink so diligently made from chopping and grating and squeezing the cassava.

Cockroaches—big cockroaches, uncountable numbers of cockroaches—invaded clothes, hammocks, food. To escape them, Kirifaka thought of building another house. But there was no escape. Kirifaka, Fawtaw, and Mamichiwa kept busy trying to control the pests in the fields. Though sensing their efforts to be in vain, they almost daily poured acid drained from the cassava gratings around their young banana plants and canes of sugar.

Beyond where they worked, their expansive field of cassava looked as if no hungry caterpillar need waste time on it. The blazing sun had seared the new bushes, and if the rains held off much longer, probably not one of them would live. Never had a field given the trouble this one did. For one thing, after cutting the trees in the stunted jungle, the men were delayed in the burning. Too much rain. Deluges kept the wood wet and flooded large sections of the field. Then when the rains finally stopped and the burning took place, the limited growth natural to a savanna provided little wood ash for soil nourishment. After the planting, the drought set in. And all these voracious insects!

There were, as well, personal discomforts to be endured. Small clouds of gnats flitted everywhere, getting into hair and eyes and ears and ingested by mere breathing; the welts they raised on the skin were painful and easily became infected. Biting flies pestered. In wet seasons and before residual pools dried up, mosquitoes abounded. Clothes frayed. As the pants of men and boys wore thin, there was the thought of going back to loincloths. It would be a last resort; the Wai Wai now considered the loincloth and bead apron as coverings for primitive people.

All during the dry season new families were expected but none came over the trail, and when the rains returned they knew they could hope for no one because travel then would be nearly impossible. Then, unexpectedly, a woman known to them all suddenly appeared, flying in, and on the same day sixteen men arrived off the trail. Excitement lifted dolorous Anaua.

Achi arrived on the MAF plane, which, banned in Guyana, was able to service mission stations in Brazil. No sooner had the plane taken off again than the men from Kanashen showed up. Yakuta and Mawasha were among them, Yakuta coming to bring encouragement to the Anaua families and to lay the ground for other families, including his own, to move in permanently; Mawasha's purpose was to lead a group on to the Atrowari.

A contact with the Atrowari had been made a few months before. The Wai Wai learned the unpredictable tribe had moved closer, two or three days' journey up river, out of the path of the new road slicing through the jungle. The Wai Wai might not have happened on to this site but for an official of Funai, the government's Fundacao Nacional do Indio, who led them to the new Atrowari village. There the Atrowari were quite friendly, even the old chief, though as usual he and his men demanded trade goods and gave little in return. For most of a day Wai Wai and Atrowari worked alongside each other in the cutting of a field. As the sun lowered, the Funai official prepared to withdraw and, much to his astonishment, the Wai Wai said they'd stay.

"They'll kill you," he warned.

The Atrowari did not harm them. As a sociable gesture, their hosts showed the Wai Wai the spoil they had stripped from their latest Brazilian victims—clothes, shoes, pots, hammocks, an outboard motor, and drums of gasoline and oil. The oil they used to plaster down their hair. They preferred the cloth hammocks of the Brazilians to their own string-knit ones of which they said, as the Wai Wai also said of theirs, "They bite." The Atrowari confided that they had learned to shoot the Brazilians in the neck—"they die quicker that way."

That the Atrowari were capable of hitting their target was in no way doubted. They'd had a lot of practice. The Wai Wai had heard that for a boy to become a warrior he must kill someone. These initiation rites occurred every three years; supposedly, they were due this year. By harsh talk and menacing gestures the Atrowari clearly conveyed their intent to kill men like the Funai official who had been in the village that day. As best they could, the Wai Wai pleaded that they not do it.

And now once more, some months after this last visit, the temper of the Atrowari was to be tested. Mawasha hoped he could persuade some in the tribe to return with him and to remain at Anaua long enough for study of their language. With an eye to the trip, he observed the abilities of the men, many of them rather young, who had accompanied him over the trail from Guyana. Reluctantly, he judged them too unseasoned to go on to the Atrowari.

"I hear the Lord telling me not to go," he said to Bahm. The trip was not made.

They were to learn later that at about the time Mawasha would have arrived on the Alalau, the wilder ones there killed three workers at the Funai post and burned their houses. Once again, heaven had protected the Wai Wai from Atrowari wrath.

The men who came from Kanashen had brought letters from kin of the Anaua families. Rather than supportive, several of the letters only stirred the internal conflict of those who earnestly wished to make this spiritual outpost succeed, but who, at the same time, felt isolated in a hostile land. One letter, short and devoid of much-wanted news, said temptingly: "We hear you are suffering. Come home to Kanashen. Here there is plenty for everyone to eat."

Yakuta urged, "Don't go back. Stay." He buoyed the little group by promising to bring three more families, besides his own, over the mountains at the end of the next rainy season. This would double the size of the settlement, no doubt adding to the food problem but helping with the loneliness. With this prospect, spirits revived.

Then, suddenly for Kirifaka, anticipation dissolved into the cold reality of solitude. Bahm, Fawtaw, and the others left Anaua and would be gone for varying times. Only Kirifaka's family and Achi remained. Banishment from the group, the Indian's worst form of punishment, seemed their unhappy lot.

Weeks, perhaps months, would go by before other people came. And was there any reason in all the world why those who had experienced Anaua's desolation should want to return?

After the last ones had left, Kirifaka went inside his house, sank into his hammock, and sobbed for an hour. When able to speak again, he said to Fehya, "*Taa,* it's all right. It's all right if my field does not grow. My Father in the Sky will have some other way to provide for my family. Do you believe that, my dear one?"

Fehya, coming to stand next to her husband, sucked in her breath and faintly smiled.

"I cannot run away from this place because things are difficult, because we are alone," he said. "My Father has something of value to give me, something more valuable than a field of cassava and bananas."

Old William also sat in the shadows of the house. What was of greater value than a field of food for his grand-children, he could not imagine. But in his son-in-law dwelt a spirit akin to his own spirit. If anyone could succeed, surely it was the husband of his precious daughter. And to prove a certain degree of confidence in his own ability, Old William left the house and hobbled to the creek where he dipped water to pour on his promising banana plants.

In time, Fawtaw and Mamichiwa returned. Then another trial struck—severe sickness. Everyone, including Achi, fell to a strange malady that covered their bodies with a rash like that of measles and fever and chills akin to malaria. They became weak and few could leave their hammocks. Achi diagnosed it as dengue fever. Even after recovering from the virulent stage, the sufferers had no strength in their hands, and their wrists and ankles hurt for a long time.

The fever hit them during the heavy rains, a season that hardly needed augmentation of its dreary character. The rains continued past their normal ending. This delayed Yakuta's coming. When he would return with families no one could know. But when the rains finally did stop, visitors were not long in arriving at Anaua.

One day the Air Force deposited a squad of soldiers to practice jungle survival. A few mornings later a helicopter appeared to carry them away. That noisy bird, of course, drew everyone to the airstrip and had them talking long after it disappeared over the horizon. At noon the villagers scur-ried again to the landing field. An MAF flight brought Achi, Kirifaka, and his daughter Meesu back from the city of Boa Vista, where they had gone for medical work. No sooner did people sit down to their midday dinners than a government plane landed, and in taxiing got stuck in the runway's mud. The Wai Wai were still at the airstrip, tugging and straining at the mired plane, when yet another arrival burst an already great bubble of excitement—Yakuta, his family, and eleven other men strode in off the trail from Guyana.

"Eight families are coming more slowly in the path," Yakuta announced. It was safe to say that loneliness would no longer be one of the afflictions of Anaua.

The men who came fell to work immediately. Under Kirifaka's leadership they built houses from the materials afforded by the jungle, cut new fields out of the forest, cleared and burned them, and planted cassava, bananas, sweet potatoes, and sugar cane. They carved out a number of canoes from tall, straight trees that were simply called "canoe trees." They penetrated the forest deeply and brought home ample supplies of meat.

The women started their work when first the day dawned and kept at it until the sun hid itself behind the trees. The number of children had burgeoned. Little boys ran everywhere, shooting their diminutive arrows at targets which might be anything moving or stationary; the birds soon learned they had lost the clearing at Anaua for either nesting or resting. There were almost as many girls as boys, but their time was more structured than their brothers'; helping their mothers and toting around younger siblings absorbed much of each day. A school was started. To teaching her pupils reading and writing in Wai Wai, Achi added basic Portuguese, a language which she herself had begun to acquire between her service in Guyana and coming to Anaua.

The church that met under Bahm's house was soon to have a new structure. Other improvements evolved in the expanding village. Anaua's troubles, however, were not over. The cassava in the old fields had failed, the victim of drought and hungry insects. At great expense to the mission, farina had to be bought at a high price in Boa Vista and flown in to feed Anaua's families. Colds, always hard on Indians, sent a number of people to their hammocks. Yakuta, in particular, suffered; his persistent cough, fatigue, and weight loss were of concern to Achi.

The chance of spreading their colds to the Atrowari concerned the men who prepared for another trip to that tribe. They decided that only those could go who had completely recovered, and that if any were caught by a cold on the trail, all would turn back. Before they departed, Mamichiwa began sniffling. Only he and Fawtaw knew the trail to where the Atrowari now lived. Mamichiwa stayed behind; Fawtaw led the expedition to the Alalau River.

There they spent two days with the Atrowari. The meeting was generally friendly, though the Atrowari lacked the niceties usually associated with hosts. The Wai Wai tried to write down the words they heard; the Atrowari grabbed their pencils and ripped their papers. Fawtaw tried remembering the words, repeating them over and over to himself, then behind a tree furtively wrote them down. Invariably he was seen, and one Atrowari or another confiscated his paper and berated him for stealing their spirits.

The Wai Wai went hunting and on return the Atrowari ate all their meat. The Wai Wai prayed, and the Atrowari lifted their heads and pried open their eyes. The Atrowari lounged in their visitors' hammocks. As the Wai Wai prepared to leave for home, the Atrowari crowded in the canoe with them until it almost sank. The final encounter was an angry shove of the Wai Wai canoe into the current, which came close to upsetting it. Yet, as he thought back over their venture, Fawtaw believed their goals had been achieved: They'd lived through two whole days with the Atrowari, and perhaps they'd taken a few small steps toward lasting friendship.

At Anaua, the nine new families were settling in. One of the wives was unhappy, however, and wished to return to Guyana. Her complaint was not about the shortage of food or lack of a river or the ever-present roaches; what she missed was her mother and mother-in-law—she had no one to hold her baby. A man huffily walked off the job of building houses. In quarreling with another man he said he would work on his house alone. The others let him.

The cassava continued to do poorly and the mango trees and banana plants still did not grow well. Three days before Christmas, the women reported to Achi that no cassava was ready to be dug.

"I thought we had enough for another month," Achi said. "Why didn't you come sooner?"

The women merely raised their eyebrows. Until today, the supply had not run out. Achi had no more money to buy farina, but she radioed an order to Boa Vista. Before the food had a chance to arrive, one of the young wives dropped in on Achi to ask a favor. Kanahmachichi, the wife of the medical attendant Emehta, was as small as Fehya, Kirifaka's wife. She was big in one dimension now, though; she was well along in pregnancy. Her shortness made her middle appear all the more bulging. What she wanted stemmed from her condition.

"I'd kind of like to have some rice," she said.

"Rice? I asked God for farina," Achi said. Rice was not a customary food for the Wai Wai. Those who were familiar with it most likely had tasted it at a missionary's table. "I can't ask God for rice."

Kanahmachichi, swinging her feet as she perched on a chair, was plainly disappointed.

"I asked the Lord for farina," Achi repeated. "If you want rice, you'll have to ask Him for it yourself."

The day the cargo was unloaded from the MAF plane, one bag differed from the others. Achi couldn't believe it. She hadn't ordered it. She'd never mentioned it over the radio. Quickly, she went in search of Kanahmachichi.

"Little Sister," she called excitedly to the mother-to-be who with all the discomforts of her condition lay surprisingly quiet in her hammock. "Would you believe it! A bag of rice came!"

"I know," replied Kanahmachichi. "I asked God for it, didn't I?"

This year the Christmas celebration was quite subdued, but immediately afterward a new source of clay was discovered and the women became hopeful as they crafted new pots. Not long into the new year, Anaua received a Brazilian visitor who said he came on a special mission.

Gilberto Pinto, Funai's chief pacification officer, was charged with overcoming the Atrowari's repugnance of civilization. The men crowded into one of the houses to hear him. With Achi serving as interpreter, he asked them to work on the new highway that progressively was bisecting Atrowari country. It would be work they'd enjoy, and they would be paid in real money, he said. When needed, they would act as go-between on behalf of the government, a contact offering them sustained mingling with the people they'd targeted for friendship.

They listened politely, some recalling threats against Brazilians they themselves had heard directly from the Atrowari: Shoot Brazilians in the neck; they die more quickly that way. Their spokesman said they would not do as Gilberto asked.

The Brazilian believed Achi had misinterpreted his request. She repeated it. Again they said no. He urged her to influence them the other way. She relayed their position very precisely.

"They do not think it wise to approach the Atrowari with Brazilians until they become better acquainted and can speak at least a little of the language. If they go with you or anyone else in the government, they are afraid both you and they will be killed."

Gilberto was a confident man. For ten years his personal relationship with the Atrowari had been for the most part positive. He was used to getting Indians to do what he wanted. Some, like the Atrowari, took a little longer to come around. And these Wai Wai, he reasoned to himself, wouldn't resist his offer for ever.

The offer of payment in money may have tempted one or two, and the man's proposition did sound reasonable. But those who foresaw danger prevailed. Yet among them, the thought could not be entirely dismissed: If we don't work with him, might we lose our one big opportunity?

10

The village of Anaua received its name from the mountain that towered over it, but Kirifaka gave it other names, names which he insisted described it better.

Old Mud Hole.

Old Place Where the Cassava Doesn't Grow.

Old Place of the Mosquitoes.

Old Place of the Cockroaches.

The Place Where God Is.

What he said was true on every count. Conditions at Anaua were still bad. More families had moved in from Guyana, and while they boosted morale they also represented more stomachs to fill. But another long dry season and ravenous insects had once more destroyed the crop, necessitating the purchase of farina from outside until prospects would mount again almost a year hence. Malaria hit hard. The village creek and the Novo River some little hike away nearly dried up, leaving pools of stagnant water that bred mosquitoes. The people were so pestered that at one time they left their houses and camped for a while in the forest. In the village they killed three poisonous snakes within two weeks. School wasn't going well, or so Achi discovered the day she heard Mamichiwa, one of her teachers, pound into the heads of his pupils that one and one equaled three.

In the church, the preaching of the elders grew stale. During the last Christmas season when the turn came for each to speak, four elders used the same passage from the Gospel of Luke, each borrowing from the others for his treatment of it.

Yet, with so many people around now, the gloom of isolation had lifted. Frustrations, anxieties, fluctuating feelings remained, sometimes the level up, sometimes down. Nevertheless, people could now laugh, and they did—at themselves and at each other.

One day the men caught sound of a pack of bush hogs off in the forest. They grabbed their bows and arrows and hurried away in pursuit. One of the older men trailed the group; he found himself alone in the lead, however, when the pack suddenly reversed itself and headed straight toward him. He saw their huge, ugly tusks and did not doubt these vicious swine would tear him to shreds. He also caught sight of the low, overhanging branch of a tree. Just in time he seized it and pulled up his legs, scrunching himself tightly, barely out of the reach of the frenzied pigs. There he hung, his survival wrapped up in a dangling ball, until a hunter shot and killed one of the pigs and the others ran off among the trees.

For days after, the old fellow was teased unmercifully.

"A monkey, that's what he was," said one after another, and each fell into a ball and rolled around in the dirt while their audience roared with laughter.

Attaching animal traits to a particular person carried no malice and produced high spirits. A gabby woman might be called a chattering jay. They named one fellow The Trumpet Bird because of his long legs; the bird could not fly and went *oomp, oomp* when anyone came near, and this they said was Wisho. Once Bahm slipped in the mud and they labeled him a wild pig.

"He looked like a bush hog taking his bath," laughed one who saw him fall.

This passion for humor in the midst of their tribulations

indicated that Anaua was, indeed, The Place Where God Is. If a more "spiritual" signal were wanted, this year's observance of Easter would surely qualify.

In the afternoon the young people conducted a service in the new church building. A group of them had memorized the Resurrection chapter of Mark's Gospel and recited it while others read from the closing chapters of Luke and John. One read New Testament references to the Second Coming of Christ. The smaller children sang songs, and this was followed by a hymn sing for everyone. Then the entire congregation walked to the creek, where Kirifaka baptized his teenage daughter, Tukuwu, and his twelve-year-old son, Fanahruwi.

Gilberto Pinto did not return. Some time went by and they did not hear from him. Had he bowed to the adamant refusal of the Wai Wai to become his agents to the Atrowari? The Wai Wai chose not to join their mission to that of the government; this stand may have even fired their enthusiasm to make Jesus known to the Atrowari. Several young fellows came from Kanashen to team with men at Anaua for another expedition to the Alalau. The two most experienced leaders were unavailable, however, so they went on their way with a prayer and much bravado. At one of the rivers they crossed they searched for the canoe the last party had tied up for future use. They did not find it. The river was too swollen to cross without a canoe, so they returned to Anaua, disappointed and chastened.

Neither Yakuta nor Kirifaka had been able to go with them. Kirifaka had taken his family to visit relatives at Kanashen. He'd heard reports that Elka was planning to leave Guyana. Would he move to Anaua, to the Cafuini, or to some other place in Brazil? He intended to ask Elka.

Yakuta was removed from all activity. The cough and fatigue that clung to him turned out to be tuberculosis. Achi took him to a hospital in Boa Vista. After three months of treatment, he was back in the village, much improved but still a sick man. It was trying for this energetic Indian to lie in his hammock much of the day; some days he was tempted to rebel against the restraints of his convalescence.

"The leaves on the roof of your house have to be tied down? Well, you can't do it," Achi said. She urged Tarishi, his wife, to make him take care of himself. One day wild pigs ventured close to Anaua. Yakuta heard them, smelled them, the look of anticipation flooding his eyes. Tarishi put up her hand to halt even his thought of joining the hunt.

"You must not go," she said. "You don't have to prove you're a good hunter. Neither of us is strong. We both have to recognize it and be satisfied."

"If you obey," Achi told him, "you'll get well and some day do these things again."

Tarishi herself had been hospitalized, though no definite cause of her hemorrhaging and weakness was determined. Like Fehya, Kanahmachichi, Yoshwi, and one or two others, she had a noteworthy concern for the conditions, spiritual and otherwise, of the women of the tribe. Unlike many women, she was not afraid to speak up to a man, especially to correct one guilty of bad talk.

"Why are you talking this way?" she said reprovingly one day to a man who had made an off-color remark in her presence. "You should be thinking about God and know He's listening."

Yakuta valued his dear wife's constancy. He felt her to be the chief cause of his home's happiness. He knew she enjoyed teaching the women at their Friday meetings and the women appreciated her loving attention to their needs. Her belief in the God of heaven was intense. Though one or two persons had hinted at the time of her serious illness that she suffered from a curse, she would not let the thought pass the threshold of her mind.

In body Tarishi was weak, in spirit strong. She and Yakuta needed each other. For her sake, he was determined to get well.

Bahm and his family and Achi were away, but after long absence Ayrin came back among the Wai Wai. The day she left Kanashen, knowing the mission was closing, Irene Benson wondered why God had sent her to South America.

At the outset of her missionary service, she meant to go to Irian Jaya. No visa was forth-coming. Her sending board, Unevangelized Fields Mission, which became UFM International, said there was need for a teacher among the Wai Wai Indians of Guyana. She answered that call. Teaching children, conducting literacy classes for adults, instructing the women in sewing, doing whatever needed to be done, she scarcely had an idle moment. That is, until her forced withdrawal from Kanashen. She went to Belem, the Brazilian city at the mouth of the Amazon, to teach American children in the school for mission families. From time to time she received reports of the Wai Wai who had moved over the mountains to Anaua. She hoped she'd be called there to teach because working with the Wai Wai was her first love.

And here she was among them again. Oh, it was just a matter of months before she would leave them because after four years on the field her furlough was soon due. For whatever time she had, however, she thanked God, then set to work teaching seventeen pupils in three classes in a new school which had a leaf roof but no walls and through which the wind blew so strongly that it seemed likely to carry some of her smaller children away.

Planes flew in and out at the airstrip, a few of them getting mired in the soft spots on the runway. A government plane flipped over one day, and despite the first word flashed through the village that all inside were dead, the pilot and his passenger emerged with hardly a scratch. Another time Brigadier Camarâo's plane got stuck, and to free it required the push and pull of every boy and man, including doddering Old William, who came in from his banana patch to help. He was hit by the propeller blast and tumbled head over heels like a weed in the wind.

Various ones came and went over the trail to Guyana, among them Emehta, the medic, whose present aim was to go fetch certain of his relatives. His little wife, Kanahmachichi, would soon deliver. Her pregnancy had been very difficult, and now that she was about to give birth, the women attending her anticipated trouble.

Tarishi, Yakuta's wife, had gathered a few banana leaves from Old William's faltering grove. These she spread on the dirt floor of the house of her neighbor. In years gone by the Wai Wai built a leaf hut for birthing because they feared the spirits hovering about would curse anyone who slept next to where a new life had been dropped. Harboring no such fear now, the women delivered in their own homes. Tarishi wiped Kanahmachichi's fevered head, spoke reassuringly to her as the pains rose and when the time arrived helped her out of her hammock and onto the carpet of banana leaves. She cried with her, too, when the baby was born dead.

Leaving her momentarily to the care of others, Tarishi ran to get her husband. Yakuta, himself spent by illness, got out of his hammock and crossed to the house of his neighbors, entered and picked up the lifeless little body. He started to speak words of comfort to the distraught Kanahmachichi, but gazing through tears at the tiny thing he broke down and wept. In a birth hut many years before he had been picked up from the banana leaves, alive, of course, but only because of the courage of his brother. Elka had defied his malevolent step-father by demanding his brother be picked up off the ground. Had he not done so, someone would have gathered up the newborn's lifeless body, its head crushed by the club in the angry man's hand.

Yakuta gently carried the little form to the edge of the village and there dug its miniature grave. He thought of Emehta. How sad he would be when he returned. He listened to the sobs of the people who had heard of the death and now were crowding into the house to console the grief-stricken mother. There was sadness here today, real sadness, but not the despair that death had once foisted on them all.

What he was hearing were cries of love and compassion, expressions of understanding and solace. The Wai Wai had their problems, the people quarreled sometimes and gossiped and engaged in petty spats. But there was something deep inside them that bound them together. Once children were valued for the security they would some day provide in a parent's old age; now even a baby born dead mattered. The Spirit of God, nesting in the pits of their stomachs, had made all the difference.

Mistokin, Bahm's brother Neill, flew in for a few days. He commended the Wai Wai for their wisdom to separate their visits to the Atrowari from those of government men. Their objectives differed. They should not be mixed. He told them, "Without question, your decision saved your lives. Gilberto Pinto is dead."

Just a few days before, the Atrowari had killed this experienced, confident Indian pacifier, along with his two companions. The ten years of his acquaintance with them, what he supposed was friendship, appeared to mean nothing to his executioners. Neill said it was Atrowari practice that when killing several people at one time, they cut off the head of their chief victim, obviously to vent their displeasure over something they connected him to.

They cut off Gilberto's head and sliced his body into many small pieces.

The three latest prey were the third group slain by the Atrowari in three months. Some may have been killed by the Waymiri branch of the tribe, perhaps angry not to receive their fair share of trade goods bestowed by the Brazilian road builders. Or, possibly, the Atrowari meant to demonstrate to men with big machines and terrible fire power that they still exercised superiority in their homeland.

Road construction would continue, Neill reported. Crews were now to be guarded by heavily armed troops. Should the Wai Wai continue their contacts? He'd leave it up to them.

"If you go, consider your timing," he said. "And watch

out for the soldiers. They're jumpy. They're young city fellows and they think every Indian is a savage out to kill them, so they're going to shoot first. Furthermore, they don't know an Atrowari from a Wai Wai."

Yakuta mustered his strength to speak.

"God told Joseph and Mary when it was safe to take the baby Jesus back to their home from Egypt, and He will tell us when the time is right to go to the Atrowari."

Another of the men spoke up.

"If God wants me to die in order to reach the Atrowari, I'm ready to give my life."

He may have spoken for others, and probably did, but the consensus was that before launching another trip they should wait until Kirifaka returned from Kanashen. With Yakuta unable to travel, Kirifaka would be the best one to lead them—if, indeed, they were to go.

Kirifaka returned home, only to be confronted by a number of problems. Yakuta was recovering from his tuberculosis, but still had to forgo most activity. For the time being, Kirifaka would have to carry the load of leadership. It was a big load.

A man and a woman admitted their adultery; there was church discipline to administer. A fractious man had to be dealt with; he was one to spread rumors and even lies and sulked when he should have been working with others. With new people arriving from Guyana, some houses were far overcrowded; work programs were needed to ease the situation. The cassava that was being dug was very small, the supply still far short of feeding the nearly one hundred persons now living at Anaua. And just as demanding in time and energy, a search had to be started for a new site for the village.

But priority of priorities was the planned trip to the Atrowari.

The decision to go at this time of Atrowari wrath was not made lightly. The people met in prayer for a day. Funai officers and mission leaders in Boa Vista were contacted and their counsel sought. There were discussions in church as to who should go. Kirifaka picked his team carefully, three of the six being veterans of earlier trips.

The first day in Atrowari territory they came upon a large house, like their own umana. It was empty. Surrounded by good fields, palm groves, and the sites of many old fires, it was at the center of several converging paths. The men went down all the trails and found no one. As the sun reached the edge of the world they turned toward their camp on a bank of the Alalau.

"*Hnnnnn* . . . Where shall we go to look for these people?" they asked themselves. "We don't know where they are."

As they lay in their hammocks at dusk they prayed, "*Ahfah,* you'll have to show us. We've come all this way. Shall we go someplace else? Back to the house we saw today? We're waiting for you to tell us."

The answer came in the morning. They paddled upriver a way and examined several paths. Then they discovered an obviously old and well-worn trail. People had been on it recently. A banana plant was freshly cut, unrotted fruit strewed the way. They followed it a long distance. At one point they felt compelled to pray again.

"Father in the Sky, we're asking you to please protect us. People may be waiting up ahead to ambush us. Help us not to come across a large group of men ready to fight. Let it be one man or a group of women. Not fighting men."

Their prayer finished, they continued on. Soon three women bobbed up in the path, walking toward them. One turned and ran, the other two continued to advance.

"Wai Wai!" shouted one. The woman had been present when Wai Wai visited before.

"*Kiriwanhi, kiriwanhi*, good, good!" called the men. The women then jabbered, and the only word the Wai Wai recognized was *maaraye*, good. Like parrots, Kirifaka and his team shouted it repetitiously, hoping to keep the women calm.

The women seemed unafraid. They turned around and, walking leisurely, led the Wai Wai to a clearing and a house. Still no Atrowari, except the two women. Did others run off to warn the men that people had come?

Someone suggested they spend the night in this house. Kirifaka said no. They would be safer in their own camp down the path on the far side of the river. They retraced their steps.

As they worked on building leaf shelters for the night, a dozen or so Atrowari men, all armed with bows and arrows, suddenly burst into view at the river's end of the trail.

"Maaraye, maaraye!" the Atrowari on one side shouted.

"Kiriwanhi, kiriwanhi!" returned the Wai Wai on the other.

Kirifaka paddled over to them, and they piled in his canoe to cross over. At first it was difficult to know whether they were angry or trying to be friendly. They spoke gruffly, snatched at Wai Wai possessions. They wrapped their arms around Kirifaka and his men and *gicha!* some kissed them like men kissed their wives. They demanded farina and Kirifaka's gun. The Wai Wai stood firm; these they would not give. The Atrowari yelled like mad men.

"Maybe they said *gicha!* in their tongue when we didn't let them have everything," one of the Wai Wai said after the wild ones had finally quieted and retired over the river.

"They walk in the forest like cats," said Emehta.

"Kofi! how scary! They'll come in the night and kill us in our hammocks."

"Kofi!" Others took up the cry.

Kirifaka sought to calm their panic. "God can protect us—if He wants to."

The next morning the Atrowari came again. This time they invited the Wai Wai to their house to eat. As both groups walked the path, Kirifaka hoped to allay fears by joking, "The smoked tapir we gave them last night, do you suppose that will be our breakfast?"

Only four Wai Wai had come; three stayed at the camp

ready to escape and report to the wives at Anaua if, indeed, the Atrowari lived up to their reputation as killers. The four were not certain how they would fare. In the house, they saw clothing and other items that quite evidently were trophies of recent conquests. The Wai Wai's tapir was put out on woven platters for their meal. Drink was provided. Kirifaka wondered if they might be killed while they ate. He had heard older ones say that is what the Wai Wai did one day long ago to men who invaded the forest in search of rubber. On that occasion there were two pots of drink. To one fish poison had been added. The hosts were careful as to which pot was passed to whom.

After eating their own tapir and downing the starch drink, the Wai Wai were offered sugar cane. When they failed to recognize the Atrowari word for it, their hosts cut each cane into short lengths and peeled them, as a father would do for his very small children.

"We're stupid, they think," Kirifaka said to Emehta. "Until we can speak their language, I guess we are."

The meal finished, Kirifaka and his friends said they would leave. Surprisingly, the Atrowari let them go, showing no interest in either keeping them or accompanying them down the path to the river. At the camp, the canoe was already packed. For ten days they traveled north, anticipation growing each day closer to home. Then, without warning, five Atrowari men appeared out of nowhere. They just popped up in the path. They appeared neither friendly nor hostile, acting as if they had been expected to suddenly appear for the purpose of accompanying the Wai Wai to their homes.

Once over their start, the Wai Wai were glad they had come. Were prayers about to be answered? For the first time Atrowari would be escorted back to Anaua and language work could begin in earnest. After gaining an understanding of their talk, they'd teach the Atrowari about God. Wasn't this what many had prayed for over a long, long time? Wasn't it for this that more than a score of men had made these dangerous journeys, only to find their contacts

abruptly ended by menacing threats and acts of belligerence? Had the Atrowari come around to want friendship?
Yet, in Kirifaka's head throbbed a troubling thought: *Our
people—are they ready to deal with a rough bunch of men
who demand everything they see?*

That night the two groups hung their hammocks near each
other at the edge of a jungle clearing.

"This night we die," ventured one of the Wai Wai ruefully.
"We won't get through the night."

They did, though. All the next day until dusk, the
Atrowari amicably walked the trail with the Wai Wai. Then,
as daylight fled, the Atrowari turned around and went back
the way they had come—just as quickly as they had
appeared the day before.

"Why did they follow us when we didn't know they were
close on our heels?" Kirifaka asked himself. "Did they want
to spy out the path to our village so they can come some
time when we are not expecting them? Why did they show
themselves but not go all the way? If just one more day . . ."

He walked sad that last day, and remained dispirited on
arriving home.

"Five times we have met the Atrowari," Kirifaka said in a
solitary lament. "This last time it seemed they would come
to our homes. We need to learn their talk so we can tell them
that Jesus cares about them. If only they had come with us
one more day!"

"*Ahfah*, Father!" he cried in a desperate prayer. "We've
done all we know how to do. We've risked our lives. We've
given away our possessions. We've endured humiliation.
What else can we do?"

Ayrin thought she had an answer for Kirifaka; not her
answer, but in a passage she'd read once in her quiet time, a
line from Oswald Chambers' devotional book, *My Utmost
for His Highest*: "One of the greatest strains in life is the
strain of waiting for God."

11

Bahm and Ferochi did not return to Anaua from their 1974 furlough; his aging mother in America required their care. Though it pained them to detach themselves from the Wai Wai, Bahm in time discovered that his translation progressed more rapidly now that he was spared the daily interruptions of life in a Wai Wai village.

The two had left the Wai Wai for short periods before, but always there was a day they could be counted on to return. Now their absence was felt at Anaua. Sixteen families lived in the village. Most were there purposely to fulfill a mission to the Atrowari. A few had come over the mountains to be with relatives. They all shared the lacks of Anaua, notably insufficient fields and no control over the roaches, aphids, and other insects that made living miserable.

Kirifaka and a young nephew one day canoed down the Novo River to look for a new site for fields. After paddling half the morning, they came upon an area they felt would not only afford better planting, but make good home plots as well. The moon went through its cycles only a few times before several houses were built there near the river's edge. Yakuta and Kirifaka were among those with a house at the new location but who kept a dwelling at Anaua as well, mainly to be handy to the airstrip and its frequent visitors. The people would come to call their new place Yawko— meaning leaf-cutter ants, because they found these hungry vegetarians rampant. If ants were the chief drawback, how much better Yawko over Anaua. Ants might be managed, stamped out—literally.

Elka made the arduous trip over the mountains from Guyana to visit his brother. He had received word of Yakuta's illness and for that reason wanted to see him. He also came to share with his brother his plans for moving to the Mapuera River, where as boys they had lived.

Their talks together were long and unrestrained. In leaving Guyana, Elka would give up his government salary. That was all right, he said. He had come to understand that some things were more valuable than possessions. Yakuta quietly rejoiced to see his brother again obeying God and enjoying his companionship with Jesus. Elka expressed his love for the Atrowari. There were others, too, on his list of tribes to be sought out and told that Jesus was missing them, the Arara for one. Other than their being on the far side of the Amazon, no one knew just where they lived. Another were the Karafou who wandered somewhere in the dense forest, perhaps to be found up or down one of the rivers the Wai Wai in their travels had crossed.

Elka's oldest son, Kurunaw, with him on this visit, was enthralled by the Karafou. Yakuta assured Elka that he, too, thought much about these people, who perhaps were their lost relatives.

"We must find them before they become dying ones," Elka said. The move to the Mapuera would reflect this compulsion to reach them with the message of God. According to the chief's calculations, locating on the Mapuera should place them near the Karafou.

Elka said he wished to see Brigadier Camarâo, whom he'd known as a colonel when the Wai Wai built the Cafuini airstrip years earlier. He asked Ayrin to contact him on the radio and say that old Elka would kind of like to see the brigadier. He wanted to seek his permission for the Wai Wai to settle on the Mapuera.

"I want to know who is living in our territory," he explained, "so I think the Brazilian chief would want to know who is living in his."

Ayrin said she couldn't radio the brigadier.

"You mean you can't, or don't want to, Younger Sister?" Elka asked.

"A little of both. I'm not one who talks with generals. Besides, our radio doesn't reach as far as Belem where Brigadier Camarâo lives."

"Then will you pray for the brigadier to come?" From experience he knew prayer reached vastly farther.

She prayed, with her fingers figuratively crossed.

"God," she said, "if you want the man to come, you will have to arrange it."

The sun rose and set several times and no general showed. It came down to the day before Elka was to return to Guyana. On her radio Ayrin caught a conversation between a passing Air Force plane and another which apparently was carrying Brigadier Camarâo.

"He'll fly over our heads on his way to Boa Vista," Ayrin reported. Elka's face lit up.

"I didn't say he is to land here."

"Oh, he will."

And the brigadier did land. He had come to drop off two guns he once had promised the men at Anaua. Among those out to welcome Camarâo was Rod Lewis, the chairman for UFM missions among Indian tribes in north Brazil, who had been visiting for a couple of days. Lewis, a convincing sort of man, pressed Irene into serving as interpreter between the Portuguese of the Air Force chief and Elka's Wai Wai. She protested; her Portuguese wasn't good enough. She knew Wai Wai very well, Lewis rebutted, and said she would do fine.

They stood on the edge of the runway, surrounded by curious adults and children, all eager to share in the excitement that visitors generated. The brigadier, handsome as ever in his carefully trimmed mustache, neatly pressed uniform, and true military bearing, began to reminisce with Elka about their days at the Cafuini. Then, through Ayrin, Elka said he had something to ask the general.

"Well, here I am," Camarâo said. "Ask it."

"God brought you here in answer to prayer," Elka began.

"Well," the brigadier said, arching his brows a bit, "if I am here because God brought me, maybe you'd better tell me what you think God wants me to do."

"You are an important man," Elka continued, not pausing to judge whether Camarâo's remark was slight sarcasm. "Many people respect you, some fear you. There are some people you fear."

The interpreter blanched. She wondered where this conversation was going.

"I'm talking of Indians," Elka went on. "You know there are good Indians and bad Indians. They know not all Brazilians are good men, but those in uniform we've seen are good."

The brigadier straightened a bit, and his short stature seemed to heighten by a few millimeters.

"But the Indians should not go about killing the Brazilians who are not good. I, too, used to be afraid of those Indians who kill. I am not afraid of them now. I have Jesus in me and He makes me not afraid. Now, I know you want to make peace among the Indians, the ones who are not peaceful. I and my people can help you in this. Will it be all right with you if we move to the Mapuera and build our village there, so we can make friends with unfriendly Indians and help those who kill to stop killing?"

Elka said he had already sent a few families to cut and plant fields at the Mapuera, and a hundred folk perhaps were sort of camping there and awaiting the rest of the people from Guyana. Hearing the chosen location was on the Mapuera, Camarâo frowned. He said it was an area of the Amazon forest that the government had selected for

"advancements." Wouldn't they be much better off to move
to the Cafuini?

Elka replied that any of his people who wanted to go the
Cafuini could—he'd put it to them—but God had called him
to the Mapuera, and there was where he wanted to live.

"This is an important matter," the general said. "It can't
be decided out here on this airstrip. You come with me to
Belem for a day or so."

"He can't go," blurted Ayrin, who for the moment forgot
her role was that of interpreting the speech of other people.
In saying this, her Portuguese was confidently clear.

"And why can't he go?" Camarâo, turning to her, asked
sharply.

"He's from Guyana."

"How'd he get here?"

"He walked across."

"I'll bring him back here and he can walk back across."

"He can't go."

"Why not?"

"He'll need an interpreter."

"You can interpret."

"I can't go."

"And why not?"

"My visa. It expires in a few weeks and I have to be out
of the country. I've got things to do for the school before I
leave."

"I'll have you back here in a few days."

"I have no clothes here." The blouse she wore was held
together by a safety pin.

"We'll be stopping in Boa Vista to pick up my son."

"She has clothes there," Rod Lewis interjected, canceling
another of her impossibilities.

"Good. You can get them while we're at the airport."

"Just get on the plane, Irene." Lewis was convincing.

Four from Anaua flew with the general, who became
relaxed and friendly. Besides Elka and Ayrin, Elka's son
Kurunaw and a trusted work captain, Tamokrana, made the
trip.

They flew to the upper reaches of the Mapuera, then followed it south. As they kept to the river below them, Elka and Tamokrana pointed out with considerable animation the features they recognized from their boyhood—the rock where they killed a giant anaconda, the pool in which they used to poison fish, Old Bead Stream, a small tributary to the Mapuera that had been named for the beads of a man who drowned in it; the man was soon forgotten, but the beads that sank with him were not. Features not evident to Ayrin and the brigadier were plainly visible to these Indians, even though of the Indians only Elka had ever before looked down from an airplane.

Soon they approached a bend where huge rocks split the river into foaming channels. New houses and fields spread out alongside the rapids. The plane dipped low over the embryonic village, the brigadier observing the ripening fruit of Elka's determination to settle on the Mapuera. All in the plane saw the hysterical waving of the people below, their necks stretched back, their faces heavenward, as they looked at the first sky canoe to buzz this remote corner of the earth.

In Belem, the general extended many kindnesses to his guests. He arranged health checks for the Wai Wai men, sent someone to take them shopping. Irene he invited to his son's welcome-home party, and one day invited the entire group to lunch at headquarters. There they discussed various places where the Wai Wai might settle in north Brazil, but came to no decision. Then suddenly Camarâo was called south. It would be five weeks before he returned to fly the men and Irene back to Anaua.

During their stay in Belem, it was a question of which stamped the deeper imprint, the city on the Wai Wai or they on the city.

Young Kurunaw wrote down some of his impressions. "The Amazon," he penned, "is REALLY BIG!" In describing the plane's night approach to Belem, he said that in seeing the lights below he wondered if someone had stirred up coals of fires all over the village. The scene was a huge campfire; would the pilot set them down in the middle of it? Tamokrana was sure they'd all die in the process.

In the city stores they encountered "lots of people . . . lots of pants and dresses." "We went to a very tall building; from the top the people down below looked like ants." On the ground again, he gaped up at the building. "People on top there think I will fit into their pockets, but I won't."

The elevator fascinated the three Wai Wai men.

"You go into a small room and the door shuts. Then you blink a few times and the door opens. But you step out to something different. You have to remember not to walk outside. It's a long way to the ground."

They found it difficult to cross the streets. Elka and his son had been in Georgetown, and there bicycles made up much of the traffic. In Belem the cars never let up. They hesitated to leave their quarters without an escort; they could travel day after day through the forest without difficulty, but in the city they feared they'd lose their way. "I was like a newly caught pet bird taken from the nest. I didn't know my new surroundings."

Ayrin guided them through the zoo. The animals they loved, but wondered why no one shot the tapir for dinner. They showed interest in the animals strange to them, but gave greatest attention to the creatures of their own forest. Ayrin took them to a number of churches. Eight times Elka testified to his faith in Jesus Christ. Kurunaw continued in his journal:

"We told the people that we love God. We were not able to understand what they said. I thought to myself, 'This is the way we are here on earth, but someday we will all speak the same language in heaven.' It makes me want to go to heaven!"

One of the churches was Japanese. There the Wai Wai saw people they deemed akin to themselves. The Japanese, the three men agreed, were *tawtaw*, real people. They meant they could pass as Indians.

During her free time, Irene asked for a six-month

extension of her visa and got it, something that had worried her because in Boa Vista her request had been denied.

The brigadier returned and flew Irene and the Wai Wai out as he promised. En route they touched down at the small town of Cachoeira do Porteira where the Mapuera flowed into the Trombetas. There Camarâo switched to a helicopter and took Elka and Irene with him on a side trip to the Howler Monkey Rocks on the Mapuera. He gave Elka's new village his nod of approval. In coming years the government would dedicate a sizable region surrounding it as an indigenous reservation, an appellation meant to immunize the area from the nation's "advancements."

12

Elka returned to Guyana only to hear that he was to be deposed as chief of the Wai Wai.

"Who is saying that?" he asked those pressing around him as he walked the sunny path from the port to his house in Yaka Yaka.

"Oh, you know, people are saying it. People—*ha tu.*"

"Mingeddi. It's Mingeddi. He says you are no longer to be chief," said another, more precise in his information.

Elka leaned his canoe paddle against the wall of his house, went inside, dropped the owchi from his back and greeted his wife, who had awaited his coming. He smiled in the semi-darkness of the house, a smile of relief that the long journey from Anaua was over and that if the source of discontent was Mingeddi, well, that was to be expected and nothing new to worry about. Mingeddi, everybody knew, wanted to be chief himself. He had no following, however, and even the government wouldn't be foolish enough to bestow leadership upon him if there was no one to obey him.

Conversation with his wife soon caught Elka up with the new pressures that were building against the Wai Wai here in Guyana. Ahmuri said much of this hounding was directed straight at him. Over the next few days he heard from various ones that the Guyanese officials would hold him prisoner if he attempted to move from Guyana. But he had made up his mind. He would go, and he knew if he went, probably as many as six hundred Indians on the Essequibo would go with him.

Attractive promises were now mingled with the threats.

"What do you want? Is there something I can ask the government for that will be of help to the people here?" The solicitous inquiry came from Lawrence Jacobs, the teacher, who just a while back had made disgruntled villagers out of the owners of the dogs he had killed. He said Elka must not leave now; the electric light plant he once sought was being shipped.

"It's too late," Elka replied. "We lived without it all this time; we can get along without it in the days ahead. I've decided. I cannot stay."

It was not only the tribulations in Guyana that made Elka firm in his resolve to move to Brazil. The call from God to seek out lost and dying Indians in the vast rain forest sounded loudly and he was committed to obey.

"It's the missionary in Brazil who has brought discontent to these people," the officials said in Georgetown as they considered the possibility that Guyana would lose many of its Indians. At least that is what the people heard from a representative of the prime minister who visited Kanashen.

"Your Bahm says, 'Come across the border and I'll meet you.'"

"He can't meet us," objected one of the Wai Wai. "He's gone to his home in America."

"Well, he's a thief. He's stealing Guyana's Indians."

It was not Bahm calling, but God, Elka assured his people.

A new administrator replaced James Calder. In the eyes of the elders, the new man lived loosely, and agreement spread widely that he set a bad example for the young people. He had an explosive temper. Fortunately, in quite universal opinion, he remained out of Wai Wai territory for weeks on end. Police, however, had been sent in. Their orders were to permit no one to leave with either a child or a gun.

The government was thought to be afraid that a gun taken across any of its borders would become a gun used against it by subversives. Practically every family owned at least one shotgun. In more trusting times the government had donated a few, but largely men had worked hard and long on the airstrip or some other project to earn their weapons. Giving them up would come hard.

The people argued strongly that Mr. Burnham, the prime minister, had said all who were born in Brazil were free to return there, and that included most of the adults. And who in their right mind would force them to leave their children behind? Who would feed, clothe, and house nearly two hundred children if not their own families? The policemen on the scene were willing to negotiate.

"Your children are in school," the officers said. "Leave them here to learn and you can take your guns." They assumed a man might be willing to abandon his children, but certainly not his gun. In answer, the Wai Wai lined up to turn in their guns.

The fire-power would be missed in hunting, but to a man the Wai Wai agreed that bows and arrows could still be used, and until in Brazil they gained guns again, the age-old method of shooting pigs and monkeys would do just fine.

Just where they were to go was now a settled matter, but for some time the topic had been energetically debated. When Kirifaka visited Guyana with his family on his well-deserved "furlough," the destination of the people was an important part of his talk with Elka.

"Uncle," said Kirifaka as they took seats in the rear of the church at Yaka Yaka, out of the path of village traffic, "am I hearing your plans right?"

Elka sucked in his breath. "You heard right."

"Then what are we doing at Anaua? Are we to be there by ourselves? We went over there because you told us to, and now you are going some place else."

"I kept back angry ones from your village, rash ones with no thought for tomorrow's food, men and women who were not walking with God. If you are unhappy, return here."

"*Hnnnnn* . . . I don't like that idea. I don't want to come back here to live. We will stay where we are. Maybe we will have more contacts with the Atrowari."

"You be there. I'll go where I'm going. Whoever in the world can know, maybe some day we will make a trail between our two villages."

"So you will not move to Anaua?"

"I asked you to look for where we might raise our village. In your letter—you remember your letter carried by Mamichiwa—you wrote that you walked around and nowhere did you find that the fields grow well. A small group is all right. Many people, no.

"From your village the Atrowari can be reached," Elka concluded. "From mine on the Mapuera we can search for the Karafou."

Mawasha, the quiet one, once wished to move to the Mapuera, but Elka at the time said he should not. He also thought of joining the companions of Jesus among the Hishkaryena on the Nhamunda River, but did not. Noncombative in nature, he came to feel he could weather the storms that Kanashen produced; thus he would stay when others moved away.

For the time, however, he was leaving the village. The Trio in Surinam had sent an invitation for the Wai Wai to join them in a special study of God's Paper. Older men and women were reminded of the shim-shim, a string tied with knots that one village used to send to another in issuing a call to come drink and dance. Every day the recipients untied a knot, until none was left. On that day they hit the trail. Mawasha was educated in dates and months and so did not need a shim-shim to send him on his way, but in anticipation he counted the days until the gathering would convene. It was to be an event unlike any in memory. Some five hundred Indians from four countries were expected. Kron was to teach, and there would be a jubilant *onahari-heh!* of once warring tribes. Mawasha and the eight Wai Wai who went with him were not disappointed. On their return home they enthusiastically recounted their experiences of making friends with believers from a half-dozen tribes, bush Negroes and young people from Surinam's capital city on the coast. The Trio, they said, planned to repeat the conference every year.

Then the tali-tali locust sang and the dawning of the year rolled around. With Guyana's dry season firmly in place, the time had arrived for The Exodus.

"Let us be like the Israelites," Elka said in church the Sunday before the planned departure. His congregation shouted *"Kiriwanhi!"* and clapped loudly.

"Let us be ones who walk the trail together. How did the Israelites travel? God went before them in a cloud, and at night He lit a fire above their heads. He cut the trail cleanly so they knew the way to go. He will lead us. Let us trust Him as we ride the rivers and walk over the mountains."

In the final days there, the light plant was flown in from Georgetown, as Mr. Jacobs promised. But, as Elka had already said, it was too late. How long would it sit by the airstrip where it was unloaded before it rusted and did no one any good?

Not everyone would be leaving, it was true.

"God has not told me to go from this place," Mawasha said, and others also evidently had not received marching orders either. Perhaps a hundred persons had elected to stay in Guyana. But from every village on the Essequibo people gathered at the ports of Kanashen and Yaka Yaka to begin the trip. In the crowds at the river were some who were temporarily staying. They had chosen to stake their future on Anaua, and would leave for there some days later.

"The land we came from lies over the mountains," Elka said to the group assembled at his village. "It is right that we go back there."

As the first of the emigrants started loading canoes, a couple of police officers rushed to the Yaka Yaka port. They accosted Elka.

"Your children are not allowed to go," one said severely.

"This is my son," Elka said, bringing forward a young man taller than he. "He is not an infant. He can answer for himself."

"I'm going with my father," Kurunaw said coolly.

"If you stay you will be made chief. You will have the salary of your father."

"No, I don't want my father's salary. He still is chief."

"The prime minister wants you to stay."

"Sir," Kurunaw said in the best English that he remembered from his school days, "I have been taught to obey people in authority. I do not want to talk bad to you or about you. But God's authority is higher than any man's. I feel He wants me to leave, to scour the forest for people who have never heard the name of Jesus. With respect, I will leave, and my sisters and brothers with me."

"All right," the officers said. This resolution too much for them, they felt they had to exhibit some mastery of their calling. "Go," they ordered. "Go today. Go now!"

This Kurunaw did. Those traveling with him shoved off, not pausing to bake bread nor to collect further possessions.

Elka's leaving was not to be so quick.

The policeman's hat and stick that had once been given to him as a symbol of authority he returned to the officers. The badge he kept; what Indian didn't like a shiny star to pin on his shirt? He was ready to go, but he couldn't leave. Where was his canoe? None knew that Mingeddi had taken it down stream and hid it from even the keenest-eyed river traveler. Why would Mingeddi wish to prevent Elka's departure, unless to please the authorities who figured that Elka would not leave without his canoe and its outboard motor? If Elka did not go, few others would. But he did leave and The Exodus was massive but orderly, the parade of canoes impressive.

Tamokrana and his family brought up the rear. He had to await his wife's return from the hospital in Georgetown. Loading his family's canoes with food for the trip and personal possessions, including a half-dozen chickens that were to be the basis of a flock at their new home, he took his family upstream a short way from Kanashen so their wait would be out of the reach of Georgetown's constabulary. The law, however, reached them even there.

Tamokrana had earned the respect of all who knew him. He and Machfu had raised three sons on hard work, honesty, love and prayer, and the boys, now married, had for their generation begun building Christian homes. There was a younger son, Ichoto, in his mid-teens, still under Tamokrana's roof—or today, out in the forest along the river under his jungle tent made of sapling poles and palm leaves. It was Ichoto who was the object of police concern, according to the informants who hastily paddled up from Kanashen.

"He stole from the government's man, *ha tu*, they say," the messengers breathlessly announced on reaching Tamokrana's campsite.

"What do they say he stole?" asked Tamokrana.

"We don't know. We have not heard."

Tamokrana, never one to tolerate the pettiest of filching among his sons, questioned Ichoto to the point that he was convinced his son had done nothing wrong.

"Will they grab us and put chains on our arms?" asked Ichoto. He was frightened.

"The ones they accuse, they take to Georgetown and throw them in a room and forget they are there," said a knowing one among those who had come to warn the family. "You must flee up the river out of the reach of the police."

"We will not run," Tamokrana said. "God will protect us."

That day two police officers motored upstream to Tamokrana's camp. Racing some distance behind were several canoes filled with curious and worried Wai Wai. On beaching their craft, the officers approached the waiting party at the edge of the camp.

"Tamokrana?" queried one of the policemen. "Who is Tamokrana?"

Tamokrana stepped forward. "I am Tamokrana."

He turned to his son and directed him to talk to the men in English, which Ichoto spoke quite well, having been an attentive student in school.

"You have not left Guyana yet?" one of the officers asked politely.

"No," replied Tamokrana. "My wife is in Georgetown. She was sick. Can you tell me when the sky canoe will bring her to us?"

They did not know. Soon, though, they thought. Would Tamokrana travel after his wife joined them? He said he would. The exchange of pleasantries continued for a good while. Then with one officer engaging the group in light-hearted banter, the other melted away into the shadow of the trees.

As the talkative policeman edged toward his boat at the river, the activity of his partner came to light. In the bottom of the craft lay a large sack, and sticking out of it were the trussed feet of Tamokrana's chickens.

In all the talk, not a word was said about thievery.

Had an eagle peered through the cover of trees sheltering the mountains where many rivers began, it would have seen for days on end a gigantic snake steadily advancing along the trail, a snake turning as the trail turned, rising up and dipping down according to the lay of the land, gliding through freshets, bumping over fallen trees, stopping now and then to rest, the pauses in the forward motion coming frequently as in each day the sun mounted higher and sent its rays to steam the shadowy domain of the forest. It would have marked this undulating creature as having four hundred moving parts, each an individual but together all making up a whole, bunched in fat nodules in some places, strained thin in others. The procession of The Exodus gained headway every day. Not without difficulties, but of course they were to be expected.

After several days, the group naturally parceled itself into single-file segments, more or less according to families and with varying spaces between. Those in the rear enjoyed an advantage. They slept in the turkey-tail shelters built and used a night or two earlier by the ones leading the migration. A ready-made roof now and then was perhaps the only prize to be collected on this long, exhausting trek. Families with young children, especially their women, found the going extremely hard. Kuhku, wife of Forosha, one of Tamokrana's sons, sometimes carried a baby on her back while she carried another in her belly. Out of necessity, Forosha shifted their younger child to her when the legs of their five-year-old son gave out, and the boy, grabbing his father's hair and hanging on tightly, then rode atop his father's bulging owchi, which was to say all the family's possessions. The only difference between this young family and others equally heavily laden was Kuhku's advanced pregnancy. Whether delivery would await their destination was of great concern every single day to Forosha.

Forosha was especially tender toward Kuhku. She was the only girl he had ever loved. A quiet, soft-spoken youth, a bit too heavy for his height, though his full, round face embedding black diamond eyes won him friends easily, he had waited patiently to get his wife; he wanted to take no risk of losing her.

Kuhku was only about twelve when Forosha, a couple of years into his teens, began to notice her. He sent her a letter by a friend.

"I think about you a lot," he wrote in the secret missive. "Do you think about me?"

"I think about you a little," she replied in another clandestine note. "Let me have some time to think how much I think about you."

Time she was given, but not another letter nor any form of

communication by her admirer. They were keeping to tribal custom, which permitted familiarity between boys and girls only to those within a clan and who therefore were ineligible to marry one another. The two would not speak to each other until there was consent all around for their marriage. In those first years of sad silence, Forosha all but gave up hope of gaining his desired one.

In due time he approached Kuhku's father. He gave his approval; her mother did not. She did not want him as a son-in-law. Kuhku's grandmother did not want him, either. People were quick to remind Forosha that Kuhku was reserved for the husband of a relative who had died in childbirth.

"I don't want to be his wife," Kuhku protested. "I don't think he's a companion of Jesus."

Kuhku was one of the youngest baptized believers. Her parents' faith was nominal, at best; her mother, especially, found her daughter's reasoning too puzzling to understand.

"You are next in line to take your cousin's place," her mother reminded.

Kuhku did not pout nor nag. To this point she had never gone against her mother's will, and she wasn't sure she could now. She did, however, quietly but persistently press her claim for marrying Forosha. All this time he walked sad, doubting the outcome, not knowing for sure that Kuhku even wanted him. One day he approached Bahm.

"What am I to do?" he pleaded.

"Go home and pray," Bahm advised. "Be willing to accept whatever God has for you."

He went home and prayed. Kuhku kept on talking to her mother.

"*Taa,* all right," her mother said. "You think you know better than I. It's your decision. Go ahead and marry the old young thing."

A few days later, Kuhku walked with a group of girls on the path from Kanashen to Yaka Yaka. Forosha happened to trail them, and catching sight of Kuhku, overtook them. Not attempting to break the community code by speaking to her privately, he asked in front of the group, "What are you thinking?"

"I want to marry you," she replied.

"I want you, too."

She hinted he should call on her mother. He did and got the answer he had long hoped for but had almost given up.

Forosha would not have subjected his wife to this hazardous trip were there a choice. Since there was not, he prayed that his Father who had given him his wife would now protect her in the rigors of walking and climbing and wading through streams. A woman up ahead died, and the news passed back was quite unnerving. She was old, however, and succumbed to the fever that sooner or later hit them all. Some children were sick, it was reported from front to back along the line. Forosha prayed all the harder. It would take two full cycles of the moon for this entire journey; he had a lot more praying to do.

They rolled up their hammocks, gathered their pots, packed everything back into their owchies and started on their way before the sun appeared. By the time it rode overhead, the heat was causing children to cry and women to implore that the pace be slackened. All were ready for the halt when it came in mid-afternoon. Stopping did not mean rest. The men hurriedly constructed leaf shelters, then fanned out through the forest to look for game. The women dug edible roots and started their cooking fires. Some had come away from Guyana without much bread. But even those well-supplied had by this time served the last of what they brought. For many meals a spider monkey, an armadillo, perhaps a bush turkey, was all they had. Whenever the hunters brought in a lot of meat, the surplus was smoked and a full pouch tied onto owchies as a welcome addition to the loads.

Before starting out on Sundays and Wednesdays, the travelers met together for worship and study, much as they had done in their home villages, except that here on the trail they were divided into smaller clusters. Elka led services for his section; Kuruyeme, the smiling one who was also gaining recognition as a "coming one," led his. So did Tamokrana and others. Every night, after the work was finally done, all up and down the line families or groups of families sat around their fires singing the hymns that had become so much a part of their lives.

At the headwaters of the Mapuera, where the river was nothing more than a narrow, shallow creek, the party was met by advance men from the new village who had brought a few canoes. They, of course, were far from enough, so for many days The Exodus paused, like the Israelites encamped in the wilderness. The men felled tall, straight trees and out of them carved new canoes. Stragglers came into camp. Sickness flared up. Whooping cough had been carried from Guyana by a few. It now spread widely. A two-year-old girl died. Would they never reach their new home? And what would they find when they got there?

At first, voyaging downstream was a pleasant contrast to the hard walk over the mountains. Tree branches met over the narrow watercourse and provided shade. Gradually, the banks moved farther apart and the water ran more deeply and swiftly. Mothers fearing for restless youngsters held on to them as best they could. Where possible, the helmsmen steered their craft near the shoreline, taking advantage of whatever shade that existed. Also ever thinking of how to meet family food needs, the men paddling kept a sharp eye out for birds and monkeys in the bordering trees and for alligators and haimara, the river's biggest fish, in the quieter waters out of the current.

Few of the people could count so far as to number the rapids they had to navigate, they were so many, but none presented danger to compare to the peril encountered at Wakri Rapids, which men who knew those things said sat directly on an imaginary line that circled the earth and was called the equator. In this cataract, the river's biggest and most treacherous, one of the canoes was battered and sank.

No human was lost, but a dog drowned. Food and knives went to the bottom. The little that was rescued was, of course, soaked.

Just after this experience, an old man died. Like the elderly woman who succumbed earlier on the trip, he fell victim to the chills and fever of malaria. Three deaths on the trail. In the old days death was the ultimate fear and if it struck as they traveled, they halted in the trail; if they did not turn and go back to where they started, they at least changed their destination. Today, despite the heaviness that death still brought, they pressed on toward Howler Monkey Rocks. The old-timers said it lay just a day or two ahead.

Forosha brightened. His confidence grew that Kuhku would make it.

The fields at Howler Monkey Rocks looked pitifully small, particularly to people coming off the trail hungry, tired, and half of them sick. Kumana and Charamcha, who jointly got this village started—the first as spiritual leader and the other as work captain—warmly greeted the flood of newcomers. Those with relatives in the advance work party crowded into their homes. The rest took to temporary leaf huts. Food and shelter were urgent priorities. The men first burned and planted a field already cut, then began cutting new fields in the forest. The work was organized by Elka, who soon proved his leadership was just as effective in Brazil as it had been in Guyana. Had Achi been there to take a census, she would have counted close to six hundred people, the four hundred who started The Exodus, perhaps a hundred stragglers who caught up to them, and another hundred who made up the advance party. It would be no easy trick to settle such a large number in one place peacefully and safely and with basic needs fulfilled.

Some the chief assigned to prepare the fields. Others he sent to a village of their friends, the Hishkaryena, two or three days' distance overland, to bring back cassava sticks for planting. The rest he put to work building permanent housing.

The houses they built here differed from those they had known in Guyana. Elongated with rounded ends, they divided into rooms more handily than the spherical houses of Kanashen and Yaka Yaka. The roofs were of the same palm leaves, but the walls had mud brick between the staves. This material was plentiful here.

The people worked together harmoniously, whatever the job. On one day a week they all dropped whatever else they were doing to join in the common task of constructing a new church. A small house near the river in which God was worshiped by the advance team could accommodate only a fraction of the people now, so until the new building was completed, services were held out of doors.

Amid new houses, new fields, and a new church came one day a new life. Kuhku gave birth to a baby boy, whom she and Forosha named Saramaw, the Wai Wai pronunciation of Solomon. The parents continued a recent trend in the naming of children. Instead of sticking by tradition to names of long-dead relatives, families now honored living kin or friends, or borrowed names from God's Paper. Running around Howler Monkey Rocks were Saromi, Saara, Ruhtu, Neyomi, Samyu, and Ishmew.

Cassava from the fields lasted one month. Brigadier General Camarâo averted disaster by sending in a plane, which alighted on the straight stretch of the river just below the rapids, the seaplane run foreseen by Elka. The Wai Wai unloaded twenty large sacks of farina. No one had to be reminded to waste nothing. Whether meal from the sack or undersized tubers dug prematurely from the ground, the staple was guarded as if it were a hunter's one remaining arrow.

The whooping cough of the trail had hardly diminished when malaria struck heavily. Even the young and healthy fell desperately ill. The government sent in a medical team, and a nurse remained in the village after the doctor left. The nurse, however, was a timid man and seemed afraid to prescribe treatment. Often when he got around to dispensing his

pills or giving a shot, it was too late. Ten children died.
Sickness hitting almost every home slowed development of
the village. Some wondered why in Guyana they had not
been dying ones, but here they were. Of course, there was a
time when the Katwena, fresh from Brazil, asked why in
Guyana death had claimed their leaders. The Katwena for a
while had thought to turn from God, but did not and some
strong companions of Jesus developed among them. Now a
few families bemoaned their present fate, not blaming God
so much as the Brazilian Air Force. The brigadier was transferred out of the region and the medical visits and shipments
of farina ceased. A few families had found it so much easier
to eat out of a sack than to dig in the ground for food.
Without that largess they were lost.

One man discovered a substitute for cassava. From his
youth in this area he remembered a wild root his people
called malia. It was big, almost the size of a pig, and the
most edible grew deep in the forest, away from streams.
Women searching for it stuck their long knives deep into the
ground in place after place before coming on it. Then find-
ing their object at last, they dug and tugged until they got it
out of the dirt. Carving it up, they carried it home in small
pieces in their owchies and there began the long process of
making it safe for consumption.

Like cassava, its juice contained a fatal acid that had to be
separated from the starch fluid. Ten times a woman would
water the starch, let it settle and then pour the toxin off the
top. When once cleansed, the starch was used for drink or to
make bread, both products far inferior to those of cassava.
Neither the bread nor drink would keep for more than a day.

Malia would have been despised had it not been so timely
in filling a very pressing need. It would get the people over a
period of insufficient fields; they looked on it as manna from
heaven—good to have, but willing enough to give it up.

Time, faith, prayer, and a little medicine got them over the
scourge of sickness. Additional houses were completed. A
whole clan living huddled together under one roof could

now separate into families; older persons recalled the beginning of family privacy when Elka moved his wife and children out of the communal house at Yaka Yaka and into his own home. Walls within the new houses were a further step in propriety.

Kurunaw, Elka's oldest son and an elder of the church, settled in his house on the Mapuera. But he vowed his stay here would not be for long. There were small rivers and creeks that flowed into the Mapuera. Up one of them, he was convinced, lived the Karafou. One of these days, when this Mapuera village was firmly established, he would take his family and paddle up one of those streams. Somewhere on its banks he would make his home. Anyone who wanted to could move there with him, just as long as they shared his vision of taking the message of God to wandering, fearful people.

Many at Howler Monkey Rocks were glad to settle down, hoping they were to stay put for the rest of their lives. So far what they had here did not equal the life they had enjoyed in Guyana. They lacked their food of choice, they had no sure source of medicine, and their children were without a teacher.

But, here, at least, they did have their freedom.

13

Yawko continued to develop as a replacement for the village of Anaua, which Kirifaka also called Old Mud Hole, Old Place of the Bloodsuckers, Old Place of Many Vexations. Set on a clean bank of the Novo River, Yawko from Anaua was an hour by trail, then an hour by canoe. It was preferred for its water advantages as well as its better soil for raising cassava. Kirifaka now spent much of his time there, and so did Yakuta—until one day he coughed up blood and Achi hustled him back to the hospital in Boa Vista for treatment of his recurring tuberculosis.

Others coughed and spat and vomited; Achi diagnosed the epidemic as whooping cough, brought over the mountains from Kanashen. She stuck the sick ones, mostly children, with her shiny thorn, blunting the problem. When finally it had largely passed, the people were eager to get on with tending their fields at Yawko or building houses there, or, for eight men, another trip to contact the Atrowari.

Mamichiwa perhaps could not add one and one to get a correct answer, but he was an expert in leading the way to the Atrowari. He and his team hit the trail just as the coughing cropped up again, this time, it appeared, from colds.

"If colds catch your men on the trail, turn back," Kirifaka

instructed Mamichiwa. "You remember we heard that's a reason the Atrowari kill people—the ones who bring them sickness."

Following a different route, the Wai Wai this time paddled down the Novo until it emptied into the Anaua River, and went further down that stream until it was crossed by the new highway. There they left their canoes for a ride on a truck that took them to where the trail to the Atrowari villages began. After speaking in his limited Portuguese to the soldiers there, one of the Wai Wai named the day they expected to reappear. Otherwise, they were informed, an Indian emerging from the forest likely would be shot and only afterward found not to be an Atrowari. Currently, the situation was that bad.

The first day the Wai Wai came across an empty house. It was evident the Atrowari had moved deeper into the forest. Two days later they discovered a new village. People were there, all right. They immediately surrounded the visitors, demanding all their beads. The following day Mamichiwa and his men returned to the village. The old chief, absent before, sat in front of the big house, engrossed in making arrow points. Those who were seeing him for the second or third time thought he looked all the more stern and mean-tempered. At their coming he had not looked up. Mamichiwa stepped forward and laid a knife in his lap. He continued to concentrate on his work. Another Wai Wai wrapped a string of beads around his neck. He gave no acknowledgment. A third placed a basket at his knee. All the time the Atrowari said to their chief, "*Maaraye*, Wai Wai; *Maaraye*, Wai Wai." He appeared to be deaf.

However, he was not. In his own good time he looked up and forced a faint smile on his wrinkled face.

"*Maaraye*, Wai Wai," he said. He got to his feet, dropped his arrow points into the gift basket and motioned in the direction from which the Wai Wai had come. Deciphering his gestures and commands, the Wai Wai realized he meant to go home with them—now.

The long-legged chief was a swift traveler; despite his being old, the Wai Wai and six Atrowari had almost to run to keep up with him on the trail. The trip to the Novo had some tense moments, one occurring as the group cautiously approached the highway and the military guard post with its trigger-happy soldiers. Others cropped up daily as on the trail or in overnight camp the Atrowari became easily angered and made incessant demands.

At the highway bridge over the Anaua River, from which point the journey would be completed by canoe, Mamichiwa moved fast to avert certain trouble. Some Brazilians waited at the bridge for a bus; the Atrowari began rummaging through their baggage, demanding everything that matched their tastes.

"Let's get them out of here right now," said a harried Mamichiwa to his men.

Just short of Yawko the Wai Wai said they should all stop and bathe in the river. The hot sun had made them sweaty. They might have said the Atrowari were very dirty, for these Indians who chose to live far from a river seldom washed. The Wai Wai gave each of the Atrowari a pair of short pants to replace the leafy belt that rode on their hips. As they paddled to within sight of Yawko, the Atrowari began to tremble. Was it the unfamiliar coolness of the water or fright? Whoever in the world could tell? The Wai Wai also trembled—from the excitement of soon to be hosting the first Atrowari visit!

Once settled on their haunches in a house at Yawko, the fear, if that is what had caused the visitors to shake like a leaf in a wind, disappeared. As the women served them food and starch drink, the Atrowari boldly grabbed at the beads the women wore, insisting on having them. They accepted as some kind of rightful homage the knives brought by the Yawko men. All but the old chief walked around from house to house, sticking their heads in at doorways, looking always for beads and knives. Later, touring the fields they dug some banana plants to take home with them. The chief, meanwhile, had settled his imposing frame on a tiny stool, and sat impassively for most of the day.

Chief Comprido, capricious to the core, let his men roam as they would, mingle with the Wai Wai as much as they pleased. He had not always been of this temper, and no doubt would again set them on a bellicose course. Without his perversity, the Wai Wai reasoned, who could tell how much further their evangelizing might have progressed?

At dawn the next day the Atrowari packed up to go home. Kirifaka suggested they wait until a bag of farina could be brought from Anaua. No, they said, they'd go now. They would leave without drinking the palm fruit juice the women of the village had hurriedly prepared. Comprido insisted on going, and that is all that mattered. People ran to their homes to grab bananas and sweet potatoes and what little farina they happened to have on hand. Though the Atrowari might go with baskets bulging with beads and knives and axes, the Wai Wai couldn't let them leave on empty stomachs. Their coming had, after all, been an object of hope for seven years, this first brief visit an answer to earnest prayer.

"Why do you go away so quickly?" Kirifaka asked.

"Wives and children," came the reply. They intended to go get them. One man walked to a spot at the edge of the village and there said he would build his house.

Uneasiness filled the minds of the Wai Wai who gathered to watch the Atrowari leave. Their unspoken fear found voice in Achi.

"Whooping cough," she said. "We have it again. And the Atrowari walked right into it."

Should the Atrowari carry whooping cough back to their susceptible village, the result could be frightening. But Achi's fears were somewhat allayed by a passage in Malachi's prophecy that she'd read the day they arrived: "And they shall be mine, saith the Lord of hosts, in that day when I make up my jewels . . ."

Suddenly without warning, four months later at the height of the rainy season when Indians seldom traveled, eleven Atrowari men led by Comprido burst from the forest through the back door, so to speak, of the Wai Wai settlement at Yawko. Their open belligerence, topped by the tall, stern, surly chief, thoroughly frightened the two Wai Wai families, father and son, living at Yawko at the time. The father slipped away, stealthily hurrying off to Anaua to give the alarm. He could only hope his family would be alive when he'd return late in the night.

Yawko lay at the end of the trail the Atrowari had followed. Anaua was two hours upland by river and trail, closer all overland, except that no direct path had yet been cut. The surprise arrival occurred on a Sunday. If the old man made good time, he'd reach Anaua as the sun started to sink, probably catch people lingering at the church after a service of hymn singing.

At Yawko, the son and his wife and mother did their best to feed the hungry Atrowari and to show them where to hang their hammocks. In surprising time, the elderly fellow returned, Kirifaka and several men from Anaua with him. Early the next morning they escorted the Atrowari to Anaua. Before they arrived, the Wai Wai had had enough time to hide their valuables in the forest.

For some little while the Atrowari danced around the village, chanting something unintelligible to the Wai Wai. Yakuta, home again from the hospital and seemingly much improved, teamed with Kirifaka to quiet their visitors and to get them seated in front of one of the houses. The women brought cassava bread and starch drink. The Atrowari grabbed at their skirts, lifting them. Did Wai Wai women wear bead aprons underneath? Such items the Atrowari were determined to take back to their own women.

With the one good eye she possessed, Yoshwi, Kirifaka's old aunt, squinted at these ruffians. They were unlike any men she had ever come upon—not like the Katwena, nor the Shedeu, though when those two tribes first appeared at

Kanashen she had thought them coarse. Atrowari talk was loud and gruff. *Kofi!* How scary! They had everyone on edge. Nobody knew whether they were for the moment angry or whether they lived in a continual state of agitation.

The men mimicked the behavior of their chief. When Comprido ate, they ate. When he made threatening remarks, they parroted those remarks. He was now ready to trade in somewhat a reasonable manner. His men offered their many steel-tipped arrows.

Knives—the Atrowari wanted knives. So eager to get a long knife, one of the men reaching for one carelessly dropped it. It sliced into his foot.

To Achi for treatment! Like the wave in a wind-blown field, the entire group surged to Achi's clinic. To their admiration, she stopped the bleeding, bathed and bandaged his foot. She could only pray that the filth that had surrounded the wound had not already brought on infection, and that the shot she was about to inject in his seat would not bring on a vengeful attack.

She asked the Atrowari if there had been a lot of coughing in their village after the last contact. By a shake of their heads, they said no, there had not been. The Wai Wai shared her relief. From her things, Achi dug out a girl's bead apron and presented it to the chief.

The white woman was good, the Atrowari said. For her service or her gift? Whoever in the world could guess their thinking?

Before clearing the clinic and shutting her door, Achi said through sign language, "Next time, bring your wives and children."

In an aside, Kirifaka whispered, "If they try to sell you their arrows, buy them. Maybe you have no use for them. Buy them anyway. We want to get rid of them."

From the clinic, Kirifaka called the visitors to the church. He got them seated and began teaching them a song. They liked it. That it spoke of the God who created them and longed so much to take away their sin and lift them to heaven was, without question, a meaning incomprehensible to them. But catching on to the tune, they sang mightily. Not necessarily the tune Kirifaka and the other Wai Wai jammed into the small church sang, but sing they did. Raucous, in eleven different keys, they bellowed out the Wai Wai words and when they ran down in the end they shouted *Maaraye! Maaraye!"*

Next they were taken to the fields to cut sugar cane for their sweet tooth. Then with much of the day still before them, they became restless. The ultimate purpose of their visit soon became very clear. The Atrowari had come this long, long way for more than beads and knives.

"That young woman," one of them said, pointing to a teen-age girl half-hiding in the doorway of her home. The rakish set of his lips spoke precisely to his purpose. He talked with Yakuta, who shook his head decisively.

"That plump one with the baby," indicated another, rolling his eyes and grinning lasciviously.

To each Yakuta said no and shook his head to emphasize his denial.

Women! Wai Wai women. The clamor grew. Each Atrowari now shouted out his demand that he be given the woman of his choice. Young girls, pregnant women—would any wife or daughter escape the rising lust that suddenly had enveloped the village? How long until these wild ones stopped asking and in all directions began raiding the Wai Wai homes, perhaps killing the men to get at the ones they wanted? Every Wai Wai man was aware of the danger, but there was no certainty their defenses would be a match for the hot blood of these brutal warriors.

"Sing! Sing! *Maaraye!"* Kirifaka shouted, and others helped him herd the Atrowari into the church. As they moved toward it, Yakuta quickly passed word for every woman and girl to run to the forest.

In the church the singing began anew. Louder. Louder. It mattered little how loud or how careless with the melody they sang. Under the circumstances, their utterances must have been an acceptable noise to the Lord. One more time! A new song to learn. Made up on the spot, it consisted of the one Atrowari word the Wai Wai knew that they knew, *"Maaraye."* Everybody sing! Again. And again. And again.

Everybody did sing—the Wai Wai to urge the Atrowari on, to steer the single-minded Atrowari from the wrong focus; the Atrowari because it was fun. They sang until "sung out." Drained of the exuberance that had posed so much danger, the Atrowari emerged from the church subdued, but hungry. The men gave them food and a sack of farina for the homeward journey, which the Atrowari said they would start in the morning.

Came dawn, however, the visitors decided to stay. They were too tired to travel and "Cutfoot," as the injured youth came to be known, said he could not walk. Two of the men accepted an invitation to go hunting. The others opted to spend the day in the village. Four of their number became aggressively hostile. Cutfoot, one of the four, asked to be taken to Yakuta's house. Yakuta refused. Cutfoot held a knife to Yakuta's face. Yakuta, who needed no further tension, agreed to his demand. But first he sent word for his daughters to flee.

At the clinic, Achi stuck Cutfoot again with her shiny needle. One of the men accompanying him grabbed a pen out of Achi's fingers and snatched a bottle containing an antibiotic off a table. Saying nothing, she simply sent him a long, hard stare. He handed back the pen. For the medicine, she pantomimed a hurting stomach, and he turned over that booty. To save him some face, she gave him an old pen and a tiny bottle of aspirin. If he swallowed all the pills, she said to herself, he'll get a stomach ache, but it won't kill him.

Later, more than one Atrowari with suspect motive sought entry at Achi's door.

"Come away," a Wai Wai said to one trying to open the door. "Achi is resting."

"She's not in her house," another said. At the urging of the Wai Wai, Achi left her house for the greater security of an anonymous dwelling. The Wai Wai were determined to protect their Big Sister from any kind of mischief.

Kirifaka felt the consequence of Atrowari displeasure. Not forgetting that an immediate goal in the contact with these people was the learning of their language, he wrote down as many of their words as he could catch. One who saw him writing gave him a telling blow on the head.

The hunters returned, and food seemed to pacify spirits as well as appetites. That second day and another night were somehow got through. Early the following morning there was another rousing "sing" and then Kirifaka, glad for the encounter but left weary by it, led the Atrowari to Yawko to pick up the trail to home.

As the canoes pulled into the port, several Atrowari men jumped out and dashed into a house. They came out carrying arrows they had stowed there. They ran to a field behind the village. Returning without the arrows, they announced they were still tired and would stay the night at Yawko.

"*Taa*, all right," said Kirifaka, knowing it was useless to argue. He went off to check on one of his fields. When he came back, all but two of the Atrowari had vanished. Comprido rose to depart. He said he would come again, but the trail was long and so would not bring his wife. Which wife was not clear; the people here had been informed he had three wives, some said five.

After the last two Atrowari started on the trail, Kirifaka left for Anaua. During that night he wondered whether he should not have stayed there. Even over the distance the incessant barking of the dogs at Yawko could be heard in Anaua. Yakuta heard them. Unable to sleep, he vowed to send a couple of men at the light of day to investigate the disturbance. Before dawn broke, however, Anaua was to learn why the dogs barked so continuously.

The younger of the two families living at Yawko stayed alone that night, but discovered they were not alone. From the shadows came whispered voices, and suddenly from nearby in the forest the piercing cry known by all Indians as the "kill" call. They rushed back to Anaua, and in the darkest hours calling Kirifaka from his house related their fears.

"The wild ones. They do not walk the trail to home."

"*Kofi!* How scary! Stay here tonight. We will keep watch."

Why had the Atrowari not returned home? Were they still intent on capturing Wai Wai women—and would they kill Wai Wai men to get them? For two days the Wai Wai had stood against their demands, and the Atrowari had been known to kill to satisfy lesser desires. That these crafty men had kept back a stash of arrows and later hid them in a field certainly showed their duplicity—likely, duplicity with a purpose. Anaua could expect a sneak attack. Unquestionably there were enough defenders to trade arrow for arrow until no assailant remained alive, and use of their guns would make short work of their attackers. But is that what the Wai Wai wanted? They were probably the only people who had not retaliated against Atrowari aggression. They had to keep it that way. More important than their own lives was the winning of these people to Christ. It would be very difficult to tell a dead man that God loved him.

At daybreak men went from Anaua to Yawko, searched in a wide arc around the settlement. They found no one, only traces that people had been there. Someone had stacked bunches of bananas and left them. Food scraps were scattered here and there. Several Wai Wai slept that night at Yawko. In their continuing search the next day one of them happened onto a new-cut trail and an empty campsite. That it had been vacated was perhaps an assuring sign.

But once again the Atrowari revealed they had not left the area. When for a few minutes no Wai Wai was in the settlement, they stole back into Yawko and ransacked the houses there. When this became known at Anaua, it was feared the Atrowari would return, bent on rape and killing. Everyone, it was decided, should take to the forest until the Atrowari indeed were gone. A bad back prevented her from running, so Achi was to fly out to Boa Vista.

Their stay in the forest was brief. In a day or so Kirifaka used Achi's radio to contact Boa Vista. Men with dogs had scouted the area, he reported. Some distance down the trail they found abandoned leaf shelters. All believed the Atrowari were gone, but had they gone far?

And when might these dangerous ones come back?

Boa Vista advised that the women and children be relocated to a place nearly a day's paddling downstream. There, much more than either at Yawko or at Anaua, they'd be safe from surprise attack. The men could tend their fields knowing their families were beyond reach. The plan was agreed on. The entire population loaded into the canoes and embarked.

Nearing this new campsite, two of the canoes struck submerged logs and sank. Instead of seeing in this an omen of evil, as in years past they would have, they merely collected the people from the water and whatever goods they could salvage and went on to the landing. It was, they declared, the place of God's choosing for today. It might, they thought as they explored the site, even become their permanent home. Situated on the river and a long distance from the Atrowari trail, it protected them from sneak attack. From here the men could work their fields upstream and meet the MAF plane on its monthly landings at Anaua. Here, if the soil were favorable, they could concentrate future fields. And if they found a long, flat stretch, a new airstrip could be built.

They called the place Kashmi, Electric Eel, after a creek so named because once one of those obnoxious, but good-eating, creatures had been caught here. They'd resettle here once assured it was The Place Where God Is.

Achi would commute to Anaua from Boa Vista once a month, at least as long as farina had to be flown in to make up for the local shortage of cassava. She would stay a few days or many, depending on the health needs of the people. She did this, and once for three weeks slept in a hammock in

Kirifaka's house; for it her back suffered great misery. Something had to be done. If there was an Atrowari raid, she could not run to the forest with the Wai Wai, yet it might be just such an occasion that medical aid would be most needed. The young men she had trained at Kanashen were now grown and had fields to tend and meat to hunt if their families were to be fed. She looked over today's youth and picked two fellows, one of them Fanahruwi, as most likely to make good medics. Fanahruwi was of a strong will, but to this point had no real purpose to his life; now he did. Achi took him and his fellow trainee out to Boa Vista for instruction, then seasoned them in another tribe before sending them home to be her surrogates.

They were still considering Kashmi as an alternative to both Anaua and Yawko when Kron arrived for a ten-day visit in which he would teach extensively from God's Paper. Bahm had planned a trip from his home in the United States, but fell sick. Coming in his place, Claude Leavitt flew from his mission station among the Trio in Surinam to Manaus, and from there rode a bus over the new highway, practically retracing in reverse the trek he and the Wai Wai had made eight years before when they walked some four hundred miles through primordial jungle.

The Wai Wai were elated to see Kron again. Hunting and fishing with him, sitting under his teaching, it was like the old days. Accompanying Yakuta and others to Kashmi, he helped them pick out a suitable site for an airstrip. That just about settled things. With promising fields, a river and the potential for an airstrip, there was nothing now to hold back their move to the new place. Nothing, that is, but a basic decision yet to be made concerning the Atrowari.

Would they ever calm the wild ones enough to learn their language so they could then tell them about Jesus, which they were convinced would bring an end to Atrowari hostility?

"We have tried and tried," Kirifaka said one day. "All they want is to kill us and take our women! How are we to reach them?"

"*Ahfah*," he prayed, "what about Comprido? Their chief is a hindrance. What will you do about him? Will you take him out of the way?"

One thing was sure. Reaching the Atrowari would not be done with the help of soldiers. More than a few in the city had suggested military aid. To this the Wai Wai quickly said no. You don't win friends by joining their foes. Protection would have to come from the Lord.

A morning of prayer was called. After literally crying to God for guidance, the people decided to remain in the area for another year or two, giving, as they said, time for God to work.

The Atrowari, everyone knew, could return at will. The prayers of ten years had kept the Wai Wai from falling prey to the murderous bent of these bloodthirsty Indians. What of the future? Even with the greater distance from the trail that Kashmi would afford, there still was danger. Having smelled blood in their recent visit, might not these wild men spill it the next time and then be free to glut their desire for Wai Wai women?

There was no question that the Wai Wai had endangered their lives by initiating contact with the Atrowari. That first entry into their village by Yakuta and his six men had started a spiral. Each time it spun around the likelihood heightened that "something" would happen. Yet, whoever in the world had ever suggested that sharing the news about God came without risk?

14

"Three men arrived today from Kanashen. Others are bringing a very sick woman over the trail."

This message Kirifaka radioed to Achi in Boa Vista. She replied she'd come as soon as a plane could fly her in. She got there before her patient and immediately sent Fanahruwi with medicines and food to intercept the party on the trail. In a few days the travelers showed up, fifty-seven of them—ten families.

All were weak and very hungry.

At Kanashen, after the departure of Elka's large group and later scores of stragglers for the Mapuera in Brazil, these ten families kept alive their intention of moving to Anaua to join Kirifaka and Yakuta. For some time they did nothing to achieve their aim. Like the Children of Israel, they were content to dwell in the wilderness but long for the Promised Land. Anticipation of the by-and-by fogged the necessity of the here-and-now. They planted no fields; when ready to move, they were already undernourished and had very little food to take with them.

A Wai Wai named Sheshwa was their leader. After Elka left, he became semi-chief of all the people remaining in the

Essequibo villages. He did not like cutting and planting fields, perhaps explaining why those influenced by him found it easy to forgo this work this past season. Always on the verge of leaving Guyana, Sheshwa finally decided to go when his wife became ill. Her only hope of getting well, he was convinced, lay in taking her to Achi.

The government officer learned of his decision. He went to Sheshwa and talked sharply.

"You cannot leave Guyana," the official said. "No more are allowed to go. If you try to take your wife to the missionary in Brazil I will arrest you. I will throw you in jail."

This threat alarmed Sheshwa. He feared the government's jail. He had heard of the jail in which Mingeddi was confined over the murder of the women and children years before. He wanted no part of it. Yet, he worried about his wife. She was so sick, and no one but Achi and her wonderful needle could cure her. If not the most ambitious and best leader among the Wai Wai, Sheshwa did have an inventive mind. He thought of a way to clear the border, to get help for his ailing wife, to fulfill his group's intention to move, and at the same time avoid landing in the much-feared jail.

One pitch-black night after most of the villagers had long since gone to sleep, the government official and the policemen among them, a number of people stole from their houses with the utmost quiet, their arms filled with pots and mats, bows and arrows, hammocks and other valuables, and made their way surreptitiously to the high clay bank of the river. Letting themselves down noiselessly to the water's edge, they packed three big canoes. Back and forth they went until all was ready. Then they carried their sleeping children to the port. Dogs barked, of course, but who here in secure Guyana paid attention to any but the most uncommon yipping of these creatures?

Silently they cast off—ten families, including Sheshwa and his sick wife. Not until far up the river did they stop to hang their hammocks by the water's edge and sleep away the little time remaining until dawn.

The food shortage at Anaua was thought to be over, then the new families arrived. Until more fields could be cleared and planted and their cassava and sweet potatoes and pineapple harvested, farina would have to be flown in from town. With most people now living at either Yawko or the new village of Kashmi, it would have helped a lot had the airstrip at Kashmi been finished. But construction lay pretty much at a standstill.

Many of the men, even Yakuta and Kirifaka, were down river at the highway bridge working for the Brazilians. There was cash to be earned there, something of significance in a community in which money was beginning to challenge the old tribal ways of self-sufficiency or barter. New missionaries had been assigned by UFM to work at Kashmi. Ruth Langer, a young Brazilian woman of German parents, came to teach in the school, succeeding missionary nurse Sharon Hinchman. Also new were Joe and Tamara Hill and their three children. They transferred from work among the Trio in Surinam. Their objective was to help the Wai Wai reach the Atrowari for Christ, particularly by gaining knowledge of the Atrowari language. For the present, however, Joe was concerned with completing the new airstrip. He worked hard, and sometimes almost alone.

In the shift from Anaua to Kashmi, another who worked hard was Fehya's father, Old William. In this new area Old William did more than plant bananas for benefit of his grandchildren. He planted three fields of cassava, and his toil day after day shamed younger men into working more up to their capacity. Three fields were all he could take care of by himself; he went further, however, toward making Kashmi food-sufficient. He located areas that would produce the most crops, often selecting land encircling a big kechekere tree, the tallest in the forest. He taught his grandsons all they'd ever need to know about growing food. He taught them other things, too—that you don't talk bad, for example, or tell dirty stories. Fanahruwi was one who learned the hard way that his grandfather, old as he was,

could chastise disobedient and sassy boys and make them
realize that God had an all-hearing ear and an eye that never
closed.

Fanahruwi, seeming to blossom from such discipline,
grew to his mid-teens and married a girl from one of the
families that came over with Sheshwa. His sister, Meesu,
married some time before him and now had a child. Both the
marriages and the birth of a grandchild delighted Kirifaka
and Fehya. For Fehya, the new baby was one more to love.
She had given birth to eight children and was raising still
another, Rasaru—Lazarus—the Shedeu boy she nursed back
from the edge of death. Fehya loved every one of her children. Busy as she was in caring for this large household, she
never let the children exasperate her. She took time to play
with them, and in their family games it was sometimes difficult to tell which was child and which the tiny mother.

Fehya's loving spirit spilled far beyond her family. Not
especially outgoing, not one to be always laughing, she nevertheless was forever concerned about people. As various
ones arrived from Guyana, she was the first to say, "Let's go
to my field. I have sugar cane for the children." And once
there, she'd say, "You won't have to ask, but feel free to dig
the cassava you need. From here to that old stump will be
your field until you can harvest your own."

Fehya helped her husband as a church leader. He would
mention that someone was sick. Right away she would make
herself useful. Or if a neighbor lost a canoe or a board for
grating cassava, she and Kirifaka would talk over how they
could help replace the item. She made sure the Friday morning meeting for the women was planned. One by one she
taught many of the young wives, and with others likewise
mindful worked on a host of women's problems.

She lugged firewood home from the forest, gathered food
from the fields, bathed the little ones, baked bread, roasted
farina, always, it seemed, while nursing a baby. She was
never sick—until a problem arose in her last delivery. Now
pregnant again, she lacked her usual anticipation of the

event. She had a feeling there would be trouble, and that worried her family.

Another weight was the talk going around about dissension over a marriageable daughter. She favored a certain boy and Kirifaka another. To complicate the matter, Yakuta asked for their daughter for a relative of his. Kirifaka refused, saying he and Fehya were fully agreed the girl herself would decide. Then people really began to talk. Speculation buzzed in Yawko and Kashmi. "Why won't he give his daughter? He's keeping her for himself, they say— *ha tu.*" Fehya naturally heard the talk. She backed her husband's denial of any wrong motive, unreservedly trusted him—but the veiled charges, the destiny of their daughter, and the unhappiness it had caused all added to the anxiety over what was happening in her body.

With her time drawing near, her house was prepared for the birth. Two poles parallel to the ground had been erected; one on which to plant her feet, one to grasp overhead and, while crouching, to pull on, a stance that aided the expulsion of the baby onto a carpet of banana leaves. The day dawned that she knew she would make use of these poles, as so often she had used such poles in the past. But to her foreboding, things were not quite the same as before.

She passed a lot of blood. Kirifaka informed their son of his mother's condition; Fanahruwi gave her a shot for hemorrhaging. At the time there was yet no completed airstrip, no nurse in the village, and no working radio. What treatment she would receive would come from her son in her own house. Nothing else was available.

About midday labor pains began. After a while she bled again and later in the day a third time. That evening she felt a change in her womb.

"The baby's not coming," Fehya murmured to Kanahmachichi, Emehta's diminutive wife who attended her. She seemed to know its life was gone.

Darkness shrouded the village. The rainy season had reached its midpoint, but tonight the sky was clear, though there was no moon. The glow of a fire and the weak rays of a flashlight enabled the shadowy figures within the house to see each other. Kirifaka and all nine children were present; the children hovered anxiously but hushed around their mother's hammock. Lying back and peering through the dim light, she focused her big round eyes on the faces of her brood. Between cries of pain, which she could not suppress, she spoke to each of them.

"My son," she said to Fanahruwi, who at that moment was her child, not her physician, "I believe I will die. Oh, son, after I'm gone, keep walking with Jesus."

How many times had she admonished him to walk with Jesus? So many nights, he recalled, they all lay in their hammocks, the fire glimmering meekly, the dogs faintly snoring on their shelves, the younger children already asleep—and their mother, in her convincing way, speaking through the darkness to each of them, teaching them about God. Fanahruwi had tried to obey his mother's voice, but headstrong and inclined to pride and independence, he often failed to be the son he wanted to be. Silently now he prayed that this, her last urging, would yield better results.

Fehya reached out for Kirifaka's hand. Gripping it tightly, she whispered her fear for the path she was to take. She had never gone that way before. What dangers lurked alongside it?

Her husband spoke calmly and with reassurance.

"Jesus will lead you," he said. "He's been over the trail and knows the way. He'll take you to our Father's home, which is better than ours."

This settled her spirit, though her body continued to convulse with pain. Kirifaka led the children in prayer for their mother. Then after another stabbing throb, Kanahmachichi got her out of her hammock in an effort to induce labor. She made no progress.

Kirifaka took her from the birth poles and, sitting on a low stool, placed her on his knees, gently drawing her to his breast. For a little time they spoke soothingly to each other.

Then, as if everything that needed saying was said and all was done, she went limp, quietly dying in his arms.

The cries now were those of her family. The chill of early morning had invaded the house, intensifying death's cold breath that blasted them so unsparingly. Though it was yet a couple of hours before dawn, and outside only the raucous roosters proved that life still existed, the neighbors nevertheless heard their mourning and soon joined the family in lamenting the loss of their cherished Fehya.

At daybreak men of the village dug the grave. It might have been one for a young girl, so small she looked in her unwaking sleep. As the news began filtering into their homes, the villagers first trickled, then came en masse to Kirifaka's house, moving in and out, sharing the sorrow of the grief-stricken family, laying aside old suspicions and gossip. Then everyone crowded the grave site in a field on the near side of the uncompleted airstrip. Before the earth was returned to the hole, it was Kirifaka's cherished friend, Yakuta, who led them all in prayer.

With his beloved daughter gone, and her baby with her, Old William lost the will to live. He himself would probably die soon, and that was all right with him. Meesu took charge of the younger children; Feero-chi, little Flo, the namesake of Flo Riedle—Achi—was to keep her father's house. Except that Kirifaka went away, sad and angry. Forgetting his own words that had comforted Fehya in her last moments, he was angry at God for taking his little wife from him.

Forsaking every familiar face, he journeyed far down the new road that led to Manaus, going almost to Atrowari country. For two months he worked for the Brazilians, to earn new hammocks for the children, to be sure, but with the more compelling purpose to obliterate from his vision that last tragic scene in his home. He returned and continued to walk sad and in a little while struck out mindlessly for the bridge over the Anaua. There he stayed another month. Again he returned home, despondent as ever. His discouragement deepened when he learned his housekeeping daughter, Feero-chi, carried in her womb the child of her sister's husband.

At the time Sheshwa's group was acclimating themselves to life on the Novo, Mingeddi was striving to succeed as chief of the Wai Wai remaining in Guyana. The government had elevated him to leadership. His theft of Elka's canoe and hiding it in hope of preventing Elka from leaving for Brazil possibly raised his stature with the official at Kanashen; so clever a fellow ought to find ways to bring the people around to the government's point of view.

As might be expected, the people brought up Mingeddi's past in their talks around their home fires.

"Why is the one who killed people our chief today?" some demanded to know.

"Will he be one to do to us what he did to his victims long ago?" others asked, and in asking seemed to say they thought he might.

One day he issued a call for workers to report to the airstrip to cut the grass. Not one person showed up. Other times he called for work to be done. His calls were ignored. The government which had installed him removed him. But that was all right with Mingeddi. They had not paid him. What was there in a chieftaincy if it brought no gain?

The people then chose Mawasha, a leader in waiting whose time had finally come.

15

Five years. Could five years have passed since Ayrin last saw the people now living on the Mapuera? This was 1976, near the end of it; it was in 1971 that she waved a final goodbye to Kanashen and with Achi reluctantly flew out of Guyana. In those five years she had taught missionary children in Belem, filled in for a few months among the Wai Wai at Anaua, and filled shorter assignments among other Indian tribes in Northwest Brazil. Once she had visited this site very briefly, the day Brigadier Camarâo landed his helicopter at Howler Monkey Rocks, where a settlement was building high on a bank of the Mapuera River. That day proved important to the brigadier's two passengers—to Elka because Camarâo gave his blessing to the new village, and to Ayrin because she stood in the place where God would call her to live and work, though she was not to know it for almost two years yet.

Only a fraction of the present population had been here at the time, preceding by several months The Exodus. In Ayrin's return today, five hundred or more inhabitants faced her. It was understandable if now and then confusion enveloped her. The youngest children she had taught at Kanashen were presently half grown. Fathers and mothers had become grandparents. Some on her teaching staff in Guyana were now church elders.

Significantly, there were other changes over the five years that had less to do with time and more with day-to-day practices.

The people looked different. Today, no woman or girl wore a bead apron, but a dress or skirt and blouse. Except when working, the men wore shirts along with their short pants, and for Sundays long pants were preferred. The men had cut off their waist-length pigtails and now cropped their hair rather closely. They sported no feathers on their heads or in their waistbands, no ear bobs, no painted faces, except on a few very festive occasions. Decorative beads had almost entirely disappeared. Arm bands, once an emblem of maturity, leg bands and necklaces of many strands—the more strands, the wealthier the wearer—were only memories now. Shoes, at least sandals or thongs, protected feet that no longer were as tough as a pig's hide.

The things they did remained quite the same: Cutting and burning fields, carving canoes out of tree trunks, the long and arduous process of turning the cassava tuber into bread and starch drink. Hunting was altered little. Even men who had managed to get guns from the Brazilians to replace those they left behind in Guyana used them sparingly; ammunition was hard to come by, and the bow and arrow still served them well. Fishing, however, was undergoing a transformation. Poisoning a pool for a fish harvest was losing favor. Several men had become convinced it was a wasteful practice that threatened future supplies, an idea making sense to a people who were evolving from a today-only complex to the longer view that tomorrow lay ahead. Besides, to the less philosophical, casting a line with weight and hook honed a new skill that was beginning to rank with the prowess of the hunter.

Early on, Ayrin would detect a more independent spirit, particularly among the leaders. The elders, she would observe, had come to realize they had no one but God to fall back on.

The day she arrived Ayrin went to the chief's house to pay her respects.

"I am glad you have come, Little Sister," Elka said. "We need you here. But I will never look to you as once I looked to Bahm and Achi."

Should she be offended, disappointed that the missionary's role was reduced to one of advising, assisting, helping out where needed? Pensively she considered his words, then nodded in agreement. What he said pleased her. She had no children of her own, but all in the school at Kanashen had been her children, and now a good many of them were grown up, married, some with children of their own. The Wai Wai had once been children in the faith, requiring much nourishment and guidance, even correction. They had passed through the partial self-reliance of adolescence. Now in these five years without a missionary, she reflected, they had attained adulthood. Not complete maturity, not perfection, nor closer to it than any other adult on earth; but they had reached a level of responsibility comparable to that of people anywhere.

How did the changes that were so evident come about?

The beads were easy to explain. Tiny beads of all colors had filtered into the jungle through Wapishana traders from the Guyanese savanna. These Indians got them from Georgetown, and Georgetown from England. Thousands of beads were exchanged for a cassava grater board, which the Wai Wai made very well. In Brazil there were no beads to be got—almost no beads; a thimbleful here was worth what a potful had been on the other side of the mountains. But what explained the shoes, the men's short hair, the clothing that replaced loin cloths and bead aprons?

Like the Israelites wanting a king because their neighbors had kings, the Wai Wai wished to mirror the people around them—Brazilians in the towns downstream and, before them, Guyanese on the savannas. The few who traveled out to the cities took as models the people in Georgetown and in Manaus or Belem. And for all, there were the military, the politicians and the academics who had trekked to Kanashen and already were descending on the Mapuera.

A Wai Wai youth was sent out to a hospital. On arriving he hid his long hair inside his shirt. The second day he cut off his pigtail. He did not want to be stared at as "different."

From Howler Monkey Rocks it was only a two- or three-day trip down river to a Brazilian settlement, and another day or so to a "real" town. People who in Guyana had never been outside the jungle found it necessary now to go to town to work for a gun, to go back to buy ammunition or to make a trip to barter farina for shoes or clothing. The women had fewer opportunities to go out, limited either to a medical emergency or to a jaunt by the entire family. Their switch from bead aprons and bare breasts to dresses was hastened more by the people who entered Wai Wai country. It was routine that when flights brought in military personnel or men to survey for gold or valued forest products, Wai Wai mothers hid their daughters. The women may not have understood the words many of these men salaciously tossed toward the females they encountered, but the leering looks accompanying the words were easily translatable.

It was no surprise that when the Canadians contributed a supply of dresses, the mothers saw to it that their daughters were clothed before even themselves.

Ayrin observed changes all about her, in the shape and materials of the houses, in the people themselves. These were not changes imposed by missionaries, but changes that for the most part had occurred when no missionary was among them.

Elka asked the authorities for a teacher who spoke both Wai Wai and the language of the Brazilians. Where was one such to be found? He knew. It was Ayrin, of course, and she was invited in on a permanent basis. It was decided that Florence Riedle, the Wai Wai's Achi, and Ruth Langer would continue to work in the villages on the Novo River, and three weeks by very hard trail to the southeast. Irene and Renate Linder, a new missionary nurse, would begin ministering at the Mapuera. When the pair posted for the Mapuera landed in an Air Force seaplane, the whole village, except for the sick, turned out to welcome them. In her luggage, Ayrin brought newly printed hymnals and copies of Bahm's translation of the New Testament epistles of Romans and Philippians. The books provided a fresh stimulus for the church.

She found the spiritual temperature generally high. The services on Sunday mornings were well attended, as were the songfest Sunday afternoons and the Wednesday morning teaching. Before going to their work, several of the faithful met at dawn to pray. The six elders were led by the devout Kumana. But six elders were not enough for all the preaching, teaching, counseling, and adjudication required of them. More would be chosen. As another measure to spread the load, a few helpers were appointed. This position was truly that of a servant.

None performed with more grace than Wisho, the old fellow some called a trumpet bird, because of his long, spindly legs and the sort of whistle he intoned as he walked. He stretched those legs to fetch people the elders wanted to talk to. He rounded up food for those too sick to provide for themselves or their families. He cleaned the church. During services he stood by the door to keep children from running in and out. All his life Wisho had worn the servant's mantle, just as wiry little Charamcha had been everyone's right-hand man. Many years before these two had guided Bahm and Kron over the mountains and Wisho further conducted them down the Mapuera to this very spot. He led them to a village that then stood on the site of the airstrip now under construction. The people of that village eventually went over the mountains to Guyana. Getting ears, they became companions of Jesus, and today were among the stalwarts of Wai Wai faith, their present life on the Mapuera contrasting to their former life like sunlight to the black pitch of night.

A few men had recently gone toward the Amazon in a futile search for the Irifikuru people. Kumana was making

plans to contact the Arara tribe on the far side of the
Amazon. The Arara—the Macaw people—were on Elka's
list to be evangelized. Elka called for volunteers to cut a trail
to the Jatapu River, a first step in hunting out the Karafou.
Missionary zeal burned brightly. It was, after all, the magnet
that drew the Wai Wai back to Brazil, a pull more powerful
than the push so clumsily administered by government pressure in Guyana.

There was of course much more to do than gather for
prayer and join in songfests using the new hymnal. To bring
fields up to an acceptable yield called for diligence. Malia,
the wild substitute for cassava, was now thankfully forgotten, though an ample supply of their precious cassava hadn't
been achieved without hard work by all. And there was the
airstrip to complete. Ayrin joined the villagers each
Wednesday and Saturday when all other tasks were dropped
to concentrate on getting this vital job done.

Ayrin's house became a center for village socializing.
Kumana, with his wife and children, stopped in one evening
to discuss his burden for lost tribes. Other families dropped
by to scrutinize Ayrin's photographs or to show off a new
baby. Children enjoyed the puzzles and simple games they
pulled from her shelves. At times, these visits brought word
of a domestic problem or the sickness of a parent, but more
usually of a child. In the last scourge ten children died.
Fever and diarrhea were making the rounds currently. One
of the very sick children was the only daughter of Kurunaw
and Fetmaru.

Kurunaw was the oldest son of Elka and even as a young
man had been chosen an elder in the church. His was a
happy family. He and Fetmaru felt blessed with their three
sons, but were overjoyed when Choysi was born. This little
girl, not quite two years old, had given the family a lot of
laughs and no little worry as in imitating her brothers she
climbed here and crawled there and got into places from
which she had to be lifted down or out of. Very quickly she
changed from a darling, squealing little energy ball to a wan,

nearly lifeless sack of bones and flesh. One day the sparkle would reappear in her eyes; the next it was gone. Sores broke out in her mouth. She was racked by uncontrollable vomiting.

Her parents prayed fervently. Kurunaw remembered his own time of sickness as a boy when his father had prayed so fervently for him. At first Elka had prayed that his son would get well, then his prayer changed to one of surrender to God's providence.

"*Ahfah,* if you want to take my child, *okwe,* how sad, you go ahead and take him. If you take him, I'll still love you. I won't give you up. I'm giving my son to you, *oklee!*"

Kurunaw had heard the details of that night many times, and now it seemed he was re-enacting the scene. Could he give up this darling daughter? He began to think he wouldn't have to, just as God had spared him to his parents. He was beginning to feel a confidence that she would live. Then the blow hit him, a blow as sudden and crushing as if it had been struck without warning by someone behind a tree, someone with full force slamming a big stick on the back of his neck. Choysi, cradled in her mother's arms, went from quick, troubled gasps to slow, seemingly reluctant breathing. Fetmaru snuggled her in the hammock in which they lay, but the loving touch of a mother was not enough. Slowly and silently the child slipped away.

The sun flashed with impertinent good humor on the thick palm-leaf roofs all over the village of Howler Monkey Rocks. Only the cracks in the mud walls let its light filter sparingly into Kurunaw's home. That semi-darkness in the middle of the morning which shrouded the room seemed appropriate. Certainly, this was the saddest day in the lives of these parents. Yet, eyeing the narrow shafts of sunlight that wouldn't be kept out, Kurunaw became aware of a light shining within himself. He had wondered if he could give up his daughter. He wondered no more. He had. He had turned her over to Jesus, who knew what was best for little children.

Choysi's brothers cried, of course, and people from all

over the village rushed to comfort the family. Many stayed
to loudly lament their loss. A few men, of practical mind,
went quickly to the edge of the forest to cut poles for lining
the little one's grave, which was to be outside at the back of
the house, under the protection of the overhanging roof.

The next day a youngster called at the house and said his
father would like Kurunaw go see him. Kurunaw declined,
saying he was too sad to talk with anyone. Then after praying he changed his mind. Shayukuma no doubt wished to
console him, and it would be ungracious not to allow him.
He slowly trudged to Shayukuma's house.

"You came?" greeted Shayukuma, a handsome enough
man not yet middle-aged.

"I came," said Kurunaw, returning the greeting. He noted
Shayukuma's wife sitting in her hammock at one side of the
house. She seemed a troubled woman, perhaps, thought
Kurunaw, because she came from a troubled family. Her old
father had been a notorious Mawayena witch doctor, and it
never was certain that after his move to Guyana he had
given up his magical charms and the turbulent existence of a
devotee of the evil spirits.

"Don't believe the talk you hear about me in the village,"
Shayukuma said, not bothering to observe the custom of
small talk before introduction of a serious subject.

"I have heard no talk about you," Kurunaw replied, surprised at this beginning.

"Old Shayukuma caused your little girl's death, they
say—*ha tu.*"

Kurunaw shook his head, frowning, his brow knit in some
shock.

"What they say is not true," Shayukuma said emphatically.

"If they say it, why do they?"

"They want to blame me."

"I don't know anything about the talk. I don't know why
there is talk as you say. I have nothing to do with charms
and curses. As a companion of Jesus I am not afraid of the
spirits."

"Will you perform *farawa* to determine who killed your girl?"

"No. Absolutely not."

Kurunaw had heard vaguely of this old practice of identifying one who supposedly had caused a death and of then killing the offender through a curse. This was his first encounter.

"No, I will not," he repeated. "If someone caused her death, we would let God gain the revenge. As it is, my wife and I are satisfied that God took her to heaven because He knew best."

Kurunaw moved toward the door, but turned back to face Shayukuma.

"If I had anything to do with witchcraft," he said, "I'd be turning my back on God. Tell me, my brother, what would you do if one of your children died?"

"I'd perform *farawa*," Shayukuma said without hesitation.

"I cry for my daughter," said Kurunaw. "I miss my daughter. But now I cry because I'm afraid I'll be missing you. I'm afraid you are not one of God's children."

"I want to help you," said Shayukuma. "Give me one of her bones—it can be a tiny bone. I'll bury it under a kechekere tree and we'll see who dies in revenge of her death."

Again shaking his head, Kurunaw spoke with a sob in his throat:

"Yesterday if we had talked I would have said it was the saddest day in my life. But hearing today what you have said, defiling as you have her memory with witchcraft, this day is even sadder. Today is the saddest day of my life."

To which Shayukuma replied, "If anything should happen to your father, our chief, you can count on me to perform *farawa*."

Shayukuma's neighbors went to Elka and reported that the young one's body was not yet cold when they heard him and his wife joking and laughing over the baby's death. The men who went to cut the poles for the grave said that on their return the woman called out to them, asking if they had got much meat on their trip. Others said Shayukuma had approached them and was puzzled that Kurunaw rejected his offer to call on the spirits. Elka went to Shayukuma.

"Don't talk to my son of sorcery and revenge," he said severely. With pain he recalled that as a young fellow just come into his armbands, Shayukuma had accompanied Kirifaka on a missionary trip to the Tunayena, but over these years he had moved from serving God to serving Seetin. And, it appeared, he wished to enlist others in his vile cause.

"My son is very sad. Don't talk to him like that."

Since he himself renounced Kworokyam, Elka had stood resolutely against witchcraft in any form. One time when his faith was still young, it was true, he succumbed to intense pressure by Muyuwa, the old chief before him, who prevailed on him to blow the hot smoke of a cheroot on his grandchild, the one-eyed Yoshwi's son, and to chant a witch doctor's songs over the ailing little body. It was a relapse that Elka never repeated, and the shame of turning from God for one evening deepened his conviction that cohabitation with the dark spirits was the worst of sins.

The elders met to consider the repercussions of this open invitation for witchcraft to reassert itself in their midst, the most flagrant example of spirit service since by common consent it had been forbidden. It wasn't Shayukuma alone who opened this pestilent box; his wife was perhaps more deeply involved in the practice than her husband. The couple knew, didn't they, that followers of witchcraft must leave the village until there was genuine repentance?

"What about my children's schooling?" Shayukuma asked as he stood before the elders.

"You should have thought of them," answered one.

Shayukuma, his wife, and four children moved to their field an hour's walk away. They could call at the clinic when necessary, but were not to enter the village on a regular basis. He, indeed, did use the clinic. Three weeks into their exile he came with a mangled hand.

He had shot at an alligator, which escaped into a hole. He reached in the hole to retrieve it and was bitten. His wound was certainly cause for a hurried trip to the village.

During his long hospital stay in Manaus, Shayukuma's family was permitted back into the village. On his return, their exile was canceled. They appeared to accept the discipline and to have renounced witchcraft, though for some time they limited their mix with other families.

Shayukuma's intention apparently opened other minds to think how a desire might be achieved without depending on God to grant it. One or another, including a work captain, dabbled in sorcery and were disciplined for it. The actions of these men, who violated the trust placed in them, was having its effect on the youth of the village.

"That's the way we're supposed to live?" they asked one another with some cynicism. "Well, that shouldn't be hard to do."

16

The trails between the Mapuera village of Howler Monkey Rocks and other Indian settlements were kept reasonably passable by people traveling mostly to visit relatives. Trips north to the Trio in Surinam were not regular but did occur, as did an occasional visit to the Wai Wai remaining in Guyana. The path to the Hishkaryena on the Nhamunda River was frequently used because their village was closest, only three days away—two when a few men hustled along with no more than light packs on their backs.

Once as Elka tramped the trail from the Nhamunda, one thought stood out from the worrisome tasks that faced him at home. Kumana, that good man, was eager to start looking for the Karafou. He had wanted to take the message of Jesus to the Arara people south of the Amazon, but Funai, the government's Indian foundation which was sponsoring the contact, had no room for evangelizing in its agenda. So instead, when the tali tali locust sang, ushering in the dry season, Kumana prepared to search for people closer to home.

His was a small party. From the Mapuera he took just five men besides himself. The group walked a new-cut trail to the Jatapu River. This tributary of the Amazon would be their highway to a land penetrated by few outsiders.

Somewhere under the spread of huge trees, up a small side stream, in the midst of tangled vines where spider monkeys played and wild pigs roamed, the gentle tapir shared food with the deer and the crafty jaguar stalked its unwary prey—there in this seldom-disturbed forest lived the Karafou, or so Kumana was convinced. Far up the Jatapu they went. Finally, they came across an old house, which looked as if for some time it had been falling before the elements. A path led them deeper inland, and soon they discovered another house, this one not so old, but similar in construction.

"Look carefully," exclaimed Kumana to his men. "Whoever built this house did not use the tools we have for building."

The men examined how the house had been put together. It was, indeed, different.

"The poles that form the frame, they've been broken off, not cut," observed Kumana.

"The leaves on the roof have been torn from the plants," said another.

"People do that when they have no knives, no axes," reasoned Kumana.

"Only stone," said Kuruyeme, who had known beggarly living in the old Shedeu villages. "I have heard that those who walked the earth before I was born had only stones for tools."

They looked inside the house and searched the area. Nothing inside, except empty dog shelves, the cold ashes of a fire, a few arrow canes strewn about, some animal pelts, two or three crude baskets, a well-worn hammock. Beyond the house there was no field anywhere, only a path on the far side. This they went down, but it ended abruptly. Satisfied that people were somewhere around, though if they were in the forest close by they were being careful not to let themselves be seen, the Wai Wai turned back toward the river. Their food was running low; they would have to return home. Soon, however, another trip would be made, now that a starting point for the search had been established.

En route to the lower Jatapu they stopped at a tiny Brazilian settlement. There they visited with an old Indian man and his daughter, who had a small child.

"Who are you?" asked Kumana.

The man knew little of his forebears, except that in the past his people had been many, and now they were just four—including his brother away from the village, hunting. Sickness had killed all but the four. The man and his brother now worked for the Brazilians. He spoke Portuguese; what little he said in his native tongue, neither Kumana nor the others understood.

"Come with us," Kumana invited, as he once had invited Kuruyeme. "We will help you. Our chief wants you to come. He will love you as we will love you. We will see that you are fed and if you get sick we will give you medicine. We will tell you about Jesus."

"No," the old man said. "Not today. Send someone next dry season. Who knows if we will come then?"

Yes, whoever in the world could tell? This ragtail remnant of a once large clan could be dead by then.

From Kashmi on the Novo River, Yakuta journeyed in the opposite direction in search of the Karafou. His party traveled several days by canoe on the Jatapu River, then three days by trail. They arrived at a camp site where they found fresh food and the bones of fish that had recently been eaten. Continuing on, they discovered a house and a field growing cassava and bananas. For an entire day they combed the area, but found no one. They believed the people who lived in the house and who had eaten at the site in the forest were hiding out.

Before leaving, Yakuta and his men placed an ax and a large knife in plain sight in the field for their invisible hosts. In the near future Yakuta would return, he said, because he was certain the Karafou couldn't remain hidden for ever.

For better communication with their fellow tribesmen on the Novo, Elka decided they should cut a better trail from the Mapuera to Kashmi. It would be a huge task, the distance was so great. Rivers and streams would help, but where they ran in the wrong direction or their headwaters became so narrow and shallow that navigation was impossible, they would have to cut away jungle. They would slash with their long knives and sharp axes. Still, man was scarcely a match for the dynamic life of the rain forest. It would take the feet of many travelers regularly trampling the undergrowth to keep it down.

The tali tali sang once again to herald the awakening of a new year, and before the dry season had much time to advance, Elka gathered a crew of about twenty men to begin cutting the trail. He asked Shirifa, Tamokrana's oldest son and an elder of the Mapuera church, to be their spiritual leader. Shirifa had once flown from the Novo over the area they would traverse, so his recall of the terrain would be most helpful. Before the party left, old Wisho took Elka and Shirifa aside.

"Look for people," he advised. Wisho, the faithful helper, was too old to make the trip, but from having lived along many of the streams emptying into either the Mapuera or the Jatapu, he in his mind could see where the Karafou, the Giant People of the Bow, lived—or in his day had lived.

"As a young fellow, I saw them at a distance. I wanted to go visit them in their village. Older ones said to me, 'You are stupid. They'll kill you.'"

"*Okwe*, too bad," he sighed, "Maybe we could have become friends years ago."

Their objective would not be specifically to look for people, but that did not prevent them from praying that God would lead them to the Karafou as they cut the new trail. That was a possibility; the trail would run through the area suspected to be theirs. In three large canoes the crew set forth, and for two weeks paddled up the Mapuera, then one of its creeks toward the sunset, and farther up a feeder

stream of that creek. At last, their craft could carry them no
more, so they hit out overland, cutting through the jungle as
they went, slowly and laboriously all day, sleeping wherever
they found themselves as darkness fell.

Shirifa estimated they were about half way to the Wai Wai
villages on the Novo. Shortly afterward the party happened
onto a large, abandoned house. Like those Kumana had discovered, it was evidently built without sharp-edged tools.
They spent the night in it. A little way along the next morning they came across a second clearing, turning up a clay
pot. For three days they extended their trail, returning to the
old house each night. On the fourth morning before the sun
had traveled far, they found a vine like the one they used in
tying the leaves onto the rafters of their houses. It had been
torn.

"There are people close by," Elka said.

Cautiously, they continued their cutting. Their route led
into an old clearing. In it they discovered a potato-like plant.
Someone quite recently had dug in the patch. Beyond the
field they came to another old house. Fresh footprints encircled it, and led to a path on the far side. It was growing late;
in prudence they decided to retreat for some distance down
the trail they had made and there spend the night.

"Tomorrow we look for people," Elka said. Tonight they
would pray.

In the morning the men put on old shorts, painted designs
on their faces, sprinkled eagle down in their oiled hair and
smeared their chests with red stain. This was their attempt to
look the classic Indian, counting on such an appearance to
lessen the shock for people who would be expecting no one.
Single file along their trail they went, Shirifa in the lead,
closely followed by Elka. As they approached the prior
day's farthest point of penetration, they heard voices.

"*Aaaaaiiiiyyyy*," Men up ahead were calling to one
another. The Wai Wai halted, listened carefully. They were
hearing their own language.

"This is the way we'll be," Elka said in a still voice as

they grouped for his instructions. "Five of us will go forward, the rest stay here in the trail. If the people we hear are wild ones, they may kill us. If they are not, we will live."

Shirifa shuddered. Just thinking about dying at the hands of unknown people sent a shiver through him. He and Elka carried guns. Elka had a word about them.

"If trouble comes, shoot your gun in the air," he told Shirfa. "Don't shoot to kill anyone."

The five started toward the clearing. Ahead Shirifa saw a man perched on the roof of a new house, tying the final leaves to the ridge pole. Others worked below.

"*Oklee!* Great!" He signaled to those behind him. "They're people just like us. Let's go!"

The house under construction sat on the other side of a garden field. On a direct line to the house two women using sticks dug cassava. The Wai Wai stopped, pulling up to silently watch them. After a while one of the two looked up, the younger woman. She saw the men in the path and, suddenly rigid, stood half bent over staring at them. Then she nudged her partner, said something to her and took off running like a deer toward the house, screaming "People! People!" Her elderly companion straightened up. She calmly walked toward the men and without a trace of fright flatly asked:

"Did you come to kill us?"

"No," Shirifa quickly answered. "We are friends. We wouldn't kill you."

"Oh, really?" She answered with skepticism, but showed relief just the same.

The man on the roof jumped down and with four others ran through the trees toward the Wai Wai, hollering and waving stone axes above their heads. The closer they drew, the less their bluster. Elka wondered how to greet someone like this. He stuck out his hand, and the other Wai Wai stuck out theirs. The axes, which had dipped in the run, were raised again. The Wai Wai pulled back their hands. The men from the clearing stopped just a pace or two short.

"Have you come to kill us?" one of them asked.

"No," said Shirifa. "We are your friends."

"Who are you?"

"We are Wai Wai."

"Are you really Wai Wai?"

"I am," Shirifa assured him. "And so are all the others."

"We, too, are Wai Wai," said the one who appeared to be their spokesman. He smiled broadly. The tension in the faces of his comrades slackened. "We are your kin."

Elka called up the rest of his party. With their "kin," they walked to the unfinished house.

The men of this village wore faded red loincloths hanging down to their knees, quite like the ones the Wai Wai men used to wear. On their upper arms they wrapped narrow strips of bark into very thick bands. Their legs below the knees they decorated similarly. Their long hair was inserted in a bamboo tube reaching to their waist in back, like the Wai Wai a few years ago. Each sported a necklace of cotton strands. The necklaces were dirty, their hair disheveled, their faces and bodies half-covered with grime of somewhat long standing, hiding much of the red dye they had applied to themselves some days ago. Their wretched appearance meant little to the Wai Wai. God hadn't told them to look for clean people, only for ones who had need of Him.

At the house, an open-sided structure, both visitors and hosts sat down on slabs of wood. Two or three more men and a few children drifted cautiously from the forest, curious as to who had come and what was happening. From a leaf shelter the two women who had been in the cassava field brought a pot of starch drink. Other women slowly assembled. Each wore only an apron strung from tiny seeds and arm and leg bands like the men. Their hair was short and disarranged. The children were naked.

One of the women edged toward Shirifa, bent down, lifted one of his hands then the other, counting his fingers, then ticked off each of her own. Next she picked up a foot, counted his toes, did the same for the other and dropping it counted her own. Satisfied the newcomers were essentially the same as themselves, she retired to the outer rim of the circle.

"They know how to talk right," one of the older men said, and his remark drew a chorus of approval from the villagers. He soon was disclosed as the headman, with the name of Faryayaka. He was long-legged and slender, his eyes sunk in and his teeth widespread. Matutah, of similar build, was next in command. He was once a village chief, but recently the two groups had merged. If all were present today, Elka calculated, they numbered less than the men with him.

"Are there more people in the forest about here?" Elka asked.

There were more. They mentioned two or three groups that roamed the jungle.

"They are afraid of people," Faryayaka said, "just like we were afraid of you until we found you to be Wai Wai. We have heard Wai Wai are good. We thought you might come. We did not expect you to come today."

"You found the knife and the ax my brother left as gifts for you?"

"We did." Faryayaka took from under a pile of leaves a knife blade that had been tied to a stick. It was not a complete blade. He explained he and others had shared the gift knife, breaking it into three pieces.

Obviously the man cherished their one metal tool. Their axes were stones sharpened against other stones, wedged in the split end of a stick and tied in place by a vine and cemented by the tar-like sap of a tree. Answering a question, Faryayaka said they had bows and arrows, but only a pointed stick with which to plant their fields.

"We cannot cut fields," he said. "We must plant where the wind has been our friend and blown down the trees."

To create fire, they rubbed dry sticks together in a pile of dry leaves. They hunted without dogs; the big cats of the forest had killed them all.

They had tried to follow their gift-giver to his village, went some way then saw no more of his tracks. It probably

was just as well; no doubt they would have been too intimi-
dated to walk into someone else's village. They were aware
also of Kumana's visit to their region. They had not seen
him, only his footprints, and observed that someone took
things down in their house to look them over but had stolen
nothing.

"We said they must be good people."

Matutah shared with Faryayaka a recital of their history.
Once they had been a proud people. There had been many of
them. Yes, they remembered their elders calling their forebears the Giant People of the Bow. There had been antago-
nism between them and the Wai Wai and after years of skir-
mishings they finally had suffered a great defeat at the hands
of their adversary. For years they had not been a settled
people. Sickness thinned their ranks, so now there were—in
their group, at least—only what were seen in this clearing
today.

Elka decided they were not his relatives, not the ones who
in a quarrel many years back had split from his tribe. They
were Karafou all right—people of the bow, but no longer
giants nor ones to be feared, thin shadows of what they used
to be. Just now hoping to gain protection, they had claimed
to be of the tribe of their unexpected callers.

Faryayaka said it was a good thing the Wai Wai had come.
They were a dying people. The house the Wai Wai had first
come across the Karafou had been abandoned because so
many people got hot and died there. Having told them this,
he laughed.

"Matutah feared more than I the visits by those who did
not find us," he said. "Frightened that outsiders had come,
he took his people and fled deeper into the forest. After
these many cycles of the moon Matutah returned, for a visit.
Wouldn't you know, it was just the time you arrived."

The headman, in a happy mood, nodded to the women,
and they brought bread and meat for a meal.

"We'd like to thank our kind Father in the Sky before we
eat," Shirifa said. The Wai Wai bowed their heads while he
prayed.

"*Kofi!* How scary," gasped one of the Karafou.

"*Kooz, kooz, kooz,*" buzzed the others, their heads together in consultation. "What ever in the world are they doing?"

The Wai Wai ate and handed back the clay bowls.

"We are going now," said Elka, getting up. "It is a long way to the house where we will sleep."

"No!" exclaimed the headman, springing to his feet. "I am not going to let you go. You must stay right here. You will sleep in our house."

He picked up an ax that lay alongside a Wai Wai and went to the edge of the forest to cut poles on which they could hang their hammocks. He soon returned, his arms laden. He grinned broadly. He liked using the Wai Wai ax.

After more talk and more food, Elka and his men began stringing up their hammocks. The headman assigned places to all. The house was crowded, with both Wai Wai and Karafou preparing to spend the night there, but it was large and being open-sided the overflow spilled to the outside.

"This may not be the safest place for us to sleep," said Elka, "but God knows that and we are here because He wants us to be here."

As the house quieted, Shirifa settled himself; it had been a long day and he was tired. Before drifting off, however, he became aware that in the dim light of a close-by night fire someone was staring intently at him. It was Faryayaka. Shirifa roused up, now fully awake. He lay back, watching the Karafou chief. Faryayaka stepped closer to him, his gaze clamped on Shirifa's face.

Whatever on earth did he want? What was he about to do?

"What is it, *Ahfah?*" the Wai Wai asked. The word "father" set Faryayaka loose from his trance. He bent over Shirifa, placing his hands on the younger man's face.

"*O mu mu ru,* my son," he said in a coarse whisper, gently rubbing Shirifa's cheeks, "you've come back."

Shirifa sat up, threw off the old man's hands.

"I'm not your son."

"*O mu mu ru*, you've come back from the dead."

"I've not been dead," protested Shirifa. "I walked the trail with the others to get here. Is your son dead? I am not your son."

For some little time he failed to convince the headman that he was not his reincarnated son.

"In the morning, in the sunlight, you will see who I am. Maybe I look like your son, but I am Shirifa, son of Tamokrana."

Faryayaka slowly retreated to his own hammock, moaning a discordant note of disappointment. Others in the room now became restive. The Karafou began to talk back and forth about their visitors.

"Are they really Wai Wai?"

"Where did they come from?"

"How did they find us?"

"Will they get up in the night and with their sharp knives kill us all in our beds?"

It was evident the Karafou meant to give their visitors no opportunity for a sneak attack against them. All night long they kept up the chatter, probably not one of them getting more than a few winks of sleep. The Wai Wai got not much more.

On the following day, a Sunday, the Wai Wai gathered for their worship service, observed curiously and at a safe distance by the Karafou. About noon the wife of the headman, the older woman who had been first to meet them in the path, became ill. Before sunset she lapsed into unconsciousness. From among the huddled Karafou morbidly eying the sick woman, Faryayaka picked out a man and beckoned him. He wanted help in untying her hammock and carrying her outside.

"Where are you taking her?" Elka asked.

"Out under the sky," Faryayaka replied.

"What will you do with her there?" Elka was suspicious of what he planned to do.

"I will blow smoke on her sick body. I will rub her arms

and chest with the stones from my basket."

"And if she does not respond to your charms?"

"I will burn her body."

"Even while she lives?"

"If my sorcery fails to cure her, how can she live anyway?"

"Wait," called Shirifa, moving to her hammock. He had got some training in medicine from Achi. He bent over the woman, pressed his fingers to her wrist.

"Her pulse is strong," Shirifa said. "Don't take her outside. She will get cold there. Let us pray and ask God to make her better."

"*Taa,* all right," agreed Faryayaka. "My charms haven't been working well lately. More people have died than Kworokyam has saved."

The Wai Wai men gathered around the woman. They sang a number of hymns, repeated verses from God's Paper, and prayed. As it came Elka's turn to pray, he placed a hand on the woman's forehead. At this, all the Karafou except the headman and his helper rushed from the house and scattered into the forest, screeching their worst fears.

This night the Wai Wai stayed awake, watching and praying. They prayed that God would heal the chief's wife; they watched that the Karafou did not steal her away and burn her body as a lost cause. The moon shone brightly and the night air was chill. Nothing stirred about the house. The Karafou were out in the jungle somewhere, probably cowering for fear of whatever magic the Wai Wai were performing in their new and thus far untainted house.

Shirifa kept raking hot coals under the woman's hammock to keep her warm. A little before dawn she began to moan and by sunup was talking, complaining that her head hurt. Shirifa had her swallow some pills from his basket. She downed them in spite of not understanding how little white pebbles could affect her throbbing brow.

Her condition improved rapidly. She was up out of her hammock, tending to her work as people drifted back from the forest. All were amazed to find her alive.

Faryayaka could scarcely handle his excitement.

"You people really know how to cure the sick," he said in genuine admiration.

"No, it was not us," Elka replied. "It was God who healed her."

"The songs you sang were strong, much stronger than the songs I got from the spirits."

"Not spirit songs," one of the Wai Wai said. "Our songs are songs of our Creator."

First one then another of the Wai Wai took a Karafou aside and patiently related the good news about the Father in the Sky who had made them all and about His son, Chisusu, Jesus, who died for their badness but who from death woke up again and some day would return to collect all of God's children and take them to the sky.

The next day the Wai Wai said they must leave. They would return home, the Karafou having assured them that trails toward the sunset already existed.

"You came to my house," Faryayaka said. "Now I will go to yours. You've seen where I live. I want to see where you live. When you go, I will go with you."

"Fine!" said Elka. "Let's go!"

Faryayaka had little to place in an owchi, only his open-weave hammock of jungle grass and vines, some smoked meat, and a small comb of palm slivers sewn onto a monkey's arm bone. Before he and the Wai Wai reached the river to board the canoes, Matutah and his grown son caught up with them. The youth would go along to help the older man.

The knocking on the sides of the three canoes brought the whole village to the port at Howler Monkey Rocks. So these were the Karafou!

"We didn't know where they were," said one young fellow to another as the crowd pushed toward the umana.

"They were in hiding, but now they've been found," his friend added.

One old man was not surprised that the Karafou had

turned up. As he was swept along with the others to the welcoming feast, Wisho mumbled half under his breath, pleased
just a mite with himself, "Didn't I tell them where they
were?"

On Sunday in church it was Shirifa's turn to preach. He
was still filled with the excitement and satisfaction of having
at last discovered the Karafou and of having two of them sitting in the congregation in front of him.

"We knew somewhat where the people were located, but
not exactly," he said, "so we are praising God for His guidance. There are so many rivers and creeks in the area that we
could have easily missed them. Many of the men who were
with me said, 'You would have thought we knew without
question where those people lived as we went directly to
their village.' God certainly went before us to show us the
trail."

Shirifa ended his message with a plea that what had been
started be continued.

"Jesus is coming soon. There are still people in the jungle
who have not heard about Him. Jesus said He will go with
us, so let us go out there and find them."

17

The two Karafou men came to the Wai Wai village just to get a gun, an ax, and a knife—so said the son of Matutah, to one of the young Wai Wai fellows. He himself cared nothing for the talk about this Jesus. Who could understand about God? Faryayaka put it less crassly to Elka:

"I wanted to see if you had food here," he said. "Now that I find you do, I want to bring all my people here to live with the Wai Wai."

This pleased Elka. Faryayaka also asked Elka for a gun.

"*Taa,* all right," Elka said. "I will get you a gun."

A gun had expanded Faryayaka's lifelong dream of some-day obtaining a knife—a whole knife, not just part of a blade. From his earliest boyhood he remembered the older folk talking about knives. Other tribes had them, but they weren't for poor, isolated Karafou, they said. Once a group of Shedeu had visited their village and left a couple of knives in exchange for a stone ax. In time these knives must have worn out or were lost. For several generations now knives among the Karafou were subjects only of legends or dreams.

At the time of the Shedeu visit, the Karafou lived near the headwaters of the Mapuera. Two main villages housed more than a hundred persons each. The numbers had diminished before Faryayaka and Matutah were born, probably declining after the Wai Wai defeated them and they retreated deep into the inhospitable forest. Cut off then from other groups, they lost the ability to trade and to equip themselves with the amenities other tribes might have offered them.

The boys grew up in separate villages, but their clans often got together for prolonged parties of dance and drink. Invariably, these ended in drunken wrangles, sickness, and sometimes death. But quarrels eventually were resolved and during one amicable period the two villages journeyed to the Jatapu to visit a relative. Having left nothing of real value behind, they decided to stay. It was not an improvement in lifestyle that held them at the Jatapu—more likely mere inertia. They broke up into small groups and scattered here and there. Reclusive living grew more pronounced, abetted by feelings of inferiority and fear of others.

In the area of the Jatapu, as at the Mapuera earlier, they fought against hunger, against nature, against their own inabilities, just to survive. Their fields were necessarily small, tiny patches of cassava or bananas or sweet potatoes here and there where a tree had fallen, opening a path of sunlight. They possessed no canoes—not even the quickly-made ones of bark—because they had no tool for felling, stripping, carving, or digging out.

Sometimes they were able to stanch the deadly dysentery by using a jungle potion. They boiled the blood of a particular turtle as an elixir for other serious or lengthy illnesses. At other times they judged the patient not worth saving.

The elderly were vulnerable to this determination. As the tribe moved from place to place, the very old were carried on a younger person's back. When enough was enough, the unwanted burden was discarded and burned. Long-term sickness could be terminated by burning. Those who outwitted the torch by dying first bowed to it later, as all corpses were burned; their ashes, along with the residue of their hammocks and other possessions, were regarded no differently than the ashes of a tree.

At the opposite end of life's spectrum, new-born twins and deformed babies were stuffed into the hollow trunk of a "death" tree. The infants were left there to die. Twins were considered dangerous; deformed infants a sure sign the spirits were angry. No one would think of taking one out of the tree trunk, either alive or dead. Whoever in all the world would want to tangle with the spirits?

Faryayaka was beginning to get ears, just a little, for what the Wai Wai told him about the One in the sky who made him and loved him in spite of all his badness. Mawalee had created the Karafou—and made the first ax—so Faryayaka had been taught. But Mawalee got angry with his creatures and walked away from them, taking his ax, never to pay them further heed. Faryayaka's feeling toward Mawalee was mutual. A loving God appealed to him. An opportunity to be rid of his badness and his guilt over it seemed too good to be true.

"Why didn't you come before this?" he asked Elka one day while they talked about Jesus dying for sin. "Why didn't you come and tell us about God before my father died?"

He wished to return to the forest to get his fellow villagers and bring them back to live with the Wai Wai. Elka said his son would escort him and his young companion.

"If you don't come back to us, *Ahfah*," said Shirifa with a kindly glint in his eye, "I will come and get you."

Kurunaw, accompanied by Forosha, a brother of Shirifa, delivered his charges to their village—except they discovered the "village" today was only an abandoned house. Not completely abandoned; two old people had remained behind. They said a woman had died. Death called for the others to forsake the place.

During that night Faryayaka and Matutah's son ran away. The next day the old people were asked why they had gone.

"Their relatives were here," they explained. "They called them."

Disappointed that they had lost the two men, and through

their defection the rest of the tribe, Kurunaw and Forosha tried to persuade the old couple to go back to the Mapuera with them. This they resolutely refused to do.

"Maybe you will take us away to kill us," one of them said.

"No," assured Kurunaw, "we will not kill you."

"*Hnnnnn* . . . I don't know."

They would not budge. The Wai Wai left with them a file, a long knife, and an ax.

Shirifa kept to his word. On his second trip to the Jatapu he brought back the two men who had come with him previously and all the other Karafou he found, a total of sixteen. They dared come, one said, because Faryayaka and Matutah's son had returned to them without harm. For these uninitiated, their first ride in a canoe was rather worrisome. Just in case they might fall out, they tied their feet securely to the heavy owchies riding in the bottoms of the boats. Shirifa hoped that in running treacherous rapids they wouldn't overturn.

At Howler Monkey Rocks an airplane sat on the runway as Shirifa's party filed up the path alongside the airstrip on the way to the village. It was of immense interest to the Karafou. They had seen airplanes before, only always high in the sky. They had not believed they were birds, that big so high overhead. Besides, what bird made such noise as they heard? As frequently one zoomed far above them, they merely called it a "thing." Like much of their world, it was something unknowable. The mystery partly unraveled as they inspected the plane on the airstrip. So this was the "thing" they had been seeing! Why was it so strangely silent now?

Like newcomers before them, the Karafou were escorted to the umana. There they were greeted warmly, the Wai Wai overjoyed because in their midst they actually were seeing the object of their prayers of many years. Before food and drink were passed, Elka prayed.

"*Ahfah,* Father," he said, "you are good, you are very

good for bringing these people to us. You made us your children, and now we are asking you to make these your children."

Anticipating their misgivings, when first he had heard the knocking of the paddles of the approaching canoes, Elka stopped to see Achi—she having come to temporarily fill in for Ayrin.

"Please do not come out of your house until I call you," he said. "I don't fear for your well-being, but the Karafou have not seen white skins, and they will be afraid."

Later that day he believed their acclimation had progressed enough that he called all the men together, asked Achi to present herself and said, "She's one of us."

The Wai Wai extended themselves to accommodate the Karafou. They built them a house, a long one where for the time being they could all live together. Women brought them bread, though it went uneaten; in cassava, the Karafou's taste differed from the Wai Wai's. Women here, the Karafou said, didn't know how to make good bread.

In developing friendships, individual Wai Wai were drawn to individual Karafou. Shirifa befriended Matutah's son. "Catch hold of Jesus," he urged. "Be like the cassava plant. When we plant it, it looks dead, but it comes back to life. You can be that way. Dead, but alive again."

This young man who had come the first time to accompany the old man and, more to the point, to get a gun, a knife, and an ax for himself, and who had no interest in learning about God, was the first among the Karafou to become a companion of Jesus.

Matutah had brought his witch doctor charms. Shirifa wasn't far in his teaching before Matutah asked his teacher to take all his witchcraft paraphernalia and destroy them. Shirifa carried them to the rapids at the edge of the village and tossed them in. For awhile Matutah feared he, a witch-doctor without his charms, would die. But he didn't. He even withstood a siege of tuberculosis.

"To keep your body healthy," Shirifa said, "Look to God and take your medicine."

Matutah did.

Elka often gathered the Karafou to teach them. One day he focused their attention on the creation of the world.

"God made the light," he said. To illustrate, he struck a match.

A woman in his class called out her question:

"Did God create matches, too?"

Not all went well with the newcomers. A young man got hot. His friends captured scorpions for treating him. It was their custom to drain the fever away by the bite of a scorpion. The medical attendants in the village warned them not to do it. But of course they did, out of sight of anyone who might object. The poor fellow died. Who knew whether of the malaria or the venom?

One day the mother of the youngest Karafou was stopped on her way to the forest with her little fellow. Asked by a Wai Wai where she was going, she replied with no emotion but annoyance, "I am on my way to kill him."

"Why?" she was asked. "Why do you want to kill him?"

"I don't like skinny, crying children."

She was turned back, but her attitude failed to change until the day she asked Jesus to come live in the pit of her stomach.

Illness swept through the group. Colds caught them. A few suffered from measles, whooping cough, and malaria. A second man died. Even the healthy had a complaint: There were too many people surrounding them at the Mapuera, too much activity, too much talk, too much noise, too much happening from sunrise to sunset. They were frightened by it all. The Karafou were accustomed to the solitude of the forest. Some began to agitate for returning to it.

Their restless spirit caused great concern among the Wai Wai. What should they do? Give the Karafou a sack of farina and a canoe and send them on their way back to the harsh and lonely forest? Should a few of the Wai Wai go with them and settle in their village? According to the Karafou themselves, there were other bands of their relatives still wandering adrift in the region of the Jatapu. Elka had a list of four groups he wanted to search out and contact. Twice he made plans to go, and twice extraordinary rains flooded the trails and prevented his going.

Elka and his son Kurunaw believed that after prayer and waiting on God they were given the answer to the Karafou dilemma. It was to establish a base in the middle of Karafou territory. From a small, permanent village they could reach out in all directions, and Faryayaka and his people could live there in a much less threatening environment, continuing to hear the teaching about God's love and concern for them.

Despite their fears, the Karafou decided to stay for the present at Howler Monkey Rocks, counting on a promise that one day a few Wai Wai would take them back and establish a village on the Jatapu. They liked the teaching and did not wish to live beyond its sound. Still, they felt little comfort. It did not help that outsiders had discovered the big Wai Wai village, especially now that the airstrip was completed. Brazilians landed their planes regularly, often arriving with no advance notice to trade with the Wai Wai or to probe their daily habits and study their tribal ways, or sometimes out of curiosity just to look at them.

A few of those who landed at the Mapuera were downright dishonest, schemers profiting from the Indian's lack of sophistication. One government employee spent less time on building an expanded airstrip and more on buying the village chickens from children for a few crackers. Another worker kept two sets of books for paying Wai Wai laborers, stealing from them each week. His thievery was discovered when Forosha courageously told a visiting inspector that, contrary to the man's "official" list, the wages marked for him did not go to him because he did not earn them. He was not a part of the airstrip crew.

Forosha, rather heavy-set and with a happy face, appeared to be soft and easily plied. He definitely was not. Along with his brothers, he had learned the lessons of honesty and faithfulness from Tamokrana, his father, and had developed a tenacity for what he believed in. Ever since his teens he had avidly studied God's Paper, hoping some day to preach in the cast of Elka and Yakuta and Kirifaka. Elka once picked him out as a work captain. This would have placed him on the civil side of village leadership, and this he did not want. Unlike most of his tribesmen, he stood up to authority and told Elka it was a position—albeit a position of honor—that he did not want. Then, with humility another of his traits, he was smitten by conscience and asked Elka's forgiveness for his sharp answer.

"I never prayed or thought about being a work captain," he said to the chief. "I don't think I would like it, but I'll try it. Maybe God has something in it that he wants to show me."

The Brazilians learned the new work captain would not bend the truth to protect himself from intimidating men.

Death, sickness, the consuming sins of lust and bitter discontent, the disqualification of too many elders and work captains, all mounted to threaten Elka's habitual composure. But he refused to remain despondent and his joy returned. He was thankful for the good people he had working with him. His son Kurunaw was a strong one. Kumana wore the mantle of church leadership very well. Young Forosha had begun to preach like the older men who were his models. Kuruyeme had become an effective elder, his friendliness and open spirit honestly earning him the title of the "smiling one." Kamfeferu was a big help, as willing today ↑s years before when he memorized the answers before understanding people's questions about God.

Others were teaching school. Older women were taking the younger ones under their wings and helping them in the establishment of their homes and launching of their families. Parents were training their children to walk the trail with Jesus. Young believers were baptized. The teaching and personal conduct of faithful companions of Jesus had an impact.

It was a happy congregation that crowded the church on a Sunday morning near the end of another dry season. Communion was to be served, as regularly it was on the Sunday nearest the full moon. Kumana preached this day, and would preside over the distribution of cassava bread, followed by the elders passing pots of starch drink up and down the rows. Communion was always so meaningful when Kumana administered it.

He had been a companion of Jesus longer than all but the older folk could remember. As a young man he, along with Tamokrana, had been among the first from this area of the Mapuera to go over the mountains to Guyana and there to quickly get ears about God. He sought out the Shedeu and led a large group of them to Kanashen. He returned to the Mapuera as spiritual leader for the advance party that began the village of Howler Monkey Rocks. Here, as everywhere he'd lived, he stayed happy, worked hard, proving his great strength, never giving into fatigue, and never was sick. In all ways, Kumana lived the definition of consistency.

This morning as he prayed on completion of his message, his tongue suddenly began to play tricks with his words. They seemed not to come out as he intended. Here and there in the assemblage before him a pair of eyes behind spread fingers surreptitiously opened, glancing his way. His words first slurred, then became totally unintelligible. All eyes were now on him.

He slumped against the pulpit. Other elders who were sitting behind him on the platform jumped to keep him from falling. Two of them half guided, half carried him off the platform and out of the church. The people sat stunned, a hush settled heavily on them all. The remaining elders looked at each other. What to do? The one who preached always presided at communion. They had no precedent for this.

Forosha rose to take the stricken one's place and the bread and drink were passed and the prayers were brief but intense and fervent.

In his house, Kumana lay in his hammock, unable to

speak, unable to move his left arm and leg. Later in the week a plane arrived to take him and a son to Manaus. In a day or so a radio message was received by the government's representative, the *chefe do posto,* that Kumana had been removed to a mental hospital.

"A mental hospital!" Ayrin exploded in her most expressive Portuguese. "Because he can't talk they think he's lost his mind and so put him in a mental hospital?"

"Well," the *chefe* said, trying to be reasonable, "people get that way, you know, from too much religion."

She looked him in the eye, giving him one of her impressive stares.

"You've been here a good long time," she said calmly, but emphatically. "You know Kumana very well. Has there ever been once, just once, that you've heard him utter a single unintelligent word?"

He turned away, escaping her gaze. She was not sure of his reaction to her disapproval. The next day, however, he reported that Kumana had been moved back to the general hospital.

It was there within a month that he died. For a week until his body was returned, the village of Howler Monkey Rocks virtually ceased to move, scarcely to breathe. School was closed, few went to their fields, silence prevailed.

"How could it happen?" little, old wrinkled Charamcha asked himself. Kumana was younger, stronger than himself. Others asked why God would take one of his most faithful. Did He love Kumana more than they did, so wanted him to live alongside Him in heaven? If so, God must have loved him a lot. Perhaps they hadn't shown their love as they ought to have.

With a few prayers the body was lowered into a grave dug by Charamcha in a corner of the house of Kumana's son. His widow did not want him to be consigned to a field somewhere, and Kumana's house was up on legs so an inside burial could not be done there. The son's house was chosen. She wanted to feel that her husband remained close by.

18

Kashmi, the new settlement where Electric Eel Creek flowed into the Novo River, was becoming a rather settled place. The last of the newcomers from across the mountains in Guyana had largely been absorbed. Long-lasting houses replaced the temporary leaf shelters. The fields were producing cassava, sweet potatoes, and various fruits at a satisfactory rate, though leaf-cutter ants, caterpillars, and assorted other insects got more than their share. A new church and school were both in use. Each was a decided improvement over the open-sided shelter that had served both purposes.

The new school met expanded needs. After the children's classes in the morning, many of the adults met there in the afternoon to learn Portuguese. Beyond the school, the airstrip was completed, and after the missionary plane landed shortly before Christmas, bringing in Joe Hill's family, the Wai Wai were encouraged sufficiently by its usefulness that they pushed on to lengthen the runway, even to delaying necessary work in their fields.

Several among the young testified to becoming companions of Jesus, and the resultant baptisms enlarged the Wednesday morning believers' meeting. The recent service at the river's edge contrasted with the single baptism of the year before. Then, at Easter, an elderly fellow who had shown no real change from his old pagan ways was the only candidate. The church leader who insisted on baptizing him was later challenged.

"Why did you put him into the water?" the skeptic asked.

"There was no one else. Without putting someone into the water it wouldn't be Easter."

But this year, Easter really was Easter! The revived spirit could be detected in many ways, one in the spontaneous singing heard throughout the village. People loved to congregate at night after the work was done to sing hymns, more and more of which they had composed themselves. There were a few deaths, several births. After the flare-up of his tuberculosis, Yakuta was doing well and became the proud grandfather of twin girls. Kirifaka still walked sad. Lonely without his Fehya, he fretted at times over raising his five youngest children without their mother.

Interest still ran high in reaching out to the fearsome Atrowari. It appeared there was a continuing interest also among the Atrowari for the new things they had learned from the Wai Wai. A young fellow who had gone far down the new road to work on a government project near Atrowari territory returned to Kashmi one day and reported the Atrowari were holding meetings, such as those they had attended in the Wai Wai church. They sang the songs they had learned in those sessions which Kirifaka hastily called to deflect the intents of the Atrowari from snatching the Wai Wai women. Someone "preached," the young man said, though the content of the sermon was not clear. The Wai Wai felt a new urgency to fill the minds of the Atrowari with the truths of God's Paper. They realized a house cleared of evil spirits didn't of itself stay clean for long. If the truth failed to occupy it, the old falsehoods would return seven-fold.

Mamichiwa got a small party together to go over the trail once again to the Alalau River. But before reaching Atrowari country, they had reason to turn around and head back home. As they were breaking camp early one morning, they heard a twig snap up ahead in the trail. Before they could draw themselves up in defense, they were smothered by the embraces of nine Atrowari men.

"To your village," the Atrowari said in sign language. They were on their way to the Novo, and they were not to be deterred.

Mamichiwa led them back. Overall, it was a friendly three-day visit.

The Atrowari were marshaled by their new chief, Maruwaga, an old fellow with deep eye sockets and haggard cheeks—a thin, angry man known for numerous killings. He had succeeded the "Long One." Compredo, some said, had got hot one day and died in his hammock. Others agreed he died in his hammock, but hinted malaria may not have been the assassin. Without a real understanding of Atrowari words, how could the Wai Wai know?

On the second day of the visit, Joe Hill, who had come to live at Kashmi for the specific purpose of breaking open the mystery of the Atrowari language, succeeded in recording a number of words and phrases. A teen-age Atrowari enthusiastically offered him vocabulary. The next day, however, the unsociably cautious Maruwaga forbade any further capture of his people's tongue. On that day the visitors decided to go home. A couple of Wai Wai escorted them for a distance on the trail, but the Atrowari ran far ahead, leaving nothing for the Wai Wai but to retrace their steps.

Almost at the end of the dry season the Atrowari again descended on Kashmi, this time for a more significant stay.

For the first time women and children were among the visitors, who numbered nearly twenty. The Atrowari said they had come to stay a year. That was fine with the Wai Wai; at last, they'd be able to learn something of this puzzling tongue. The price of their learning would be steep, however. Though coming peacefully and for the most part seeming to be happy, the Atrowari had lost none of their arrogance. Even in getting there they had been demanding.

"Send canoes to fetch us," had been the word they sent to

Kashmi from the bridge over the Anaua River. Emehta and Fawtaw went to get them.

They were put up in the umana. Indeed, it became a miniature Atrowari village, immediately taking on a disorderly look and the smell of many unwashed bodies, both of dogs and humans. Like their fellow tribesmen who had come before them—and for some it was a repeat visit—the Atrowari grabbed at the few strands of beads remaining to the Wai Wai. They whined for knives. They were very hearty and frequent eaters, testing the adequacy of the village food supply. But these annoyances aside, the Wai Wai were beginning to get something in return—the Atrowari language.

From previous encounters various ones had learned the meaning of a few sounds in the strange tongue. Twefu, more than the others, had a good ear and was able to string together several words. A limited knowledge of Portuguese on the part of both groups also helped bridge the language chasm. And more than at any previous time, the Atrowari cooperated in the venture to systematically record their speech.

The Wai Wai escorted their visitors to church. There the Atrowari sang lustily, though Kirifaka likened their screeching to that of parrots. They aped Fanahruwi when in leading the singing he clapped his hands. Later in meeting him on the path or in the clinic they greeted him by clapping. In their minds, he'd probably always be the fellow who banged his hands together.

The men went hunting, the women harvested food and baked bread. Children of each tribe played with one another. Still, it was not long before the Atrowari grew restless. Every day they said they'd leave, but two weeks passed, then three, five, seven. Perhaps they stayed because all was not well in their own country. Piecing together what they could, the Wai Wai understood there had been internal warfare on the Alalau. Or was it two tribes fighting each other? Not even the Atrowari seemed certain whether the Waymiri were a separate group or just a subdivision of their own tribe.

"We will go today," said a fellow by the name of Maiko, as others had said on other days. "We will go home and bring back our entire village."

An entire village? A few could be handled, like the group present now. But fifty people, perhaps a hundred—surely the Lord wouldn't saddle the Wai Wai with an unmanageable number of wild, unpredictable people.

Shortly before Christmas they wondered if, as a matter of fact, He had done just that.

Some twenty Wai Wai men took Maiko with them as they went deep into the forest on a twelve-day hunt to get meat for the coming celebration. Among the Atrowari remaining at Kashmi was a man named Tamoshi, who had brought along his pregnant wife. He and Maiko, both about thirty years of age, were thought to be brothers, or perhaps cousins. Maiko had brought his two wives and mother and three boys who called him uncle. Despite the presumed kinship of the two men, it did not follow that they shared the same feeling for the boys, two of whom were brothers and the other a half-brother, having the same mother but different fathers. Maiko assumed responsibility for the boys. Estefen, the half-brother, was in his mid-teens; the other two, Prara and Shikin, about twelve and eight. Maiko said they were orphans. He had brought them to Kashmi for their protection. In the current upheaval in the Atrowari villages, boys like them could easily get killed. But were they safe here at Kashmi?

Tamoshi confided to a Wai Wai that when the two younger boys grew older, he would kill them. He had nothing against them personally, but a relative of his had killed their father, and it naturally followed that someday they would retaliate and in revenge kill him.

But right now it was Maiko whose life was in jeopardy, though away in the forest he would not know it for certain. Still, he probably thought from time to time that one day his enemies would overtake him. His mother was the first to learn of the danger. She was at the river leisurely bathing when she looked up and caught sight of more men across the river than she had fingers. Men she recognized. And what frightening men they were!

Her heart pounded as she scrambled out of the water, snatched up her scanty apron and, trying to watch the path while at the same time looking back at the men, she ran, stumbling, panting, fearful she'd never make it to the main part of the village.

"Killers have come! Killers have come!" she shouted to the first person she encountered. Kanahmachichi, the little, industrious wife of Emehta, worked in a leaf-hut kitchen preparing starch drink for the forthcoming Christmas festival. She raised up from her pots as the Atrowari woman rushed up, screaming her warning. Kanahmachichi did not comprehend her words, but knew from the terror in her face that some disaster impended. Others, hearing the woman's shouts and her wailing, quickly gathered. One or two got the word "killers."

She spread her fingers, then pointed down the path toward the river.

"They've come to kill my son!"

Yakuta had come up. He had not joined the hunters this year, still restricting strenuous activity. He also was needed to prepare the village for the celebration. Better than most, he understood what the woman was saying.

"Why should anyone want to kill your son?" he asked.

"I know these men. They are bad. They will kill my son."

The Atrowari crowding among the Wai Wai accepted her dark prophecy for Maiko. They began to moan as if already mourning for their dead tribesman. None was more shaken than Tamoshi. Overbearing and demanding up to this point, he now clung to Yakuta, trembling like one in the chill phase of malaria. Was he afraid for Maiko or himself? One of the Atrowari women said she had known the Waymiri would come. Maiko had been in a war party that killed members of their tribe, and it was to be expected that the offended ones would track him down.

Maiko's mother continued to scream out her fears.

"They will kill my son!"

"No," said Kanahmachichi, trying to quiet her. "God is in this place. We will pray and He will protect us. We do not believe your son will die today."

The old lady sobbed. Then, spying a bow and a couple of arrows propped against a kitchen support, she grabbed them up and started running toward the path that led to the river and the men she so much feared.

Yakuta sprang after her. Catching her, he stopped her.

"*Yemeh*, Mother, where are you going?"

"They're bad. You kill them first or be killed. I can shoot a bow and arrow."

"You said there were as many as your fingers. Can you fight all that number?"

"I can try." She tried to shake off his hold on her arm.

"No," he said, trying to calm her.

"I can shoot straight. I've been in war."

"No, that's not the way we do things here."

She broke loose and ran down the path. Yakuta caught her again.

"At least we'll talk to them," he said. He shoved her in the direction of the village. Her bravado spent, she stumbled submissively back toward it.

Yakuta saw the Waymiri approaching. He hailed them. Twefu, the Wai Wai who was most fluent in Atrowari, now stood beside him.

"Do you come to kill people in my village?" Yakuta asked.

"No," replied a spokesman. "We want only the one who killed our relatives. He is the one you will see dying."

The Waymiri took Maiko's absence stoically, content to wait for his return. Yakuta took advantage of this mood to steer them to the umana where he called for food and drink. He recognized the leader of the group as one he had encountered on the first visit to the Atrowari some years ago. He talked to him at length. He learned their deadly mission was

in earnest. Proof was in their recent action. With all the emotion of slapping at a mosquito, they admitted to killing a
brother of Maiko and the man's wife before setting out to
track their quarry here.

Matching their dispassion, Yakuta said that killing of anyone in this village would not be allowed.

The Waymiri—there were actually eleven of them—settled down in the umana, hanging their hammocks next to
their Atrowari kinsmen. They appeared to pose no threat to
Wai Wai women or to any of the Atrowari present. The Wai
Wai realized, however, that when the hunters returned,
Maiko among them, war could break out. For this reason
they pushed active trading with the newcomers, hoping to
get possession of the bundles of arrows the Waymiri had
brought with them.

The arrows, made of the almost weightless, stiff and
strong arrow grass, were as long as the Wai Wai arrows; it
was their points that differed. The Waymiri tips were steel
barbs, like giant fishhooks, fashioned from knives—explaining the penchant on the Alalau for knives. As quickly as any
passed into their hands, the Wai Wai hid them. They hoped
that before the hunters returned they'd have them all.

Ordinarily, the return of the hunters became the joyous
start of the Christmas celebration. Yakuta intended that it be
that way this year, though in everyone's mind was the fear
of what the avowed killers would do when Maiko showed
up. Responding to the unison whacks on the sides of their
canoes and their happy yelps and whoops, Yakuta inter-
cepted them before they entered the village. He warned
Maiko that men had come to kill him. His best defense was
to stick close to the Wai Wai. Further, only a few arrows
remained to the Waymiri. But, of course, it would take only
one rightly aimed to snuff out his life.

The hunters' entry was grandly ceremonial. Their faces
daubed with gaudy red and black designs, they tramped
to the umana single-file, toting their owchies filled
with smoked alligator, pig, bush turkey, howler monkey,

armadillo, and many kinds of fish. In a clearing in front of the workhouse they pranced to the beat of a drum, greeting loved ones as they circled about before them, stomping, shuffling, rhythmically clapping their arrows on their bows. At length, the Wai Wai women passed around the circle, lifting big pots of thick palm fruit drink. One by one the hunters dropped their trophies into a pile. What a feast they'd have this year!

The party moved into the umana. Several Wai Wai men formed a protective circle around a frightened Maiko. He soon learned of the murder of his brother and sister-in-law, and his fear hardened into anger. Across the big house, the eleven Waymiri gathered in an isolated knot. Their eyes were only for their intended target. The few arrows they still possessed were in their hands, along with their bows. It was clear their goodwill of the last several days had given way to their original thirst for blood—Maiko's blood.

Maiko said he would kill the Waymiri. The Waymiri already had vowed to avenge themselves on him. If the shooting started, who could tell where it might end? Both parties began to hurl insulting calls across the center of the house. Arrows were fitted into bowstrings, and though no string had yet been drawn, it would take only the blink of an eye and the war would start. As the tension mounted and violence seemed inevitable, a gun shot exploded.

Yakuta held the smoking gun, pointing it to the roof of the workhouse. He had discharged it, shooting through the leafy ceiling above them. The cursings and threats ceased immediately. All in the umana was eerily silent.

"There will be no killing," Yakuta said, raising his voice only so slightly because his blast had got their full attention. He lowered his gun and stepped toward the drink pots in the middle of the floor. The Waymiri bolted for the door. It was blocked by Wai Wai men.

"Nobody leaves," yelled Twefu.

"There's good drink," said Yakuta. He held a pot out toward the Waymiri. Their leader accepted it.

"*Taa,* all right," he said. "Let's be friends."

Soon the pot was being passed from one to another, and other vessels were lifted to thirsty lips all over the house. The Waymiri cluster began to dissolve, broken up by a general intermingling. Where only minutes before there were raging catcalls and grisly threats, there now were laughter, a playful slap on a shoulder blade, a sharing of drink pots.

"It was God who turned them around," one Wai Wai after another said that evening as the friendly spirit continued.

"There might have been war. But there was not."

"The fierce ones became happy ones."

Maiko, however, was not happy. He thought not about the killings of Waymiri he had participated in, but about the slaying of his brother by these men housed with him in the umana.

"I will kill the old things," he said to Twefu and Fawtaw. "Tonight when they sleep, I will stick my knife in their throats."

"No," said Fawtaw. "God doesn't want us to kill. We will protect you."

What the Wai Wai said about God was beginning to sink into Maiko's inner self. He was getting ears—just a little. There was much that he did not understand, and thought to himself he never would, but if God said for him not to kill, well, perhaps, he should obey. Somehow, he and his adversaries slept quite peacefully that night. The Waymiri stayed one more day and night, then headed home.

They asked Yakuta for the return of their arrows. He stood firm.

"You use sharp arrows only to kill people," he said.

On the day before Christmas Eve from sundown until early morning, the Waymiri chanted and danced on the airstrip, then docilely hit the trail for the Alalau.

In a few days Tamoshi's wife stole across the river to the jungle and there gave birth. She buried the baby. Was it born dead? Or had she killed it? Or buried it alive? Probably no one would ever know, nor seemingly did Tamoshi and his wife care.

If a baby could be buried with no apparent remorse by its parents, how could orphans be expected to survive in Atrowari society? That the three boys brought by Maiko had lived to their present ages was, indeed, a most unlikely achievement. Perhaps it was because their mother, before her death, had placed them under the protection of old Comprido, the "Long One," who as chief was obeyed out of fear if not always respect. Though their guardian, he turned the boys over to a subordinate, an old man who looked after them day by day. With the boys one step removed from Comprido, people dared torment them and often did, especially Prara and Shikin, the younger ones.

"This little old thing," a swaggering youth said one day of Shikin, then only about seven, "he's too much trouble to take care of. It's better to kill him."

This fellow and his brother tried to do just that.

Viana was the son of a leader in one of the Atrowari villages. About eighteen and already proud, vain, and never forgetting his own importance, he and his brother Maryo were constantly on the lookout for malicious activity. A fresh opportunity came the morning Shikin and Prara hunted birds with bows and arrows longer than they were. Not far into the forest they sighted a band of red-bellied macaws feeding noisily on clusters of bright orange palm fruit. Carefully Shikin circled under the waving fan palms. He raised his bow and arrow for a shot at an unsuspecting bird, but was thrown off his mark when someone suddenly yelled at him. Before he and Prara could trace the sound, Viana and Maryo had grabbed them and with bow string tied them to a palm tree.

With cruel pleasure, Viana pressed a sharp arrow point to Shikin's neck.

"We'll be back soon to kill you both," he said, and laughing he and Maryo went off to shake their thirst with a pot of thick banana drink.

The little boys managed to worm lose from the tree and

scampered off into the woods. Viana and Maryo were right behind them. The boys circled around to the house where their old stand-in guardian lived. He would protect them. Their pursuers chased into the house after them.

"For shame!" the old man said to the assailants. "You're picking on mere children."

Viana and Maryo had dropped their cynical smiles for dark, evil frowns. The scolding of an old man was not to deter them. Ignoring his protests, they dragged the boys out of the house and to the river. There they sought to drown them by holding them under the water. But the boys would not die. Neither tormentor could understand the resilience of these two mere twigs of human flesh. Finally tiring of the effort, they shoved them into deeper water and left.

Like all Atrowari boys, the three orphans learned early in life that some of their own people could not be trusted. They were also taught that even more to be hated were the Waymiri, the "cousin" tribe, and the Brazilians—especially the strange-looking, strange-talking, strange-living Brazilians.

Brazilians, they had always heard, were bad. They would kill you. Grown-ups kept children in line by threatening to expose them to the Brazilians.

"Kill them before they kill you," was the tribal motto. Stories were frequently told of Brazilians having wantonly killed Indians, so both Atrowari and Waymiri prowled about where Brazilians lived, looking for an opportunity to gain revenge. When the road construction started, the enmity grew. One day the Atrowari wrapped the builders' earth-moving machine with a vine, indicating their animosity toward this noisy monster that gouged great mouthfuls out of the land. In return, the construction crews replaced the vines with charged electrical wiring. In this game, curiosity could kill their opponents.

The Atrowari did not know what to think the day Yakuta and his men first visited their village. These outsiders were not Brazilians, but they were outsiders and so posed a prob-

lem. The women, of course, fled to the cover of the forest.
Each time the Wai Wai came it was the same. Shikin remembered a group coming when he was very young. He was told
to go off with the women. He disobeyed. One brazen little
boy went out with the men to meet these fabled Indians.

Fabled the Wai Wai were, for among Shikin's earliest
memories was their reputation as the Owners of Beads.
They impressed him, not for the beads they wore until giving them over to the Atrowari, but for the looks on their
faces. The Wai Wai seemed to be happy ones. Why should
they be when people he knew were more often not happy?
He was convinced there were no bullies among them like
Viana. Probably not one of them would kill a small boy's
father, like someone of his own relatives had done. He wandered freely among them. Later, his brothers said how foolish he had been. At one point the Atrowari had decided to
kill the Wai Wai; had they carried out their plan, he, too,
might have fallen with those surrounding him.

He was, of course, older and perhaps wiser when Kirifaka
later came, but his trust in the Wai Wai remained.

"Walk the trail with us to our village," this Wai Wai had
said. And now with his brothers, years later, here he was in
the land of the Wai Wai. He might not have got here but for
the turbulence that had seized the numerous Atrowari and
Waymiri villages. After Comprido's death, there was great
upheaval. People moved around, never stopping in one place
for long. The Waymiri hovered close to the new road, the
Atrowari pulling back away from it, and then reversing their
positions. Groups which had been together for years split up.
Sickness struck hard. There was no medicine. Those who
were well often fled out of the reach of the sick. Estefen, the
older half-brother, traveled from village to village, learning
what he could. He returned to his own people and reported
the turmoil to Maiko.

"The days are ripe for killing people," Maiko said. "The
safest place for you boys is with the Wai Wai." Thus, a party
was quickly formed and off over the trail to the north they
went.

After the vengeful Waymiri left Kashmi and peace reclaimed the Wai Wai village, Maiko grew restless. Once again he spoke of leaving. But wouldn't he be in danger back on the Alalau with no one there to forbid the Waymiri to kill? This was not in his mind. What pestered was the realization he had not told his in-laws he was going to see the Wai Wai, and now he felt rather strongly the obligation to present himself to them. But he insisted the orphaned boys should remain at Kashmi.

For a long time Twefu had prayed that God would send them two Atrowari boys without parents as the means to learning the Atrowari language. Why orphans? Because there would be no one seeking their care in old age. Why two? Because one would get lonely. And now he had given them three! Why three when two would be enough? Twefu admitted he didn't always understand God's ways.

Sickness again erupted in the village and, as the Atrowari complained, there were no longer any wild bush hogs in the nearby forest. Maiko was the first of the Atrowari to leave. With his two wives and mother, he just disappeared one day. Eventually Tamoshi led the remaining ones away. Only the three boys were left.

They first lived with Yakuta. As they learned to speak Wai Wai, the Wai Wai in turn began to decipher their strange tongue. The boys were especially helpful to Joe Hill, filling up his tapes and notebooks with significant sounds and words and phrases. Achi had a big part in their adoption into the Wai Wai community. As much teacher as nurse some days, she often sat between the younger boys, teaching them to read.

"Is it possible," she sometimes asked herself, "that I am sitting here between two Atrowari for whom we have prayed for years?" It was reality, however incredible it might one day have seemed, that three Atrowari were getting ears about Jesus. Three different personalities, the brothers provided a tiny peek into the make-up of this tribe that to outsiders had been nearly inscrutable. Estefen was serious and responsible. He understood the desire of the Wai Wai to learn his language and eagerly cooperated. Prara, a restless, moody wanderer, reflecting no doubt his tumultuous past, was slower to learn. Shikin, a warm, loving boy, soon became everyone's favorite. The native skills they had learned on the Alalau applied equally on the Novo—hunting, fishing, slashing away vegetation to create a new trail, using the vines and leaves of the forest to make all the fasteners and containers they needed.

The brothers accompanied Mamichiwa and Twefu on a hunting trip that took them far from Kashmi, downstream and across country toward the Anaua River. There in the warm sand of the creek banks they dug turtle eggs; their arrows brought down from the treetops the tasty spider monkeys; bush turkeys were fair game. One morning Mamichiwa cut down a particular vine, stomped on it, beat it with a rock and threw the pulpy mass into a still bow of the stream on which they were camped. The sun would not move far in the sky before the vine's toxin would deliver up all the fish they could eat and carry. Fish poisoning was not yet completely abandoned.

But Mamichiwa's plans did not include sudden illness. Estefen had awakened hot and with a pounding head. The symptoms of malaria often appeared among the Indians, whether at home or somewhere on the trail. If they were too far from Achi and her medicine, the stricken generally stayed in their hammocks until they felt like traveling. Estefen's fever, however, was of no ordinary variety.

"This boy is hot!" pronounced a worried Mamichiwa after feeling his head and cheeks. "We'd better go home now."

Mamichiwa and Twefu prepared to carry Estefen back to the stream where they had tied their canoe. Being of a practical mind, however, they were not about to let sickness rob them of an anticipated bounty. Mamichiwa instructed Prara and Shikin to stay there, wait for the fish stunned by the poison to surface, to club them, gather them up and bring them along later in the day.

At Kashmi, they hailed Yakuta, whose house was closest to the river.

"This boy is really sick," Mamichiwa announced as they lugged Estefen toward Achi's clinic. She treated him. The village prayed. In a couple of days Shikin and Prara arrived with their fish catch, and were told their older brother might not live.

He did not live. Succumbing to the disease that ravaged the entire Amazon forest, he seemed to burn internally until nothing more was left to waste away. The people of Kashmi were greatly saddened, for in the little time they had known him they saw in him a youth of great promise.

"He was beginning to get ears about God," said one of them, offering a bit of hope to people whose vision extended beyond the grave.

"Maybe Jesus wanted him close by," another ventured.

"What will his people think?" asked one.

"Oh, what will they think?"

It was a new thought fraught with uncertainty and possible danger. As once the Wai Wai did, the Atrowari believed that death seldom "just happened." Someone had to bear the blame. Would they say the Wai Wai had killed one of their people? Would they charge that some man or woman had eaten the lad's spirit, and now in revenge the Atrowari must declare war on the Wai Wai?

Mamichiwa made special effort to comfort Estefen's younger brothers. The boys responded by saying they accused no one. They had been with Estefen when he came down sick, and it might easily have been one of them.

"What will your relatives say?" Mamichiwa asked. More importantly, he meant, What will they do?

They were now down to two orphan boys, the number Twefu had prayed for.

While malaria was the prevailing illness, it was not the only malady to strike at the homes of Kashmi. A month after Estefen's passing, the wife of Yakuta died. It became

Kirifaka's turn to comfort his lifelong friend. His own Fehya and Yakuta's Tarishi had been as inseparable as sisters—and now, after only a few months, they were united again and were walking the paths of eternity together. Before she died, Tarishi made Yakuta promise he would marry again. She knew her husband—he couldn't manage without a wife. By insisting that he not be without one she showed just how much she loved him.

In the months the surviving brothers Prara and Shikin had lived at Kashmi, each had been very helpful in Joe Hill's study of their language. They in turn had got good ears, both about God and for the Wai Wai language. Shikin, the younger, responded more freely to what they learned in God's Paper, but the teaching was nevertheless beginning to show up in Prara's life as well.

As the dry season settled in, nine Atrowari men, among them Maiko and Tamoshi, returned to Kashmi. The big question on every Wai Wai mind was the reaction they would have to Estefen's death. An Atrowari dying under a Wai Wai roof could threaten the tenuous cord that had begun to link the two tribes. The Wai Wai feared that if the Atrowari became angry over Estefen, and if they did nothing in revenge, they would at least take the two boys back, thwarting another attempt at winning the tribe to Christ.

The nine arrived unannounced. Because they were without their wives, they probably would not stay long. With some trepidation, Yakuta broke the news to them that Estefen had died of malaria.

"Oh, he died from sickness?"

"Well, we die from sickness in our village, too," they said.

Some among them helped Joe Hill in learning new words and more structure of their complex language. In this Mamichiwa was of material aid. He approached the Hills' house one day, a firm grasp on the arms of two Atrowari.

"Joe, Joe! *Oklee!*" he called, grinning widely and shoving forward his daunted wards. "Get out your tape recorder.

They'll give you language."

Writing to friends in the United States, Joe said of his work:

"At this point, analyzing the Atrowari language is like trying to put together a five-thousand-piece jigsaw puzzle when you have only five pieces and almost no idea what the picture as a whole looks like."

He was laboring over their sounds at the same time he was still trying to become fluent in the Wai Wai language. In a letter about Wai Wai he said:

"I will shell nuts. I am shelling nuts. I just shelled nuts. I recently shelled nuts. Some time ago I shelled nuts." All these tenses. Whoever said there was such a thing as a primitive language? This one contains hundreds of verbs in five tenses divided into four classes, each revealing an interesting cultural tidbit."

"Though they know nothing of carrots or spinach," he wrote to another, "it is quite Wai Wai to admonish your son to eat up all of his cooked tapir's nose so he will develop a good sense of direction on the trail."

Fanahruwi had eaten the nose of many tapirs. Good at music, languages, and medicine, he also was a natural woodsman. He could speed through the forest, pick out the trail that to a less keen eye might appear as having never yet been cut. He took a half-dozen Atrowari on a quick trip over the mountains to Guyana, simply because they wanted to go, and had them back in Kashmi in plenty of time for the Christmas festival.

After the celebration, Yakuta learned that the last of their visitors were about to leave. They intended to take Prara and Shikin with them. The boys could not be held against their will. Shikin seemed content to stay, but the fidgety Prara missed his relatives. If he went, undoubtedly his younger brother would go with him.

A few days into the new year Mamichiwa escorted the nine men and the two boys out of the village and on their way toward the Atrowari's home. After a couple of days on the trail they surprisingly met up with Emehta and Fawtaw, who some weeks before had gone to the Alalau and now were bringing a very large group of Atrowari to Kashmi. Those going south turned around and joined their tribesmen heading for the Novo.

In the midst of the Wai Wai readying fields for planting, cutting the forest for new fields, repairing houses in the village, settling problems and trying to fend off others, ninety-two Atrowari descended on Kashmi.

They came with all their belongings—men, women, children, grandparents toting or leading or trying to keep up with dogs, pet monkeys and parrots, macaws and chickens. They were burdened with bows and arrows, knives, axes, wooden stools, flutes, packets of feathers, cooking pots and smoked ham joints.

"We come to stay," said Maruwaga, the chief. He was smiling this time. Except for one or two really cross fellows, they all appeared to be happy. Well might they be. They had escaped, their Wai Wai escorts reported, from a land riven with sickness and where the government, whose presence was otherwise felt, lacked the necessary medicines. Thin and pale, the Atrowari had many among them whose flesh went from hot to cold and back to hot. Fanahruwi and his co-workers at the clinic treated countless cases of malaria.

Suddenly, the population of Kashmi had nearly doubled. How could this influx be fed?

The Wai Wai had prayed for women and children to come with the men, assuring a peaceful and more prolonged visit. The twenty who had been there the year before had made up a convenient size. Then Maiko had said he would bring his whole village. If he was to be believed, they wondered if they could ever manage that many newcomers. Well, they'd now see how the Lord was going to fit them for the task.

Ninety-two Atrowari meant constructing new houses and hastily throwing up leaf shelters until they could be built. Farina would have to be flown in from Boa Vista until new fields could be cut, dried out, burned, and planted and there was time for crops to be brought to harvest. Should school be attempted for the children? Should they set up a church service just for the Atrowari? Nobody had yet learned enough of their language to delve deeply in spiritual things.

As usual, the Atrowari demanded everything in sight. Some foods were strange to them, but they insisted on tasting it all. One woman drank the dishwater. They did try to return the hospitality shown them. A Wai Wai woman went out to one of the leaf huts to visit. The day was hot; she was asked if she'd like a drink. Her hostess seized a gourd of palm-fruit juice from her thirsty dog and whisked it to her guest. The occasion called for both Christian grace and God's protective hand.

But they'd bear up. Hadn't they asked for this day?

Filth, obscenities, superstition, language barriers. A host of new temptations and trials came in on the heels of the Atrowari. Spiritual battles between light and darkness that the Wai Wai had fought and won thirty years ago loomed before them once again. Like many of the Wai Wai in that earlier day, a few Atrowari today showed themselves willing to be taught about a God they hadn't known, and who had only been the vague subject of idle speculation.

Young as he was, Shikin caught many a listening ear as he told them about life among the Wai Wai. For a whole year now he had called Kashmi home. Nine, perhaps even ten, he was growing taller than his brother. He was more reliant and confident than Prara.

"I wake up in the morning and I am not scared," he said.

"Not scared?" How could that be? he was asked. The nights among the Atrowari were always scary, and when one awoke after a restless night he knew there were angry quarrels left over from the day before, and if they did not explode into greater trouble, the day would in a little while give over to night again, with new fears filling the dark all around.

"I'm not scared because the people around me aren't scared."

The Atrowari watched the moon go through a complete cycle and a few days later a great many of them hankered to go home to the Alalau. First one then another voiced his discontent.

"I am missing the palm fruit I can get only in my own village," one said.

"The Wai Wai are stingy ones," said another. "They say, 'Don't eat the bananas until they're ripe. Don't dig the cassava until it grows bigger.'"

"*Gicha!*" said still another, spitting out the word of disgust he had picked up from the Wai Wai.

Maiko and Tamoshi, who had begun to get ears the previous year, said they would stay. Several others were also reluctant to leave. But some seventy went back, lugging with them the things they had brought. Tamoshi built a permanent house and found time to help Joe Hill in his analysis of the Atrowari language.

Four months after the seventy left, however, the remaining Atrowari went back to the Alalau. To the disappointment of the Wai Wai, they took Shikin and Prara with them.

"We'll come back next year," Maiko promised. But would they? Could they?

A government official landed at Kashmi one day and said the group returning from the Novo had contracted measles on the road somewhere and when they got home many Atrowari came down sick and twenty-one people died. The man was asked if it was known for certain that their recent visitors had carried in the disease. Well, he admitted, a boy had returned from the Indian house in Manaus, where there had been an outbreak of measles. It was either the boy or those who had visited the Wai Wai. He chose to believe it was the fault of the Wai Wai.

There would be no more Atrowari visits to the Wai Wai. The government, with its heavily armed soldiers, would see to that.

Not long ago at Kashmi there had been two Atrowari for every three Wai Wai. Now there were none, not even the two boys they had come to look on as their own. Some among the Atrowari had begun to get ears—a little. But could you expect them to stand in a hostile environment? And boys as young as they were, even having got ears quite a lot, what would happen to their faith if a Maruwaga or a Viana ground it down every day?

Had their opportunity to win the Atrowari to Jesus come and gone? With the door shut, was there a window or even a crack through which the light of heaven could filter into the dark, dark house of the Atrowari?

Right now, with perhaps fifteen years of hopes dashed, no one among the Wai Wai saw even the smallest crevice.

19

The fence of threatening soldiers which the government erected around the Atrowari had endured for almost a year. Five Wai Wai penetrated it once and to their surprise Prara and Shikin were permitted to return to Kashmi with them.

The brothers had tried to live according to the teaching from God's Paper. They found it hard. Life among the Atrowari was hard for everyone, tribal chiefs being no exception.

Since their father's violent death, the old chief, Comprido, the "Long One," had been the boys' protector. He died, and after he did life was especially hard and fearful for the two young orphans. Had they known at the time just how Comprido died, they would have feared even more for their own lives.

Comprido died in his hammock, it was true. He died while asleep, that was also true. But, according to what Prara learned during his recent stay with the Atrowari and revealed one evening after returning to the Wai Wai, the old chief was murdered.

Of course, Comprido himself had killed many people, and in his savagery were sown the seeds of his own villainous death. One day while he slept fitfully during an attack of malaria, one of his own men stole into his house intent on perpetrating Atrowari justice. In the semi-darkness, Comprido's very old father sat on a stool near his son. His presence made no difference to the intruder. A quick stab to the chest and the chief was dead. Comprido's father, shocked by this sudden assault on his son, picked up an arrow and thrust it into his own body. He, too, died without complication.

Once the Wai Wai had prayed, "Father, are you going to change Comprido, who is a hindrance to his people getting ears about you? Or will you take him out of the way?"

Until now they had not known that when death removed him his own wild tribesmen had contributed to the answer to their prayer.

Prara and Shikin were glad to be back with the Wai Wai. Here they were able to sleep through the night; no waking up to the screams of women as their men were being killed by raiders and the women were dragged away as the victors' prize. The brothers again listened attentively to the teaching of God's Paper, and Prara said he had caught hold of Jesus. Then Maiko and Viana came to take them back to the Alalau.

A strange pair for such a mission: Maiko, who may have been an uncle and who had sought refuge for the orphans among the Wai Wai; Viana, a budding chief now, but unchanged from the cold, contemptuous youth who had tried to kill the orphans a few years back. This time, however, Viana wore a smile and spoke kindly. He said their cousins were missing the boys and he had come on an errand of family cohesion.

"You have lived away from your own people long enough. I will take you back."

Once again Prara, still moody and restless, was only too pleased to hit the trail; Shikin seemed content to go along with him.

Shikin soon realized he had made a mistake. In this second year that he lived among the Atrowari he was ridiculed, persecuted, and despised for holding to his faith in the God of the Wai Wai. At times he was denied food. His tormentors included not only Atrowari, but the Brazilians he met while living near the road.

In this settlement close by the government post, there was no school. He missed Ruth Langer's classes and the additional teaching from Joe Hill and Achi. He complained there was nothing to do; he had grown out of childhood and its simple satisfactions. Prara, however, was content—something new for him. He talked of soon taking a wife.

"If you go back to the Wai Wai," Prara said to his younger brother, "I'll not go with you."

The *chefe do posto* asked Shikin why he wanted to return to the Novo River.

"Why are you not happy with your own people?" he asked the youth.

"Nobody here teaches us about God," Shikin replied.

"No. That's not the Atrowari way. It's the Wai Wai way, and it's not right. The Atrowari way is not to look to God. You need to forget that way."

Shikin refused to forget, and back to the Wai Wai he went. He took along another youth about his age, Gilberto, not to be confused with the murdered and mutilated Indian service agent. They settled in at Kashmi. Gilberto a little and Shikin very much paid attention to God's Paper.

In previous stays, Shikin had listened carefully as every day he learned of God, and he listened now. He heard Yakuta and Fawtaw and others speak from God's Paper each Sunday and Wednesday in church. Yet it was a dream one night that answered his enduring question, "How ever in the world can Jesus come into the pit of my stomach?"

One day he heard people talking in shocked terms about the death of Kumana, a man at the Mapuera whom he had never seen. This man, they said, was a companion of Jesus. There was no question—Jesus certainly lived in the pit of *his* stomach. Jesus came down and lifted him up into heaven. His young mind taking in all the talk about Kumana, Shikin thought of little else as he climbed into his hammock that night and went to sleep. He dreamed, and his dream was as if it were no dream but were really happening.

Jesus came down over their village. He reached out His hand to Shikin.

"Son, let me lift you up."

Shikin looked around Him. He saw many of God's people going up into the sky. They were happy. Shikin wished he could be as happy as they.

"My son, all the bad things you have done—let go of them."

Shikin wanted to.

"*Hnnnn . . .*" he said, but got no further.

He woke up. Jesus was no longer in front of him. What did it all mean? He thought he knew, and it frightened him. He hadn't gone up to heaven like those others around him!

The next day he told his dream to Yakuta.

"Little Body," said Yakuta, "God revealed Himself in a dream to you. Only God's companions will go through the air. If you want to be God's child, you must do what He told you in your dream. Let go of your bad ways. Let Jesus come into the pit of your stomach."

Strange—now he understood that if he invited Him, Jesus would come in and make His home inside him. Though unable to see it happen, he would know for certain it had.

"Read some in God's Paper every day," Joe said.

"When you learn what it teaches," Achi counseled, "you will grow strong as a child of God and won't become discouraged."

This Shikin endeavored to do. As he became familiar with it, especially the book that John wrote, he discovered that what people had told him about God they had not made up. It was all there, just as they said, right in God's Paper. That made him very happy.

On a hunting trip he found God to be as dependable as His Paper said He was. It had rained all day and as Shikin thought of lighting his night fire, he discovered he had only one match, and all the wood around was very wet.

"Father in the Sky," he prayed, "how will I dry out tonight and keep a cold from catching me? I have only one match and the wood is wet."

He gathered his tinder, which was rain-soaked, and struck his match. To his amazement, the little pile of twigs blazed up. He put on a small piece of wood, then a larger one. He had a fire for the night!

If what he had experienced wasn't a miracle, it was the closest he'd ever come to one.

"It's true," he said when he got back to the village and spoke of his fire, "God really does protect and help us."

The Atrowari were barred from visiting the Wai Wai and almost two years passed since there had been any witness to them, except to the two young brothers and now the teenager, Gilberto. That door effectively shut, the people at Kashmi felt God was turning them to focus on the lost tribes of the Karafou. Yakuta had tried to find these stone-age Indians; he was determined to take the words of God to them. He communicated with his brother and nephew at the Mapuera and together they planned another foray into the forest bordering the Jatapu River.

For ten days under Faryayaka's direction the search went on. The explorers had come upon a number of abandoned houses and fields, some old and some recently lived in. But they found no clue as to the present whereabouts of their elusive target. Their food supply nearly exhausted, the two groups were forced to turn homeward—Yakuta to Kashmi, Elka and his son, Kurunaw, to the Mapuera.

Another year another trip was made, Faryayaka's little band of Karafao again pointing out where they believed their relatives lived. Still they found no one. This time the people from the Mapuera brought cassava sticks and banana plants; if the seedlings grew well, the next time they would have a source to replenish their supplies, giving them a longer time away from home.

And somewhere in this vicinity, Elka and Kurunaw

vowed, one day soon they'd plant a village. It would become the base for contact with the Karafou.

After seven years, life along the Mapuera began to settle into a pleasant, placid routine. Early one evening Ayrin relaxed in her office, a screened end of her house under wide, extended eaves. Starting a letter to friends in the United States, she wrote the date, September 1983, then, dropping her pen, sat back to enjoy the entertaining life of the village.

She looked out over the river; countless times as she worked at her desk or waited for the daily radio contact with the MAF pilot or his wife in Boa Vista she took note of the changing colors and moods of the Mapuera—cool blue or green in the morning, dark and mysterious under lowering skies, a glaring white mirror when the sun rode high, a shimmering orange as the big, liquid circle sank each evening into the trees beyond the far bank. The river ran several meters below the level of the village. It had risen almost to the top of its banks in last year's rainy season, and the rocks which gave their village its name were all but lost under the swift-flowing flood.

Now, the river was back to normal, quiet and serene, at least from her distance, until at the lower end of the village the huge rocks broke it into a dozen channels of thrashing, swirling jets of white foam. The rocks were favorite places for the children to play and for women to beat out the dirt from the family's clothes on laundry days. With sunset advancing swiftly, the village was beginning to close down the day's activities. Between Ayrin and the sinking sun a silhouetted row of chickens, macaws and a big-billed toucan lined the ridgepole of a house. Families headed for the river for their daily baths.

"*Ah nah muuchi,*" Ayrin called in greeting two women passing under her window, heavy owchies filled with cassava strapped to their backs. "Where are you going?" did not really intend to be inquisitive, but friendly.

"A chey fo ko mai, Yemeh," the women called in return. Literally, they had asked, "What are you doing, Mother?" but they meant no more by it than the question in English, "How are you?"

The women said their heavy loads were a welcome change from the previous year when, once again because of drought, they had brought home from the forest floor the despised but nevertheless life-saving malia.

The improved fields were not the only signs of progress. From where she sat, Ayrin saw a new house going up for the *chefe do posto* and next to it a new clinic. There was an urgency to complete the clinic because there in October they would hold their first training course for medical attendants. Other building projects would soon start. Under her house a stockpile of palm slats was growing, materials for another house when one might be needed. The enlarged air strip was now finished. Beyond it stood the new school with its several divided areas accommodating the wide range in pupil ages.

Six or eight young men flung a greeting to *Yemeh* as they sped by the corner of her house toward the school's playing field. Their soccer game was a daily ritual.

"*Yemeh,* I'm on my way to my old aunt's house," a young woman said as she ambled by. "She borrowed my grater board and now I need it to shred my cassava."

Others announced they were going fishing or hoped they'd have time before dark to dig some cassava or cut a few canes of sugar. A group of children played around the steps leading to Ayrin's front door, waiting for her to open it so they could swarm in and take the puzzles and books from the shelves and spend a happy evening under the dim light bulb that hung over her living room. Ayrin's house had been fitted with a solar panel, and from it batteries were charged and a few lights were lit.

She turned back to her letter. There was a death to report, a Katwena woman who was lost in childbirth. It had been months since Easter, but she had yet to describe to this correspondent the happy times of the five-day celebration, of the baptisms and the singing. And since then there had been the National Day observance in which the school children marched with the Brazilian flag and sang the national anthem with the solemnity of patriotism. As school head, Ayrin meant to instill in her children a respect and loyalty for the land in which they lived. They were Indians, yes, and their first recognition was as Wai Wai; but in a few short years their isolation here, however incomplete it might be, would break down further, and she was determined that the young generations should be equipped to walk the bridge to the outside world when necessary and to cope with the world when it crossed into their own village.

Closing her letter, she turned to school work. Always there was school work. The making of books, posters, flash cards; curriculum planning; staff training; scheduling of health examinations; ordering of medicines; filling out reports, reports, reports. . . .

"Good evening, *Yemeh*," said Forosha as he walked by. This young man spoke Portuguese rather well and also a little English, remembered from his schooling in Guyana. Wai Wai children and youth called their mother's sister "mother," and because many of the women addressed Ayrin as sister, she became *Yemeh,* mother, to many of the young. Forosha was a special "son" to Ayrin; she had other "sons" and "daughters" among the young men and women whom she first taught, then later supervised, as teachers in the school.

Mornings when Forosha walked past her house, it usually meant time neared for a service in the church. The first there, he would pick up the cow horn hanging inside the door, mount to a small hill next to the airstrip and blow the long, moaning signal for assembly. She'd still have a few minutes, however, so she'd open her door and stand aside as the children, gathered from an early hour, poured in. They'd skim through the books and puzzles and she'd have opportunity to talk to a couple of parents or so, and still everyone would get to church—almost on time.

Forosha and Kurunaw were two young men who had risen to positions of responsibility. Outwardly, Forosha was a picture of the old Indian; Kurunaw of a newer, more sophisticated breed. Though different in appearance and personality, they were much alike in character. Sons of leaders, they were driven by vision. Dependable, resourceful, vigorous, each felt his duty to God was best expressed in service to his people. Both were in their thirties, Kurunaw perhaps a couple of years older than Forosha.

Kurunaw had grown taller than Elka, his father. He was slimly built, but strong and quite handsome. His face was serious, displaying dignity, though always his slow-developing smile was genuine. Had his flesh been a little lighter, he could have passed for a Brazilian from Sao Paulo. He was soft-spoken, his voice pitched a little higher than one would expect. Kurunaw acted slowly and with deliberation, which perhaps he inherited from his father, and seldom became agitated. That he appeared to be a person of no nonsense did not argue against his kindness. He was a reasoner given over to logic.

Forosha was a bit pudgy. His round face broke easily into a broad smile. Intuitively he believed in people. More folksy than Kurunaw, he nonetheless was basically serious and thought things over more than his quick responses implied.

Forosha and Kurunaw were both skilled in ways of the forest and both were intent on raising life above the level of merely surviving. The outside world might have called them progressive.

Kurunaw was the oldest son in his family and none of his brothers exhibited his dedication to God. Perhaps it was because, when in his deathly illness as a boy of seven, Elka had relinquished him to the Lord. Once given, the gift was not retracted. The morning following the crisis in his illness Elka had said to his son, "God saved your life. You are one who has not wanted to talk about God. Maybe that is why He let you get so sick. If you do not accept Jesus, what will happen to you will be far worse than sickness." That day Kurunaw asked Jesus to come into the pit of his stomach. He began a steady walk down the path God would lay out for him.

It took an act of petty thievery at about the same age for Forosha to start his walk with God. He was a believer, but had not always matched his conduct to his talk. Caught red-handed, he confessed, incompletely at first, but came around to admitting he was wrong. At that point he wanted God to direct his life.

The two young men were asked by the government to be part of a team to make contact with a tribe very few persons had laid eyes on, the Gojodoa. Far up the Japura River, which was fed by the snows of the Andes, this tribe might be hostile or timorous and reclusive; the government wished to know in order to plan for its domestication. The Gojodoa turned out to be not timorous, but both reclusive and hostile. It was a harrowing experience for Kurunaw and Forosha and a third Wai Wai accompanying them, a fellow named Taruchi. The wild, totally naked, but hideously painted Gojodoa spat on the three, ripped off their clothes, slashed pants and shirts to shreds, tested Wai Wai strength by forcing the three into superhuman feats, cut off Kurunaw's hair to the scalp and, before the trio escaped, shot at them, with only the restraining hand of God causing the deadly arrows to miss by a hairbreadth.

On their return, Kurunaw said, "I think of the Gojodoa as people who need Jesus."

"I've been there and seen them," Forosha said, "and now I have a love for them. If God makes it possible, I'll go to them again."

For both Forosha and Kurunaw, the contact with the Gojodoa reinforced their commitment to the will of God. Kurunaw would be starting over as he led Faryayaka's people from the relative comforts at the Mapuera to a new village hacked out of the forest near where fragments of the Karafou had last been seen. Forosha would return to the heavy duties of a church leader. Each knew he could count on the attacks of old Seetin, whose arrows would be even more deadly than those of the Gojodoa. And no doubt he was a better marksman.

Some little time after their return, the Wai Wai received payment from the government for taking part in the venture. Each was given two pairs of pants. None came close to a fit.

20

The distant, vibrating hum of an engine pricked the ear of several Mapuera villagers going about their daily routines. Among them were a woman roasting farina, another tossing flat circles of cassava bread onto her house roof to dry in the sun, a man shaping a canoe paddle, and children picking out words in a first-reader book. For those hearing the throbbing purr, the day at that moment ceased being routine. Abruptly dropping what they were doing, they hurried to a point of land jutting out to the river. There they peered upstream, lifting their eyes and shading them against the water's glaring reflection of the noon-day sun, searching the clear, still sky. The speck they saw, or imagined they could see, had to be a plane; and judging by the increasing resonance it sent toward them, it would soon arrive.

"He's coming!" one shouted, and the others picked up the cry.

Rushing back to pull the burning sticks from under the farina or to snatch up a small child or to pop in a doorway and alert anyone in the house, these heralds of anticipated visitors scurried toward the airstrip, others not far behind them.

"Bahm's coming!"

"How long we've waited for this day."

Bahm had flown in many times before. Always the entire village turned out to greet him as he stepped from the plane. But this time there was added excitement, even before he landed.

It was over what Bahm was bringing.

A book in his suitcase bore the Wai Wai words for That Which God Gives Us Free of Charge, a phrase that in English meant "grace." It was this book that was generating such great commotion. The rather cumbersome title—but one nonetheless apt—was the Wai Wai way of saying The New Testament. For thirty years its on-going translation into Wai Wai was a book in the making, a Gospel one year, an Epistle the next, each a separate small volume. Now, up there in the on-coming sky canoe was God's Paper in a form they had only dreamed of.

The MAF plane soon came within view. As the pilot circled the field once before landing, the last of the stragglers hurried along a half-dozen paths that converged on the spot where the planes stopped. Well-trained by the various pilots to hold back behind an imaginary line until the engine shut off, the villagers waited for the propeller to die. Then, led by stampeding children, they surged to the side of the plane. After what seemed an interminable length of time, the door opened, and Bahm unfolded his long legs and stepped down to the ground.

Holding aloft a thick volume, he raised his voice over the welcoming hubbub:

"For a long time I've talked to you about God's Paper. This is what I was talking about."

He waved his book and smiled broadly. His greeters waved back and shouted approval.

"One day soon there'll be a copy for everybody."

The people were ecstatic. They pressed tightly around Bahm, reaching out to touch the book as if trying to assure themselves it was real. He opened it to show that it did speak Wai Wai. One young man read a line, then a woman twisted her head around to read another. Children cried, "Let me! Let me!"

Three other passengers emerged. UFM leaders, they had come to take part in the dedication of the Wai Wai New Testament. Sickness prevented Bahm's wife from making the trip, a keen disappointment to both Bahm and her because in this work Ferochi's language talents had gone far in deciphering the meanings of many difficult Wai Wai expressions and reducing abstract ideas in English to Wai Wai words of everyday usage. Tomorrow, a plane would drop off numerous copies of the New Testament at Kashmi on the Novo, then fly on with a boxful for the Mapuera dedication. Kashmi's dedication and distribution would have to await Bahm's arrival there. On the day the volumes came into their hands, the believers at each village would together express their thanks and ask for God's blessing.

Bob Hawkins had felt his call to missionary service encompassed a three-fold task: Translate, teach, and send out the believers as missionaries. From the beginning he had taught God's Paper to the Wai Wai. From the start of their walk with God they had been evangelists with a mission to the jungle tribes around them. Now, at last, a significant milestone in translation had been reached. The task had been shared by many of the people. Elka, Kirifaka and his son Fanahruwi, Totore, Kaukma, Yafoma and his wife Chana—these among others, had altered or refined Bahm's transformation of the English text into Wai Wai. Besides Ferochi, co-workers Achi and Ayrin had helped importantly. Unlike the irrelevance of subject matter to an interpreter or typist, the content which these translators handled was of great importance to them. They sensed the need for utmost accuracy; after all, it was God's words they dealt with.

If in Bahm's language God's Paper said "eat," what exactly did it signify in Wai Wai? One word meant to eat bread, another to eat meat, still a third to eat pineapple. Depending on the chosen word, "we" included or excluded the speaker. Unless the right words were selected, the translation would

be the talk of a small child. Who wanted the apostles or the
prophets to sound like that?

Each language informant brought his own particular
strength to the project.

"If thy right eye offend thee . . ." Had anyone ever
plucked out his eye? Elka in practicality asked one day.

Whatever Totore said, it was straight and to the point.
Kirifaka strove for perfection. Young Fanahruwi was
perhaps the most helpful. He had a way of seeing things in
perspective and of expressing them so people easily understood.

Thanks to Bahm's basic work of turning their oral language into writing and to their various teachers through the
years, all but a handful of the Wai Wai could read. The many
small books that had been their canon and a hymnal of some
two hundred songs were counted by most families as their
dearest possessions. Now the Book itself had been fixed, as
Yakuta said of its publication. On receiving it, the people
would have an even more precious treasure.

The dedication at Howler Monkey Rocks took place the
day after Bahm's arrival. Because a new church was under
construction, the service moved to the umana.

"I couldn't speak Wai Wai when I first came to live with
you," Bahm in light vein reminded them. That was right.
The older ones playfully poked each other, recalling how
they had doubled over with laughter when Bahm and his
brother first tried to talk their talk. Those strange white men
had asked for words of common objects and on hearing
them made scratches on their paper. Then amazingly they
made those papers talk back to them. When the brothers
spoke to each other in their own odd tongue, the Wai Wai
said they sounded like buzzing flies.

Crowded into the umana, decorated with jungle foliage
for the occasion, the people sang their favorite hymns and
several prayed. The visitors spoke. Elka expressed his
appreciation to Bahm for his long years of hard work. Then
he admonished his people:

"Don't lay God's Paper on the ground; it will get wet and dirty. Don't use it as a toy to amuse your children in church. Above all, read it every night before you lay in your hammock."

Turning to Bahm, he said, "We are grateful to you and God for giving us this half of His Word. We have only half. Now we want you to give us the rest."

The women then served a big, festive community meal, a joyous *onaharineh!*

There was one hitch. The box of additional copies had not arrived. Ayrin knew why. She had missed much of the service. The radio had kept her in her office.

"An aborted take-off," was what she heard in the crackle of the receiver. The MAF pilot had touched down at Kashmi, dropping off Achi and Ruth Langer from Boa Vista and unloading that village's box of New Testaments. Then bound for the Mapuera, he sped down the runway, but before lifting off an explosion rocked the plane. As the engine died he braked to a stop, just short of the trees at the end of the runway. Had the blowup occurred two seconds later he would have plowed into the jungle thickets; five seconds later he would have been in the air, and for certain a pilot, a plane, and a village's supply of New Testaments would have plunged disastrously to the ground. Had it happened before the stop at Kashmi, two other missionaries and the rest of the New Testaments would also have been victims.

A cracked engine, Ayrin was told. Now an utterly useless piece of junk.

The pilot related what Achi had told him as they had flown from Boa Vista to Kashmi. "Something is bound to happen," she had predicted. "Satan doesn't let people get near the Word of God without putting up a terrible fight." On which he was later to comment: "I think the Lord told Satan, 'Yes, you're determined to do your dirty work. Go ahead and do it. But I'm the one to tell you when you can do it.'"

The box of New Testaments arrived at the Mapuera on another plane a week late. The distribution brought great excitement.

"To think," Elka said, "I've lived long enough to have God's Paper in my hand today!"

Kurunaw held his copy in his arms as he was used to holding his infant son. After a while he gently passed the book to his wife.

"It's your turn," he said, "to hold our precious new arrival."

Kurunaw was eager to read the Book of Revelation. The rest he'd read from his little volumes. They had not had Revelation; they had only heard Bahm preach it. To one elder, his copy was a "priceless gift." He checked to make sure it was complete. He was especially glad to pore over the Book of the Acts. Before, he'd read it in story form, now he had every bit of it.

"Those people were very much like we are," he said.

Tough little Charamcha sat down to peruse his New Testament. He wished to make sure that the teaching they'd had was actually in it.

Forosha disappeared inside his house. The following morning he spoke to Ayrin.

"*Yemeh,* I didn't sleep last night."

"Oh, is one of the children sick?"

"No. I waited all my life for this book. So I couldn't lay it down on the shelf." He had stirred up his night fire and sat by it on his little stool, reading all night long.

A couple of the children proudly showed Ayrin the pictures in their family's copy.

"What do the words say?" she asked them.

"Oh, we can't read it."

"Why can't you?"

"The book's too big."

She had to convince them that the thickness did not matter. The print inside was the same as that in their simple workbooks and in the little volumes of God's Paper they had read before. One of the girls gave it a try.

"I can read it!" she exclaimed. And so could most of the villagers.

It was to be the same at Kashmi.

Achi happily watched as the elders there sat on the front palm-slat bench in the church, thumbing through from Matthew to Revelation, looking up verses they'd memorized, comparing pages. As the service started, they smiled as they searched for passages read from the pulpit.

Some readers were confused at first; with their little books, they had only to pull from the stack the particular book under study. Now the Gospels were followed by Acts, then the Epistles and finally Revelation. To find any one of them, there was an order to be learned.

Yakuta penned a letter of appreciation to Ferochi, giving it to Bahm to carry.

"God really helped you and Bahm to fix the book well, *oklee!* The thick kind is now in our possession, so now we are very happy, *oklee!*" He was pleased, too, that groups of women in Bahm's land had made plastic bags with handles for carrying their new books.

Fawtaw read to his children every morning. At night, after they were asleep, he and his wife shared a chapter together, each taking alternate verses. For his own reading, he started at Matthew, laboring over the begats, and went on through Revelation.

The churches at both villages breathed new life. Now all within a single set of covers, God's Paper took on a new cohesiveness. Many of the believers felt that what they had learned until now was only a small beginning. More than one person asked God to give their poor minds an understanding that matched the profoundness of their new books.

Before leaving the villages, Bahm taught the people. Still, they felt they needed more. In particular, Kurunaw, anticipating the opening of a new village in Karafou territory, wrote an open letter to Christians in North America, circulating it through a UFM publication. He spoke of his plans to resettle in the forest where groups of Karafou were believed to be roaming.

"I would like missionaries to go with me," he wrote, asking especially for teachers and medical workers. "We would like many people to come help us. Who will the Lord send? Perhaps some Americans, perhaps some Brazilians."

Bob Hawkins returned home. He sent more boxes of New Testaments to both Kashmi and the Mapuera, and also a supply to Mawasha in Guyana. Then with Yakuta's letter to Florine fresh in his mind, he contemplated the challenge it contained: "Here's what else Bahm told me: 'There's another one, my brother, and I will now turn to working on it.'"

That other was the Old Testament. Bob settled down in earnest to tackle its translation. He had completed many of the historical accounts, some psalms, and other selections. Now he would start at Genesis and systematically work his way through Malachi. He had learned much about translating from his work in the New Testament; he expected the Old to go more quickly.

It had to. There was much else to do—a grammar, a dictionary, a book on Christian doctrine. Nothing he could do in his remaining years, though, could rival his translating the full Bible. Having God's Paper in their own tongue, they could read and study for themselves what God had to say; it was essential to life, the nourishment of growth in the Christian faith. Outside teachers could come and go—like Mistokin, who had recently died—and missionaries might not always be with them. But if the Wai Wai had unrestricted access to God's own words—which meant hearing God speak in their own language—they could, if need be, go on alone. The church deep in the Amazon forest would remain integral to the church universal.

Bob hoped that in his lifetime he'd take part in another dedication, the whole of God's Word, from Genesis to Revelation.

21

Kirifaka traveled to Surinam, going back to where he had had a part in starting God's work among the Trio. There he married a Trio woman. Several months later he returned to Kashmi to ask his children to join him for an extended visit there. His wife did not come with him. She was pregnant; it appeared he meant to start a second family, adding to the eight offspring and the adopted boy which he already had. But while at Kashmi, one of those nine children died—a married daughter. The type of malaria that took her life was a strain the people had not experienced before.

For some time the mosquitoes had been bad, due to the paucity of rain in the customary wet season. The Novo River all but dried up, leaving pools of water where mosquitoes bred. Many nights the people fled their infested houses and slept in the forest. Fanahruwi and his fellow health workers treated more than fifty persons a day with quinine, the only effective medication, and between the disease and reaction to the treatment the villagers were extremely weak and languid.

Kirifaka buried his daughter. Then after the rains finally came and went and the village settled down once more to normal times, he and his family left for Surinam.

If God allowed it, another family would leave Kashmi, this one to stay away a long, long time. Fawtaw wished to head in the opposite direction, to the Atrowari. Following the return of the large group of those capricious people to the Alalau River, the Wai Wai had had very little contact with them. But Fawtaw had not forgotten them. Everyday he thought about them, prayed for them. He remembered how his own people, the Katwena, one day had fought among themselves, killed their enemies if their enemies did not kill them first, were suspicious of all people not of their own village, feared the uncountable evil spirits of the forest—the mirror image of the Atrowari today. He looked on it as nothing short of amazing that God's message of love and forgiveness had penetrated through the jungle to their village, though they knew nothing about Him.

Fawtaw and his family eventually joined the other Katwena and walked the trail over the mountains to Kanashen, the Wai Wai village that was so different from the meager settlements of the Katwena. There, one by one the Katwena began to get ears about God. Fawtaw, in his teens at the time, was glad when Jesus entered the pit of his stomach, and felt secure and satisfied as others of his people asked Jesus to take away their badness. Then one day a young Wai Wai friend pointed down a trail and said at its end lived a tribe of cruel killers who hated people because they did not know that God loved them.

Fawtaw had wanted to start out that very day to find the Atrowari and tell them that if they became companions of Jesus they could be happy as he was happy. From then on, the Atrowari never left his mind. With Kirifaka's and Mamichiwa's, his was one of the first three families to leave Guyana and settle on the Novo in order to reach out to the Atrowari. Several times he had made the trip to the Alalau, and whenever the Atrowari came to visit the Wai Wai he made it his priority to minister to them.

But the contacts had all been too short. The Wai Wai had been able to learn some of the Atrowari language, but other than the two young brothers who remained at Kashmi, none of the Atrowari had got much understanding about God. When the ninety-two had come prepared to live for a year on the Novo, Fawtaw 's hopes soared. But they quickly plunged the day the last of the group trooped out of Kashmi.

Another way would have to be found to acquaint them with God's Paper.

One night Fawtaw lay in his hammock quietly praying for the Atrowari.

"*Ahfah*, what about the Atrowari? I have been reading your words. What is it you are saying to us—to me? Should we just forget about them? Have you forgotten about them? I visited them. You were the one who led me to them. Later, many of them followed me back to our village. *Okyo!* great surprise! More than ninety people came. *Okyo!* But after awhile they all left. *Okwe!* how sad! Surely, you are still mindful of them. You couldn't have forgotten about them. If you are still concerned about them, speak to me. Make it known to me, *Ahfah*, I want to hear your voice. It's true, I am unworthy, just a nobody really, talking to you. Nevertheless, if you would burden our hearts for the Atrowari, that would make us happy.

"My spirit is stirred. I know you hear me, *Ahfah*, for you are present here."

Then Fawtaw drifted off to sleep. He dreamed.

God showed him an empty field, its trees slashed and burned, ready to be planted. But no one could approach the field because it was guarded by a giant, ugly seven-headed alligator. The beast devoured many Atrowari, until Fawtaw cut off each head, finally killing it.

"Plant my word among the Atrowari," God said to him. With the dreadful inhibitor now gone, there now was no reason not to plant it.

"Plant the field of the Atrowari as you do your own."

In his field there at Kashmi, Fawtaw had planted cassava and bananas and pineapple. Each crop was growing beautifully. If he planted God's Paper among the Atrowari, why shouldn't it thrive even more?

He then awoke, overwhelmed. His heart pounded. His body was covered with sweat. "It's really true," Fawtaw said to himself, "God did speak to me."

Fully awake, he prayed, burdened for the people in his own village who consistently heard God's Paper but just as consistently did not obey it, and for his renewed concern for the Atrowari.

"The evil one who was killing others wanted to kill me and, it is true, when I faced it I was afraid. But you destroyed the beast. *Ahfah,* in the same way help me when I am actually living among the Atrowari."

Fawtaw had encountered God during the night; with the coming of the day he was determined to go as soon as possible to the Atrowari. That morning he shared his dream with his wife, and she pledged to help him fulfill the task God was giving him.

"I'll go with you," she said. "We need to obey God without delay."

They did not doubt that they would live among the Atrowari and one day would see God gain victory over old Seetin, the beast that was devouring the people. But how could they go, with the government fencing off the Atrowari from people such as they? This Fawtaw could not answer. But trust God; he must certainly have a way.

With faithful old Charamcha, Kurunaw had planted a field deep in the forest, and he was depending on it to feed him and his family and several other people, including the Karafou who would accompany him from the Mapuera to a village to be established near the Jatapu River. There were those at Howler Monkey Rocks who advised him not to take women and children at this time. He should wait until houses were constructed and fields definitely could be counted on for their food supply.

His fellow elders pleaded with him not to go.

"It is good that you should seek out the remaining

Karafou," one said to him. "But the time is not right for you to go there to live."

Was there a wrong time to do God's bidding? Kurunaw asked himself.

Whether because of faith and vision or youthful rashness and stubbornness, or perhaps some of each, Kurunaw would not be deterred. He had asked for a missionary to go with him, but none was forthcoming. Alone he led his group to the Jatapuzinho, the Little Jatapu, a river that flowed into the main stream. There almost on the equator and about half way between Kashmi and Howler Monkey Rocks, these frontiersmen began yet another settlement.

Getting there had not been easy. The Karafou's canoe sank in a rapids and all their goods and a lot of farina were lost. Despite this setback, the Karafou were happy to be going home to their region in the forest. It had been good to be among the Wai Wai on the Mapuera where they learned about God and enjoyed good food and had the tools to produce it, but there simply were too many people there in one village. The Karafou never got used to the crowded conditions. Here on the Jatapuzinho they would have no such problem. Some twenty-five persons made up the village initially. In several months Elka planned to join his son, so with the people accompanying him the population would about double.

The immediate problem was how to feed the present number. To Kurunaw's distress, the cassava in his field had not grown. There were bananas and sugar cane and, of course, game in the forest and fish in the river, but without their staple, the people would suffer.

News of their plight eventually reached both Kashmi and the Mapuera. Despite his having spurned their advice, Wai Wai leaders and the people alike respected Kurunaw and felt his experience counted for a lot, so the two villages willingly sent carriers with sacks of farina. Charamcha led the team from the Mapuera, and from Kashmi Yakuta himself walked the trail to the Jatapuzinho in order to aid his nephew.

Missionaries from Boa Vista tried without success to find the new settlers; they left their food bags at a place on the bigger Jatapu river where they believed Kurunaw would eventually find them.

That their new village sat in the midst of yet unvisited people became clear one day when Kurunaw's wife harvested bananas in their field. Alone there and on hearing voices, she looked up apprehensively, knowing they were not those of her own people. Kurunaw and the others were some distance away, cutting a new field. She caught a glimpse of several persons, but could not see them distinctly. Whoever they were, they circled the field, keeping back in the shadows of the trees. In a few minutes they went away, but planted pointed sticks in a path, a signal that they did not want the newcomers to go down it.

Once the men of the village went out to gather Brazil nuts. On their way home they came across a very large turtle, over which they smacked their lips in anticipation of the meal it would make them. They were already loaded down with owchies of nuts, however, so they tied the turtle to a stake in the path. Later in the day a couple of the men went back for the turtle. The big fellow was gone, but in its place a much smaller one was tied.

There was no question, people were around, people they had yet to see.

On another occasion Kurunaw heard people talking in the forest. He called to them:

"*Kiriwanhi,* Good. Come to our house. We have food and gifts for you. We want to be your friend."

If they were Karafou, they would understand him, Kurunaw reasoned. But they evidently were frightened off. He did not see them.

Yakuta and Cohki, the fulfillment of Tarishi's dying wish that her husband marry again, found a challenge in the enterprise Kurunaw had begun. They would return to Kashmi but in a little while come back to the Jatapuzinho.

"For three years I will stay here to help you get started,"

Yakuta pledged to his nephew. Kirifaka had for some time been in Surinam, and Fawtaw was eager to move to the Atrowari; at least one other family would go with his. All these moves would leave Kashmi's leadership quite thin.

Some of its people were beginning to wonder if the village's days were numbered.

22

The church leaders at Kashmi encouraged Fawtaw in his determination to live among the Atrowari. Hadn't God spoken to him in a dream, just as He had to Joseph, Daniel, and the apostle Paul?

They recalled someone had pleaded with Paul, "Come over into Macedonia and help us!"

In Fawtaw's dream, God had shown him a barren field of the Atrowari and instructed him to go and plant it. That there would be terrible dangers in planting and tending the field there was no doubt. The monstrous alligator with seven heads was proof of that. It killed many of the Atrowari and would have killed Fawtaw, too, but was rendered harmless by God's intervention. Would Seetin's attacks be any less? Or God's protecting hand shortened?

"Go quickly," the elders counseled Fawtaw.

The paralyzing attack of malaria on the village, however, delayed Fawtaw's move. Not until the epidemic eventually passed could he prepare to leave. Mamichiwa would go with him, just the two of them making the trip. They would seek a plot in an Atrowari village, build their houses and then return to the Novo to get their families.

Viana, who had become chief of all the Atrowari,

welcomed the pair, distinctly remembering them from his visit to the Wai Wai. He showed them a location where they could construct their homes. Everyone was friendly. Fawtaw, especially, increased his understanding of the Atrowari language. Then before their houses had actually been started, the two Wai Wai were told they would have to leave.

"Viana has declared you must go back to the Wai Wai," several people said to them. The messengers were apologetic, some openly expressing disappointment that they would hear nothing more about the God the Wai Wai had come to share with them.

"The *chefe do posto* warned Viana that if he lets you stay, he will get no more gifts from the Brazilians," a knowing one explained.

Fawtaw did not doubt the truth of this revelation. Everyone knew Viana loved gifts. All the Atrowari desired things—they had snatched beads from the necks of the Wai Wai, had seized their knives and axes. But Viana more than anyone thirsted for the new and fascinating objects the Brazilian officials were beginning to give the Atrowari. For Viana there had been a gun, a radio, clothing for himself and his wife, food that came in boxes and cans rather than by hard work in the fields and long days in the forest. There was the promise of a house like the ones the Brazilians lived in. Oh, yes, the Brazilians had much that Viana wanted.

Viana could be much more amiable than his predecessor chiefs, and the display of this attitude toward them had given the Wai Wai hope for good relations between the two tribes. But now friendship with the Wai Wai would cost him more than he cared to lose. If the government wished to fence the Atrowari off from the Wai Wai and their Christian behavior, it had certainly discovered how to lock the gate. The Wai Wai or government gifts? No genius in predicting which Viana would choose.

The much younger Viana differed from the old chiefs. Maruwaga, the most recent, was surly and it mattered not to him that his disposition won him no friends. Comprido, the Long One, had been an Indian through and through, a rough and often angry man, a killer, fiercely independent, a denizen of the forest, one who looked on outsiders (especially white men) as his enemies. Viana had grown up with Brazilians often around. He became rather fluent in Portuguese. He readily took to the Brazilians' softer style of living and grew used to some of civilization's gear. He was like Comprido, however, in having a hot temper, and people came to expect wide swings in his moods. But where Comprido killed with his own hands, Viana liked to have others perform his dark deeds.

"Viana says you must go," was the way he conveyed his orders to Fawtaw and Mamichiwa. Indirect as it might be, it was an order to be obeyed.

For several months after their return to Kashmi, Fawtaw waited patiently before suggesting it was time to try once more to live among the Atrowari. Surely, the message from Funai must be wrong, that if he returned he would be killed. He believed Viana would relent, would allow him to build a house and take up residence. After all, hadn't God instructed him, Fawtaw, to plant the gospel in the Atrowari fields?

Who would share his vision this time? Mamichiwa would not return to the Atrowari, but Twefu would. Twefu had made three trips to the Alalau, once with his uncle, Kirifaka, and twice with Mamichiwa. It was he who had prayed that God would send two fatherless boys to Kashmi so the boys would be free to stay with the Wai Wai and become their teachers in the Atrowari language. One of them, Shikin, lived for a time with Twefu and from this daily contact Twefu's concern for Atrowari souls deepened.

"My brother," Fawtaw said to Twefu as arrangements were being made for this second attempt, "You need to realize they are companions of Seetin, and life there won't be easy."

Fawtaw and Twefu decided to take their wives and smaller children, but leave their teenage sons and daughters to the safety of Kashmi. They went by river to the highway bridge and from there by truck and the Manaus bus. For a long way they rode in comfort, the women and children amazed that this thing on wheels sped so swiftly. It took most of the day to reach the government station that marked the northern boundary of the Atrowari reservation. On the opposite side of the road stood a military post. For the through traveler, these facilities would be the last evidences of security until the highway passed out the far end of Atrowari territory; for the Wai Wai they were the gateway to what they hoped was their new home.

"Who are you letting out here?" a voice called from the station's sentry house. A man sauntered from the building toward the bus. A Brazilian, he was short and somewhat thin, but swaggered with a confidence from knowing he was the nation's highest civilian authority for a vast territory around. "What do you mean by letting people out here?"

"I brought you some Indians, Senhor," the bus driver said, helping the Wai Wai to alight. His indulgent tone indicated he'd had run-ins with this official before. A couple of soldiers from the military post strolled across the road to join the circle.

"They can't get out here," the official said.

"You can't keep Indians out of an Indian reservation," the driver said, and the two soldiers nodded to support his thesis.

Fawtaw and Twefu stood next to their wives and the children clung to their parents. Speaking in the best Portuguese he could muster, Fawtaw told the official why they had come.

"Viana once showed me where we could build our houses," he said.

"Well, Viana is angry at the Wai Wai now. He doesn't want to have anything to do with you people. It's dangerous for you to be here."

"It is?" answered Fawtaw. "I'm still going to stay."

The bus pulled out on its risky run south and the soldiers

ambled back to their post. Joao, the Indian agent, had nine Wai Wai on his hands. With little else he could do, he gave in to the situation, and in his Jeep drove them into the Atrowari forest as far as the road penetrated. Leaving them there, he turned around and went back to his office. The Wai Wai began walking the trail to an Atrowari village.

The sound of the vehicle had drawn several persons to the path. Meeting their visitors, they escorted them to the village clearing where many others streamed out of the one large house and the various kitchens and other outbuildings. All appeared happy the Wai Wai had come. Maiko and Tamoshi, the Atrowari who had spent the longest time at Kashmi and whom the Wai Wai had saved from the murderous intent of their Waymiri pursuers, gave the two families a warm welcome.

"We are glad you brought your wives and children," Maiko said as he settled the travelers onto stools and mats in the house. "But your big children—where are they? Don't you love them anymore?"

"Our chief is an angry one," Tamoshi said, looking out the corner of his eye at Maryo, Viana's brother, who stood quietly in the shadows. "Maybe God can protect you."

"Yes," joined in Maiko. "We went to your village to kill all the Wai Wai. We saw how God protected you then."

The Atrowari had come to Kashmi for the purpose of killing them all? *Okyo!* Fawtaw arched his brows in great surprise. Then it was true what everyone believed, that the Atrowari had meant to kill the men and steal the women, and perhaps after violating them to kill them, too. What a great protector the Wai Wai had in God! Would He do less for them now?

Maryo stepped forward and gave a sign that the visitors should follow him. He led them to the edge of the clearing and to a rather dilapidated house.

"Why did you come with your wives?" he asked in somewhat of a pout.

Twefu stepped inside.

"*Okwe!* Oh dear!" he exclaimed. "We tie up our hammocks here and the posts will fall on our heads."

Some of the village men came around, bringing new posts and patches of leaves and vines for tying materials in place. Maryo, headman of this village, stood around to more or less supervise, and as the work proceeded said he would go find Viana.

"My brother lives in a village near the road, at a spot where the trucks speed through," he said.

And where Atrowari shoot at trucks and carry away their loads, Fawtaw added, to himself.

"My brother will probably be very angry that you came."

He wheeled a bicycle out of a small hut and walked it down the path toward the Jeep road. Three days later he returned.

"My brother is very angry," he said, confronting Fawtaw and Twefu in early morning near the entrance to their house. "He wants to send you away—today. If you do not leave today he will be extremely angry. Do you know what Atrowari do when they become angry with people? They kill people. That is just the way we are."

Fawtaw looked straight at the chief's brother.

"I did not make up this idea of coming here all on my own," he said. A crowd had gathered. How did Fawtaw, how did any Wai Wai, dare talk to the chief's own brother as if he had no fear of him?

"It was God who sent us," said Twefu.

"Do you know that God is living, and that He loves you very much?" asked Fawtaw. "I've heard you people are fierce ones. But you are strong because God made you that way. You say you are strong and fierce. Yes, you are because God created you. My brother, God is the one who made each of us. We didn't just happen to exist. We are all on this earth because God created us and put us here. Even though you do not know God, He still loves you. Why do you think you are still alive? Why hasn't someone killed you?"

"We were like you once," added Twefu. "Me, I was running

away when I did not know God. I tried to run from Him, and people frightened me, too."

"What do you think, my brother?" persisted Fawtaw. "Did God make us or did we just exist?"

Maryo's eyes met Fawtaw's. He had understood perhaps half of what was said, a mixture of Atrowari, Wai Wai, and Portuguese.

"You're right," he said, "The sun and stars and the moon and the sky—they didn't just happen. I see all those things and I know they didn't just happen, yet I talk bad to you."

He placed a hand on Fawtaw's shoulder and with a half sob in his voice said, " I'm beginning to like you, to like you a lot. But I talked with my brother, and he has said you must leave."

Maryo turned to those gathered around.

"If Fawtaw and Twefu do not leave," he said, as if giving an order, "you protect them. If their children want bananas, give them bananas."

He soon left, saying he was going to another village down the Alalau River. Within the hour someone else came, someone whom the Wai Wai knew well. Evidently having run a long way, he rushed into the clearing short of breath, his eyes popped wide with excitement.

Recognizing the runner, Twefu called: "Oh, look! It's Prara." Prara was one of the two orphan boys adopted by the Wai Wai, the one who when taken back to the Atrowari by Viana had chosen to stay with his kin while Shikin, his brother, returned to Kashmi.

"Little Body!" exclaimed Fawtaw.

Prara had no time for the pleasantries of a Wai Wai greeting. Speaking in Wai Wai, he burst out with the news he had to tell.

"*Kofi!* how scary! You know Viana. You know Showowo—he's a real killer."

Fawtaw sucked in his breath.

"I know them. Showowo came to Kashmi one Christmas," he said. He led the gang that had swooped down on the Wai Wai village intent on killing Maiko.

Twefu passed a pot of palm fruit drink to Prara. The youth took a long swallow, set the pot down, and wiped his lips.

"I heard Viana talking to Showowo," he continued. "'The Wai Wai have come with their wives,' Viana said. 'They're getting more bold. These people talk about God. If we let them, they will pull people away from us with their talk about God and we will not be as strong. We must send them away—or kill them.'

"Showowo said killing the Wai Wai would be no problem. 'There are only two men,' he said. 'I'll take as many men as my fingers and the toes of one foot—I'll not need more.'"

Fifteen Atrowari warriors for two Wai Wai men. No, thought Fawtaw, he'd need no more.

"Showowo means to kill you all. He said none would live to take revenge."

Prara sat down. He dropped his face into his hands and cried.

"They've already chosen the ones to kill you. They will kill you, your wives, and all your children." He glanced at his friends and sobbed. "I'm going to be missing you."

"Little Body," said Fawtaw, bending over the young man. "What you tell us is scary, *Kofi!*. We are only men, so it frightens us. But today we need to look to God and see His strong arm of protection. You be one to watch. If God keeps us from dying, you will see His great power. It will make you want to really serve Him."

Prara looked up. "They will come at daylight tomorrow. If you leave today, they cannot kill you."

"Son, we did not come on our own. Just by ourselves, we did not make up the idea of coming."

Prara went back home to Viana's village. With their wives, Fawtaw and Twefu began to pray. Twefu then spoke to the women:

"You heard what Fawtaw said to Prara—we did not come here on our own. Our travel was not just a trip."

"*Ahfah*," Fawtaw prayed, "you made the Atrowari. You

sent us to tell them about you. We place our lives in your hands. Will we see the sun rise tomorrow, and the day after? Only you know, *Ahfah*."

Taking no time to eat, yet all day long feeling as if they had just finished a big meal, they prayed and sang reassuring hymns until some time after the sun sank below the trees. Then they took to their hammocks, cuddling the children, and slept peacefully through the night.

Just as Prara had warned, Viana's warriors tumbled into the village clearing at daybreak.

"*Aaaaiiiiyyyyiiii!*" yelled Showowo. The villagers, up and about already, scurried back to the cover of the main house or took shelter behind scattered huts or among the trees. Their curiosity demanded they see what would happen, but they wished for no part of the action.

Showowo and his carefully chosen fifteen, raising high their bows and steel-tipped arrows and brandishing heavy war clubs, skirted the big house and headed straight for the house of the Wai Wai. Fawtaw and Twefu, waving back their women, stepped outside. They stood quietly, each remembering they had committed their safety to God. They waited for Viana's men, who now approached more slowly, though keeping their weapons in full display.

The Wai Wai stepped toward Showowo, seeking to shake his hand. He refused their cordiality. They turned to the others, but none would shift his club to make a hand available. Instead, the warriors encircled the Wai Wai and Showowo himself, standing shoulder to shoulder in a tight ring. They placed their war clubs between their knees or at their feet and inserted arrows into their bows. Penned in with them as he was, it was obvious Showowo had a message to deliver before the execution took place.

Fawtaw, however, spoke up first, silently praying that God would give him enough of their language to get his meaning across.

"*Ahfah*," he said, addressing Showowo respectfully. "Why have you come to see us like this? Other times, you've been friendly and happy. Other times, I saw you as a different one. What's the matter today?"

Showowo, perhaps surprised by Fawtaw's questions, said nothing. He was a big man. Wearing only short pants, he exhibited strong muscles in his legs and arms. His shoulders were broad, his neck was full and firm, his chest well developed from a rigorous life. To kill, he needed no weapon beyond his two hands. Like the men with him, he had cut his hair short and he wore a necklace of monkey teeth and a bracelet of woven vine. A few of the others also wore shorts, but most only a grassy belt.

When Showowo did not answer, Fawtaw continued speaking to him.

"Jesus wants to take you away from this kind of life, away from revenge and killings. You've lived like this for a long time. Fighting. Killing. Afraid others will revenge your killings. God wants to deliver you from all this."

"Tell me more about God," Showowo said, his first words since the curdling scream by which he entered the village.

Now it was Fawtaw who was silenced by surprise. How was he to express the concept of God in a language he was just learning? Back in Kashmi Shikin had told him words that might reveal God to the Atrowari. Now these words were only a jumble in his brain. He looked Showowo in the eye, trying to peer down into the pit of the man's stomach.

"*Ahfah*, I want you to be a different one. I want you to become a companion of Jesus. He came from God to pay for all your badness."

Showowo relaxed the hold on his weapons. In a muted tone, he answered Fawtaw:

"I've not heard these things before. But I like what you say. To think we came here to kill you!"

He took the arrow out of his bow and pointed it to the ground. His men did the same. As best they could in a composite tongue, Fawtaw and Twefu spoke to the Atrowari about Jesus, and the villagers brave enough to emerge from their safe havens also heard that Jesus, the Son of God, came to earth to die in man's place for the sin of the whole world.

"Jesus lives in heaven today," Twefu said. "Someday when He comes back to earth you'll see him and know we're telling you the truth."

"He'll take all who are His children to live with him in the sky forever," added Fawtaw.

The bows and arrows were now loosely grasped in each man's hand, and the clubs lay unnoticed on the ground.

"We were bad," Showowo said. "We were going to do just what our chief told us to do. Our intention this morning was bad."

The men had broken up their circle; they started talking, one above the other.

"Viana ordered us to do a bad thing."

"Why did we think we should obey him?"

"We should go kill him."

"No," Fawtaw said. "Don't kill Viana."

Showowo quieted the crowd. There was something further he wanted to say.

"I don't know why I could not kill you two this morning. It was as if I had forgotten how to pull the bowstring. Almost as if I did not know how to shoot an arrow."

The others echoed his confession.

"This happened to me once before," Showowo said. "I went all the way to the Wai Wai village only to kill Maiko and Tamoshi. But I couldn't kill them then, and I couldn't kill you today."

Before they left the village, the repentant warriors insisted on leaving their steel-tipped arrows with the Wai Wai.

"We won't kill you. We think kindly of you. We are loving you."

Maryo returned to the village later that morning; he had come to view dead Wai Wai.

"I think some of the things you are saying must be true," he said to Fawtaw. "Showowo is really a killer, and you are still alive."

After the sun had reached its peak and began to recede,

Viana came to see the Wai Wai.

"My brothers," he said, "God protected you today."

He said killing them had been Maryo's idea. Fawtaw said it did not matter, it was God who had kept them alive.

In a direct about-face, the chief said the Wai Wai were free to visit the Atrowari villages and tell the people about God.

"Tell anyone who wants to listen to you. Just don't tell me."

On another note, he asked Fawtaw:

"How long do you plan to stay?"

Answering his own question, he said, "Maybe you will stay fifteen days."

For fifteen days the four Wai Wai adults and their children traveled from village to village and spoke to the Atrowari about God and His Son, Jesus. Viana had appointed Showowo to be their guide. He heard the story over and over.

"I want to wake up and live forever in the sky," he said one day.

"If you will tell Jesus about all your badness, He will take it away and some day you can live with Him," said Fawtaw.

"*Hnnnnn . . .*"

At the end of the fifteen days, the two Wai Wai families returned to Maryo's village. A visitor dropped in as they made ready to leave the area. Joao, the *chefe do posto*, said he'd heard the Atrowari had plans for killing the Wai Wai, so had come to see if it had happened. Two weeks and he was just now investigating? Oh, but he had been prompt in sending a radio message to Kashmi that perhaps all in the Wai Wai party were dead.

Fawtaw felt disappointment that his mission to the Atrowari was cut short. But surely if their lives were in God's hand, so was the length of their stay. He counted eleven persons who had spoken personally with him, saying they were beginning to get ears about God. He would have to entrust them to the Lord.

For four days the Wai Wai stayed at the government station on the road, waiting for the north-bound bus from Manaus. Many people came around to say goodbye. Viana dropped by one day and talked confidentially with Fawtaw.

"I sent you away before because of the government man," he confessed. "The *chefe* said, 'Don't let Fawtaw come back. He teaches you different. What he teaches will make you want to change your ways and not be like Indians anymore. Fawtaw and the people from Kashmi are not like Indians. You are fine just the way you are. You dance, you drink strong drink, your women like to play. Why do you want to change?'

"He asked me if I wanted the Wai Wai to come and I said I did. 'Then we will leave,' he said. 'Do you think the Wai Wai can give you money and medicines and clothes and all the good things we give you?' "

Somehow sure that Fawtaw would return, the *chefe* had instructed Viana to assemble a war party to kill the Wai Wai a day or two after their arrival. This Viana had done, running his men by the government station to report his obedience to the order. It was at that time that Joao had radioed Kashmi that presumably the Wai Wai were dead. It mattered little to him that his message upset people on the Novo nor that it would take two weeks for him to personally verify if the tidings he had sent were true.

"As chief of the Atrowari, I will ask that he be removed from our land," said Viana, putting forward the friendliest of manners.

He really had meant to kill Fawtaw's party, but hearing of the resolute stand the men took in face of his warriors he changed his mind.

"God caused you to spare us," Fawtaw said.

"God protected you," Viana allowed.

He could not explain why, if fifteen days had been good, an unlimited stay might not be better.

"I took you to a lot of places," he said defensively. "Already I am seeing people living in a different way. Men

you taught are staying by their own wives and not running
after other women. One said to me that he had thrown away
his wife and taken another, but he would not be that way
anymore."

He confessed he had talked bad about Fawtaw, but he did
not want to talk that way again. "You walked around and
told people how God loves them. That is the way we want to
be."

The day the bus came many people gathered to see them
off. Showowo was there, so were Maryo and Maiko and
Tamoshi and Viana himself.

"Come see us again," the people shouted after them as the
bus roared off toward the north.

The soldiers in the military post across the road looked on
with amazement. Two weeks ago they would have sworn
these visitors would not live past the second day. And there
they were, riding away in safety, having taken leave of these
wild, dangerous people as if they were all related and close
friends.

Viana did succeed in getting the *chefe do posto* transferred. And at Kashmi, on hearing the report of the return
home of the families, Joe Hill took heart that his longing to
live as a linguist and teacher among the Atrowari might be
realized. But like the Pharaoh of the Nile, the chief whose
domain covered the forest on both sides of the Alalau was
capable of changing his mind. Viana sent word to the Wai
Wai that Shikin, the Atrowari youth who so unmistakably
had become a companion of Jesus, was not to set foot on
Atrowari territory. If he did, he would be killed. Neither
Fawtaw nor Twefu nor any Wai Wai was to come back, ever,
even for a visit.

Mining had followed the highway to their reservation and
several Atrowari got jobs in the operation. A large hydro-
electric project had also started, and some of the Atrowari
villages would be moved for the flooding of a huge reser-
voir. The key to this economic progress was pliable Indians.

No Indians with ideas of God-given standards or promptings of conscience. None whose minds entertained the notion that every man and woman and down to the youngest, most helpless child was due a chance in life and his worth as an individual was incalculable. Money, food handouts, and lots of mind-numbing drink, unabashed revelry, gifts of many descriptions—these purchased peace in the forest and paved the road to submission.

Quite some time before, Viana had made his choice. Hard on the heels of an interloping moment of candid insight, when his vision briefly elevated to take in more than his gods of pleasure and power, he once again had come down on the side of getting things from people. How many of the Atrowari followed their chief toward the promise of an easy life? And there was Prara, the one known believer living among them; how was he standing today?

Often Fawtaw wondered about the eleven who had begun to get ears.

23

Murder was suspected at the Mapuera when an old man mysteriously disappeared and the next day his body was discovered snagged on some boulders downstream from Howler Monkey Rocks. Elka had reason to suspect foul play and evidence pointed to Takatutu as the killer. Before governmental authorities could be contacted, Takatutu fled with his family, making his way to Manaus where he was able to dwell anonymously and with immunity.

With Takatutu out of the village, the hubbub over the likely murder subsided and life settled down. Among the people, that is. For Elka and the church and civil leaders, the crises seemed never to wane, crises arising from nearly a thousand persons living in a limited clearing walled in by forest. Elka and the elders particularly came under attack by government personnel who were hostile because the Wai Wai chose a biblical way of life over a pagan, and abuse from a small but assertive network of villagers, some of whom made an outward show of solidarity with the brethren but who never truly gave up the old ways. Others, younger ones, wished to resurrect the dark practices of their forebears. If no specific deed could be found for assault, a disgruntled person might fan a breeze of innuendo into a tropical storm of malicious defamation. When thunder rolled, the Wai Wai said the sky was talking. The village thunder clapped hard on the ears of Forosha.

Since the departure of Elka's son Kurunaw to set up a new village on the Jatapuzinho, the people in general looked on Forosha as leader among the elders. He possessed many of Elka's settled qualities and shared the progressive optimism of Kurunaw. To many much older than he, Forosha was wise beyond his years, more perceptive and capable of doing the right thing than they ever were or would be. Still, he was not immune to distracting barbs shot his way. Once he was so slandered he felt he should quit as an elder. But Forosha was a man of prayer, and through his communion with God felt he must continue.

His decision pleased Elka. It was men like Forosha who made his own work easier. Another he came more and more to depend on was Forosha's father, Tamokrana. Elka made him his assistant, and the villagers happily ratified his choice for a stand-in and prime helper.

Tamokrana had long been a leading figure among the Wai Wai. Committing himself to Jesus two weeks after crossing over the high mountains to Guyana, he remained loyal to his faith and raised his children in the ways of the Lord. Three of his sons became elders of the Mapuera church. Increasingly, Elka turned over tribal responsibilities to Tamokrana, and the heavy-set, hardly handsome deputy gained widened respect and the following of the people.

One area Elka did not delegate—his vigilance against witchcraft. He personally led the elders in attacking it whenever and wherever even a suggestion of it appeared.

"The spirits of the Evil One are real," he once said. "We know. Our lives were once ruled by them. They are the enemies of Jesus, and it is He whom we now serve. We will neither work for the evil spirits nor play with them."

Some said what they did Christmas night was just another game, coming on the heels of a variety of games the people had played in their week-long celebration. Elka thought otherwise.

Christmas preparation started many days ahead. While hunters went out for a week or even two to shoot the choicest of birds and animals, the women labored in their kitchens to make huge stacks of cassava bread and countless pots of drink. The festivities began when the men, laden with huge owchies of smoked meat, made their ceremonial return from the forest. For days afterward the entire village gathered in the church to hear the Christmas story read once again from God's Paper, and then contests and games and communal meals filled the hours with good-natured neighborliness. Adults as well as children wore animal costumes, some invading the village as a pack of big bush hogs, a couple running through the crowd like the little pigs that go about in pairs. Others masqueraded as anteaters, jaguars, tapirs, dogs, and armadillos, and the sounds they made turned the place into an animal Babel.

Everyone then went to the airstrip for a soccer game and to run races. Then they trooped to the river for canoe races. There they also watched young men wrestle on the sandy beach and others try to throw an opponent from the rocks into the river. In the umana a carved bird was hoisted to the high ceiling by a vine thrown over a rafter. The village's best shots lined up, and one at a time aimed their arrows, trying to hit the target as someone rapidly jerked it up and down. Outcries of joy and admiration greeted the successful marksman.

The slow dance of a women's circle inside a larger men's circle, rotating in opposite directions, drew anyone possessing a sense of rhythm. Those owning a bamboo flute or drum provided the music. Sometimes the dance lines wound outside the work house and filled the open space in front of the building. As the festival recessed each night, their hammocks looked pretty good to the tired but happy revelers.

A few young men sought to recreate a dance that was a throw-back to the tribe's pre-Christian days. Late on Christmas night the last game ended and the drums and flutes were laid away. But not everyone retired to his hammock. Some young blades asked the *chefe do posto* to extend an electric cord from his generator to the umana so they could prolong the high spirits, and he in turn asked that they fashion a costume some idle talkers had described as something integral to their old spirit-worship days. Mingeddi, the failed chief in Guyana, was visiting and happily led this effort. A young fellow roaming through the village saw the unusual light in the umana and heard shouts of laughter. He strolled over to see who still carried on. It was not who, but what he saw that startled him.

A human haystack stumbled out the door.

"Whatever in the world is it?" he asked.

What he saw was someone in a concealing robe of palm leaves, his face masked and his head covered with bark.

"The Yamo," said one of the creature's attendants. The explanation meant nothing to him.

Someone considerably older and more knowledgeable about such things also saw this leafy being. Wisho, sometimes called The Trumpet Bird because of his long, wiry legs, set those legs in the direction of Elka's house and with real effort sped them there. He knew the costume well. Hadn't he been a witch doctor once, and the Yamo a part of his devil worship? He called out the chief. Learning what was going on, Elka needed no prodding.

"Round up the elders," he directed. "If you need to, pull them from their hammocks."

Seeing the uncanny costume in the light streaming from the umana, Elka was reminded with more clarity than he wished of his days when the Yamo was a wearying but inescapable part of his life. His people had been engaged in a month-long Yamo dance when Bahm and his brother first set foot in their village back on the Essequibo. Unlike the shuffling, rhythmic rings of pat-patting the Wai Wai still danced, the Yamo was personification of evil. It was the Evil One himself communing with the people.

The wearer of the costume must not let any of his body be seen, just as the spirits hid themselves from sight by borrowing the body of a jaguar or humming bird. He was not allowed to talk, but made his commands known by shaking a gourd rattle. He drank only the strong fermentation of chewed cassava bread spewed into a pot of water. He had to dance all night.

Neighboring villages had been invited in for these night-time frolics. During the dance, the men in the party fed drink to the Yamo. This offering granted a man the license to snatch any woman he desired and in the sight of all to subject her to his passion. The Yamo never lacked liquor. Finally felled by odious intoxication and utter exhaustion, the Yamo gave up his costume at daybreak. Another would pick it up that evening. Elka recalled that some of these carousals had gone on for three full cycles of the moon, and ended only when the fields had been stripped of their cassava, ensuring hunger in the days ahead, and fights scarcely short of killings sent visitors back to their own villages.

It was for this personal history that he refused to accept the scene before him as a game.

"Take off the costume," he ordered its wearer. The fellow did as he was told. Some of the elders, gathered now along with a crowd of villagers, were satisfied, relieved when the costume was thrown aside. They could deal with the issue in the morning. They were eager to get back to the comfort of their hammocks.

"No," said Elka. It was a matter they had to address then and there. He reminded the older ones present that God had freed the Wai Wai from the shackling vines of witchcraft. Why go back to it?

"Yes, why?" echoed Wisho. "That old stuff we left long ago."

Elka warned the youths in the circle around him that to cohabit with the evil spirits only boded tragedy. He elaborated neither on the Yamo nor the other elements of witchcraft that today were so abhorrent to those who once had been entrapped by them.

"Witchcraft is bad," he said, "too terrible to talk about."

And because he as chief had said it was something to reject, they rejected it. For this night, anyway, they did.

The next day the dry leaves of the Yamo burned quickly.

Elka keenly fought the spirits of evil. But his weakness was the weakness of so many—the flesh. Once again he was accused of an illicit affair with another man's wife. He denied it, admitting the appearances were condemning, but swearing innocence. No one seemed to believe him. This loss of confidence among his people, possibly added to a guilt he would not confess, appeared to hasten his move to join his son Kurunaw and the Karafao on the Jatapuzinho.

Kurunaw and the nearly fifty persons with him still lacked sufficient food. For this reason, the church leaders, missionaries, his oldest friends, all advised Elka that he and family members who would accompany him should not move to the Jatapuzinho until new crops had grown.

"August," he said, "I'll move to my son's in August."

Some now had calendars and some wore watches on their wrists. They were learning to use the rows of numbers to project days, weeks, and even longer periods ahead. They flipped over the pages from January to August and were satisfied that by August the food crisis at the new village should have ended.

That settled, Elka unsettled it. He would leave in February. But on a Sunday morning between the short and long rains when many of the people were up or down the river tending to their fields, he announced in church he was leaving right away—this week. Who would go with him to help with his load?

Shock rippled across the thin congregation. His eyes swept back and forth; no hand in the church was raised. He repeated his request for volunteer carriers. Still there was none.

"*Taa*, all right!" he snapped. "If you want to, you be the lazy ones. I will find helpers. I have just decided I will leave tomorrow."

Tomorrow! Ahmuri hadn't baked bread enough for that long trip. People didn't out of the blue say they'd go on a trip tomorrow. Elka had always been a man who thought things through, wrestled with both sides of an issue, then, having made up his mind, stuck to his decision. How strange he was acting. How surprised people would be when they returned from their fields and found their chief had left them. The abruptness of it all had immobilized them, had kept their hands in their laps as he asked for volunteers.

Why was he going so suddenly? Could it be true he sought to escape the accusations about him and another man's wife? Was he running from Takatutu?

This suspect in the death of the old man in the rapids downstream from Howler Monkey Rocks, spent some time in Manaus. There his wife died from an illness, and Takatutu returned to the Mapuera without incident. But not all had gone well between him and Elka. The chief's canoe sank mysteriously, his outboard motor with it, and Elka believed the evidence pointed to Takatutu. Some people agreed the motive could be there. Wasn't Takatutu still angry that he'd been singled out as a murderer and Elka had tried to keep him out of the village?

Some even said that Takatutu was into witchcraft. He had been among those bringing back the Yamo at Christmas, and it was reported—*ha tu*—that Takatutu had placed a curse on Elka. To those who believed this, Elka's decision to leave the Mapuera so suddenly hinted at a change in his character. While in Guyana Elka had been threatened with loss of his chieftaincy, with imprisonment, and even, some said, his life was in jeopardy. His response to it all then was unyielding resolution to take his people across the border into Brazil. But perhaps leaving this place now was different. It looked as if he might be running away, like a frightened agouti trying to escape the jaws of an alligator.

Elka found five men willing to aid his move. Monday morning the group pulled away from the port and, soon eclipsed by the bend in the river, were lost to those bidding them goodbye.

"That's no way for a chief to go," said one who watched them go. He shook his head sadly as he retraced his steps homeward.

"How will the children be fed?" another asked and did not expect an answer.

One who all his life had been close to Elka did not go to the landing this morning. Saddened by his chief's strange behavior, Charamcha, everybody's handyman and Elka's faithful trouble-shooter, kept clear of the river by working a field in the opposite direction. A few like-minded men went with him. Later that day families began returning to the village from their fields. A number of men said that had Elka waited they would have been glad to help him.

The shock of his leaving—the way he left—was quickly blunted when a night or so later the community was pitched into the grim reality of the present. As her family paddled back to the village from their field, a five-year-old girl, a precious youngster known to so many, died unexpectedly, and no one could tell why.

Kirifaka hauled into sight at the Mapuera one day, bringing his new wife and baby from Surinam. His children who accompanied him on a visit to the Trio either came back with him or had preceded him and were once again in Kashmi on the Novo. Shikin, the Atrowari youth, had accompanied the family and returned ahead of Kirifaka; on his way to Kashmi he stopped over at the Jatapuzinho. A girl lived there he liked very much, and before departing that new village he would marry her. Kirifaka decided to go no farther than Howler Monkey Rocks. He'd heard people were leaving Kashmi, so decided to set up his new household on the Mapuera.

One of the four original church leaders and possibly the second Wai Wai to become a companion of Jesus, he had served God in many capacities—elder, preacher, teacher, missionary, translator, and Christian father of a large family. At present, there did not seem to be an official duty for him.

But that was all right. He wished to fit in wherever the Lord might have a need.

It was a new era for this large body of Wai Wai and associated tribes. For the first time the guiding hand of Elka was absent. People were sad that he had departed under a cloud and that nerves were on edge among both those who went away and those who remained. Elka had been a good leader, natural in his dealing with people. He worked hard, never ordering a man to do something he wasn't willing to do himself. He seldom got angry. Fair-minded, he understood the arguments on both sides of a dispute. He was a good organizer—his work teams knew what he expected of them and he saw that the work got done. Elka was a wise man. His failings were of the flesh. He hadn't admitted the latest charge, but few, if any, believed his denials.

The man who succeeded him as chief discovered that going from the second rank to the top was not easy. At first, Tamokrana went at the task timorously. He half expected Elka to come back, so performed his duties with a tentative touch, as if he were holding the position only until the master's return. How would Elka do this or decide that? Gradually, he gained confidence and began being his own man. But did people want Tamokrana to be Tamokrana? A few months into his chieftaincy there were plenty of doubts.

"Our new chief yells at the men," one complained as his crew rambled across the airstrip to make improvements at the school on the other side.

"He does not talk like a smiling one," a companion conceded.

Other villagers complained that Tamokrana often scolded them.

" 'You're all lazy. You don't want to work,' he tells us."

"He thinks up things for us to do, but he doesn't do any of it himself."

Tamokrana had been a stalwart believer, a good father, an exemplary citizen, falling into adultery once and suffering a painful disease from it. He had been a dependable assistant to Elka. But now some of his friends were advising him to step down. Their saying so made him angry.

Teams of men readying a field by slash and burn aired their discontent with the chief. Women grating cassava or slowly stirring the meal as it roasted over a hot fire discussed all phases of life, but sooner or later focused on the change in village atmosphere. Family groups gathered at their doorways at sundown spoke of the tension and lack of a happy spirit, whether it was in church or at an *onahariheh!*, the communal dinner that brought groups or even the whole village together. Wherever they went, people kept hearing the name Tamokrana.

"Tamokrana. . . " Then a shake of the head.

What kind of a leader did they want? This question was also given voice more and more.

"A young man," someone offered. "Not one who is untried, but one who knows things."

It was time, consensus ruled, to replace their chief. But who would organize the effort?

Kirifaka, more than one person suggested, was a man used to speaking out. Why couldn't he be their spokesman? A number of the men met with Kirifaka and persuaded him to abandon the reticence he had practiced since coming from Surinam. They impressed on him that for the good of the community, someone had to act. And who better than he, one of the original four, one who over the years had taught many of them much of what they knew about God and His ways?

"If anyone can convince our chief to step down, certainly Kirifaka can."

He spoke to Tamokrana.

"My brother," he said in a very private conversation, "I think it would be better for you, for everybody, if you'd step aside and not be chief anymore."

Tamokrana refused.

Wisho—stooped and seemingly made up more of spindly legs than torso, his front teeth missing, but his eyes still dark and piercing—approached his stocky, strong friend of many years.

"Better for you not to be chief," he said.

"I am chief," said Tamokrana coldly, "because the people made me their chief."

But all this unsolicited guidance had its effect. Tamokrana asked three men, one of them an elder, to circulate among the people and determine exactly their feelings. He would have found out for himself had he attended a meeting of the villagers on a Monday morning in the umana.

Tamokrana selected Chownyon to conduct this session which, he figured, would end with a vote of confidence. Neither he nor the elders, except Chownyon, would attend, but wait in the church for the outcome. Chownyon had come a long way from the day he schemed to leave his Katwena village for the Wai Wai settlement in Guyana by hastily marrying and thus becoming eligible to accompany Yakuta. Today he was rather tall and slender, of light skin, his facial bones pronounced, his hair hanging in bangs over his forehead. He had matured into a responsible person, and now more than any other was trusted by the chief as his go-between with the people.

In bright sunlight that bathed the village with peaceful splendor, Chownyon walked alone past deserted houses from the church to the umana. For some days he had held out against Tamokrana's insistence that he meet with the people this way. The chief pleaded that he needed him, assured him that all would go well, that the men would be in their fields long before the sun rode to the middle. He gave in. Then there in the church just now, the elders, with one or two absent, spoke unanimously on how Chownyon would bring unity to the village. With this confidence ringing in his ears, Chownyon neared the workhouse. All the children, it appeared, played outside the building. Stepping inside, he saw that adults crammed every bench, and many stood. He pressed through the fidgety crowd to the middle of the big, round room. Turning slowly, his hand raised, he at last quieted the people. Then with his first words he unwittingly set the stage for immediate rebellion. He asked what he thought was a simple, rhetorical question:

"Do we want Tamokrana as our chief?"

It set loose a deluge.

"Tamokrana made me fall in the river late at night. I stood in the end of my canoe and his bumped mine, making me fall."

"I made many artifacts and sent them with the chief, who promised to bring me money for them so I could buy teeth for my wife. He never brought the money and she still walks around without teeth."

"He talked very strong to me when once we had a disagreement about a canoe."

The talk was plain. Because they were unused to such direct attacks in public, always instead having favored round-about hints of dissatisfaction, the charges were like blows of a war club to the head. The children pushed in at the door to listen.

"Once I wanted to visit the Trio. He was angry with me because I wanted to go."

With rapid fire, the invectives flew across the big room. Not one person stood to say anything good about the chief. The other two community probers selected by the chief wrote down what everyone said, with names. Their notes grew and grew.

Finally Kirifaka arose.

"My brothers and sisters," he said. "The list of complaints is so long that it seems to tell us we don't want Tamokrana as our chief. What would you think of . . ." He hesitated to pronounce the name ". . . Forosha?"

He was pitting son against father, but this he could accept if it would bring a solution to the grave problem they faced. He was more concerned with the reluctance Forosha had expressed earlier to this suggestion. Forosha was a leader in the church, and that is precisely where he wanted to work. On mention of Forosha's name, the umana became stone silent. Then someone broke the stillness by crying out, "Yes!"

"Yes, yes," came from various parts of the room. Then a resounding "YES!" thundered from one side to the other and back again. The older children, who had elbowed out their younger siblings at the doorway, bolted to the open spaces, ran up and down and shouted "Yes! Yes!" The little ones took up the cry, having a lot of fun in this new game.

Chownyon waited out the clamor. Then, striving to be loyal to the one who had assigned him an impossible task, he asked:

"What would it be like if we told Tamokrana that his son must be assistant chief?"

"No! No!" This cry was as loud and expressive as the yesses had been. The crowd let it be known that nothing less than Forosha as chief would satisfy.

Word was quickly slipped to Forosha, who had not been feeling well and had remained home, attending neither the community gathering in the umana nor the little group of elders in the church. Forosha said no, he would not become chief. He was adamant in his refusal. The emissary returned with the disappointing news, but the meeting had broken up, the people having already filed out to their kitchens or fields or off to the river or forest with the extraordinarily good feeling that under Forosha's leadership all was going to be well.

24

Before Chownyon could tell him and the elders about it, Tamokrana learned the details of the meeting that took place in the umana. The tell-tale wren, in the form of a human ally, had sped to the chief with the report. So, as the would-be mediator entered the church, he was pummeled by the chief's wrath.

"I should have sent a bush turkey to conduct the meeting," he yelled derisively as Chownyon and the two recorders trudged to the front where the little group was assembled. Besides the chief, who sat apart, six church leaders were present, two of them the chief's sons, one his brother, and one a brother-in-law.

"You did it all wrong," one of them said.

"We gave you a responsibility," joined in another, "and you were an unwise one in the way you talked."

"Such harsh feelings coming out into the open!" censured a third, still in shock at the report he'd heard.

The two who had recorded the complaints displayed their several sheets of paper. Tamokrana brushed them aside.

"You should have asked, 'Who do you want as Tamokrana's assistant?'" This from the chief himself.

"The people wanted to talk about their leader," returned Chownyon.

"You were sent to get them to like me."

"The way it came out," one elder lamented, "so many hard feelings—why couldn't you have kept the pot from boiling?"

"Now there will be division," another added. "Will the village stay together?"

"Bringing in my son's name . . ."

"It was not I who mentioned your son," Chownyon protested.

"We know who did," said an elder, nodding his head.

"It has been said—*ha tu*," began Tamokrana, standing up, "that my son wrote a letter to the one who proposed his name while that one lived in Kashmi, and that my son complained he was not happy with his father. Now that that one lives here on the Mapuera, perhaps my son asked him to suggest his name as the next chief."

Even the chief's staunchest supporters did not believe this of Forosha.

"Are we to talk about the things the people said?" asked Chownyon, pointing to the lists still in the hands of his associates.

A son of Tamokrana got up and in open anger stalked out of the building. Tamokrana, looking at the pages just enough to see there were several, followed. He, too, was angry, but brushed away the tears that wet his cheeks.

"What is there to talk about?" an elder spoke up in a belated answer to Chownyon's question. "If you'd done things right, there wouldn't be a list."

Having lost the confidence of his peers, Chownyon stepped down as a church leader. Kirifaka, roundly criticized by a small faction in the village, became withdrawn and introspective. In great part, however, the people stuck to what they had spoken so loudly and clearly: They wanted Forosha as their chief in place of his father. In spite of all, Tamokrana seemed determined to maintain his position. To any who would listen, he spoke venomously against Forosha.

"He's probably not even my son. If he truly were my son, he'd say 'I don't want to be chief.' I haven't heard him say that. I doubt he is my son."

His hearers blanched. Forosha a bastard? Machfu an unfaithful wife? Tamokrana appeared beside himself. Still, he went on.

"My son is playing. He flips from one job to another. Work captain, church leader, chief. Who knows what he wants next?"

Tamokrana's struggle against his son becoming chief was no keener than Forosha's effort to keep from being chief.

"I can't do it," he protested to the many who urged him to lead them. "I'm not the oldest son, nor even the second. The village is too large for me. I've never done anything like that. I'd walk sad. Teaching God's Paper, preaching, sharing in problems—this I was called to do."

Also, being a dutiful son who really loved his father, he did not want to hurt him.

There would be a new chief, he was assured by some who sought to persuade him.

"Then let them pick someone who wants the job."

He resisted the pressure a dozen times a day. Worn by it, he said to Ayrin that he wanted to leave the Mapuera.

"Fawtaw needs help in the church at Kashmi," he told her one day.

"You can't run away," she admonished. "Stay and see what the Lord wants."

His wife backed him. "You give people the message of God's Paper," Kuhku said. She was a resolute woman with a great deal of command in her eyes. She had good teeth, a clear face, curl in her hair, full breasts, strong arms—she looked like a chief's wife. Yet she did not want to become one. "If you become chief, I am not going to help you."

The villagers certainly didn't help to make life enjoyable for Tamokrana. He called out work crews; they went to fields other than the ones he assigned. He issued rules; they were largely ignored. He still was chief, yet he was not the people's leader. Howler Monkey Rocks had entered into a era of rather uncivil disobedience. Tamokrana continued to govern, Forosha to preach, Kuruyeme and others to search the forest for lost people; babies were born, children crowded into Ayrin's school, families went farther and farther up or downstream to clear land for new fields; men hunted, women baked, girls took care of their younger siblings, and boys complained of overwork when their play was interrupted by an order to carry water home from the river; preparations proceeded for a coming conference to study God's Paper in a concentrated way. But underneath all was a subterranean flood of roiled waters.

Some three weeks' distance by trail, Kashmi was no place of certainty, either. People there generally felt the end of the village would come soon. Yakuta had moved to the Jatapuzinho to help Kurunaw with his new village. Others had also gone to the Jatapuzinho and some to the Mapuera. The church was down to one elder, Fawtaw. On coming back from the Atrowari, Twefu had become enamored with a woman not his wife; his adultery set him aside from a role in the church. Kirifaka's son Fanahruwi, the medical attendant who through his translation work with Bahm had gained considerable insight into God's Paper, shared the task of preaching and led in the singing. Nevertheless, it was felt he was too young to be made an elder.

Kashmi missed Joe and Tamara Hill, too. Their absence, however, kept alive the flicker of evangelism directed toward the Atrowari. After long and unremitting effort, they had won appointment by the government as linguists, and they gratefully accepted the task to teach the Atrowari to read and write in their own language. Not that they were permitted to engage formally in more than literacy, but they could demonstrate in their daily experiences what it meant to be a believer in Christ and through friendship share their witness of God's grace with those who wanted to know.

The friendliest of relations was not difficult to establish. It appeared everyone welcomed the Hills, availed themselves of the classes, were eager to help teach these teachers their spoken tongue. Even Chief Viana came around. He had caused their predecessor to be expelled when the man did not give him the gifts he wanted. Thus far, the non-material benefits the Hills brought seemed enough, even for him, and after a period of testing the couple, Viana toned down his haughty pride.

The workers crowding the desks in the bureaus in Brasilia, however, were not so sure they would tolerate two North American missionaries among Amazonian Indians.

Another loss at Kashmi came in the retirement of Florence Riedle. For thirty-four years the Wai Wai's Achi had been their nurse, in many ways their doctor, trainer of medical attendants, teacher, translator, counselor, and confidante—their Older Sister. A New England Yankee, she nevertheless took readily to her jungle surroundings, first on the Essequibo in British Guiana before it became the independent Guyana, and then in Brazil.

At times she commanded Elka to stretch out his arm for a shot and browbeat an old incorrigible Mawayena witchdoctor into swallowing his malaria pills, and at other times spent sleepless nights hovered over a fragile newborn. Once she saved the tribe from probable extinction because against their will she made the people put down their common drink pot, separate into families, and stay inside their homes until a deadly measles epidemic passed. Yet under that professional toughness was a tender love that touched almost every Indian who knew her. The women especially—young mothers; wives of difficult husbands; old, hobbling, spent grannies—but men, too, could thank Achi for the love, hope, encouragement, and direction she had brought to their lives.

But now Achi herself was getting on in years. Her back became a problem; no longer could she hike the trail or travel any distance in a canoe. She'd suffered malaria, hepatitis, dengue fever, ailments of the tropics. She could stay in the village and chance that others would someday have to care for her, or could return to New England and nurse her aging mother. She slipped away without any recognition of her leaving, probably because for a year she didn't go far—only to Boa Vista, where she took as her personal responsibility the welfare of the growing number of Indians coming to the city for medical attention.

Achi's retirement left only one missionary at Kashmi, and Ruth Langer would soon obey the call of God to another field, a work which held a growing rather than a diminishing need of her service. The remnant at Kashmi chose Emehta to lead them. But Emehta's chieftaincy was to be short lived. Kashmi's time, indeed, had ended.

Prior to their leaving, the miscreant sons of Yarka, a dour, square-jawed, acerbic man, did their dirty work. They sold an electric generator to the area prefect down river from Kashmi. Not theirs to sell, the generator had been Bahm's and when he left the village he gave it to the people. The youths pocketed the money but were unable to deliver the rest of the power plant as some of the people in moving to the Jatapuzinho carried it with them piece by piece. Esura and Sakaraya had other tricks to play as they abandoned Kashmi. They chopped down all the fruit trees and burned all the buildings.

Kashmi gone, its prior settlements up the Novo abandoned and overgrown, the village on the Jatapuzinho was on the rise. Perhaps it was true: Anaua, Yawko, Kashmi—their purpose had been fulfilled. Beginning their outreach to the Atrowari when the main body of the Wai Wai was still in Guyana, their people had experienced more than a score of contacts, both on the Alalau and the Novo, and the seed of God's Paper had been planted in that hostile tribe, the clearest evidence showing up in the lives of the two Atrowari orphan brothers, Prara and Shikin. A combination of government antipathy and Chief Viana's eagerness to sacrifice friendship with the Wai Wai for gifts from the government had effectively stopped communication between the two tribes. It was hoped Joe Hill could keep open a dialogue, but this would come from his living in an Atrowari village. There seemed no reason for anyone to eke out a subsistence from land on the Novo that was the poorest the Wai Wai had ever tilled.

Kurunaw's village on the Jatapuzinho had evolved into the spearhead for tracking unreached people in the forest. Search was still being made from there for Karafou and possibly other groups. If someday a trail reopened to the Atrowari, it would start at the Jatapuzinho. This village, which had no name, lay about as far from Brazilian settlements as had Kashmi and as Howler Monkey Rocks did on the Mapuera. A hard canoe trip—a half-day down the Jatapuzinho to the confluence of the Jatapu and then almost two days against the current of that larger river—delivered the traveler to the end of the perpendicular arm of the Manaus-Boa Vista highway. Alternately, a day's trek through heavy jungle and then along a partly finished extension of the road connected the village to an outpost of Brazilian life. On the red-dirt road itself, plowed out of jungle and small savannas, stood a number of towns. They sprang up to service the many cattle ranches now reaching back from the road to primeval forest.

Kurunaw had laid out his village as a narrow strip bordering the small river. Behind it stood numerous fields of cassava and fruits, which at last were bearing quite well. Someday when the soil played out and further cuts into the forest were made, the old fields could be turned into an airstrip. But today there was no airstrip, and with no air service, no communicating radio. Despite this isolation, the Jatapuzinho village enjoyed street lights.

A visiting politician gave a new generator; it was coupled with the old power plant and hooked to wires that looped from pole to pole the length of the village. On moonless nights, six dim bulbs threw out enough glow to guide the stroller around the holes and hills of "Main Street." A line ran to the church, giving light and also power to blast hymns out over the village from a public address system.

Kurunaw and Yakuta, nephew and uncle, made an effective team in leading the village. The older man deferred to the younger.

"You, my son, were here first. You are the head and I am here to help you."

They looked to the legacy in leadership that Elka had passed on to them, harking back to past days when he, their father and brother, had met many of the challenges they faced today. Elka was not of much help now. He was a very sick man.

Since his arrival, he had fallen a number of times and some days could not leave his hammock, and when he did he leaned heavily on a stick. His eyes burned, he coughed, his breathing came hard, nerves and muscles degenerated. Weakness in body and at times in mind forced him to relinquish all but elder statesman's status, and he finally arrived at the point that he got up only to attend church. His back hurt dreadfully, his work-hardened body turned into flabby flesh and retained fluids, giving him the look of a carelessly fat man.

He confessed to his brother that yes, he had sinned with another man's wife. It was a confession he'd had to make a couple of times before, and each admission seemed harder than the last. He also said that the way he left the Mapuera was wrong. He was, he said, in a hurry to leave because by admitting his adultery there, the church leaders would have insisted he stay around to get things straightened out, and if he had stayed longer he might never have been able to join Kurunaw at the Jatapuzinho.

"It was not the best way to leave," he said contritely to Yakuta. There remained, however, some misunderstandings with Bahm. And the quarrel with Mawasha on his departing Guyana had been merely brushed into the recesses of his mind.

This once-strong branch of God's Vine clearly had need of more pruning. But the Elka of other days would not be easily forgotten. Hunters brought him meat. Women washing clothes at the river or squeezing the poison out of their cassava juice often spoke of him as a good one, a strong one.

"He was our chief." The emphasis indicated he had stood alone in their estimation. "Now, *okwe*, he is sick."

The one-eyed Yoshwi visited him regularly and in his presence prayed for him. She was unable to forget the difference his stand for God had made in her life.

One of the missionaries who knew him best thought perhaps he had made the difference between the Christian faith's progress among the Wai Wai and its slow pace in other tribes; Elka accepted the light God gave him, and as a result God gave him more light. But more times than his people wished to count, he had proved himself human, an imperfect piece of pottery that just as often the Potter had to smash and start shaping again.

Would he die a broken man, one foot still dragging in the mire of defeat, or would God once more lift him up and equip him to accomplish new tasks?

Confusion continued at the Mapuera. Tamokrana hung on to his position, but it was as if the village had no chief. The work was in disarray. Orders given had no force. The chief seemed not to know what should be done, how to do it, how to rally the people to the need. Families pretty much went their own way, but in truth longed for a leader who could give them direction.

The church elders were beginning to connect with the people again and most sought to make peace with Forosha, Chownyon, and Kirifaka. Tamokrana, however, maintained his role of Saul to Forosha's David. He read intrigue and betrayal in every action of his son, while Forosha, like David, had purposely refrained from injuring "the Lord's anointed." If what a visiting Trio elder had once said was true, that it was God who controlled the destinies of chiefs, both in lifting them up and setting them down, then it appeared that the Lord at last was about to show His hand in Mapuera's difficulties.

In the early months of 1989 the elders realized that the church would not be large enough to seat all the visitors expected to gather at Howler Monkey Rocks for an intensive study of God's Paper. The roof needed replacing, too. As it was now, whenever it rained everyone had to crowd to the front of the church. The big rains would come in about a month, then as they tapered off, the conference would start. In the little time available, how were they to enlarge the church and cover it over with a new roof?

The task fell to Forosha, generally thought of as first among church leaders. He did some figuring then said the job could be done—in one month.

"One month!" His father, attending the elders' meeting, nearly exploded. He ridiculed his son's projection and said the job would require at least three months, which is what it had taken him a few years back to build it. Forosha was not deterred.

"Tomorrow," he said quietly but confidently, "we'll take the end off the church. The next day we'll set the poles in their new position, allowing for a much longer building. Then the day after, no man who can breathe and walk will stay in the village. Everyone will go to the forest to collect leaves."

He established collection points up and down the river, and used all the motors in the village to speed the laden canoes to the village port, and designated teams to carry the leaves on to the church site. The collection done, on schedule, he said, "Tomorrow everyone in the village—including women and children—will either fold leaves or take care of babies."

The day was a festive one, as much fun for all as Christmas.

A fine new roof and a large extension caused the villagers to almost believe they had a new church building. All the work was completed in one month.

Tamokrana was quick to say, "I knew we could do it!"

But the people hardly heard him. It was Forosha they credited. They talked about his organizing and his execution of the project, talked on the trails, shouted their satisfaction from one canoe to another, spoke of it in circles before the doors of their houses of an evening and in their hammocks at night.

Saul hath slain his thousands, and David his ten thousands.

There was no way that Forosha would not become their chief. It merely was a matter of time.

The rains came and the people in church kept dry. The rain continued to fall and the river rose. As usual, the sand bar at the port quickly covered over. The rocks in the rapids then disappeared beneath the surface of the water. Driving rain pelted. The sky flashed with jagged lightning and thunder boomed like a giant kechekere tree falling in the forest. The river continued to rise, and the current sped immeasurably fast. Day after day the villagers gathered at the high banks, though the banks were not so high anymore. Half the steps that had been cut into the clay path down to the port were swallowed, and the bluff's height of eight meters or so had been reduced to three or four.

On their calendars, the people marked off April, and May gave way to June. Still the rains did not let up. The waters roared down from the north. Across the river the lower land had completely vanished from sight, the trees appearing like so many reeds shooting up out of a backwater. On the village side the steep bank had all but disappeared. The river spilled into a lower spot near the government house. The *chefe do posto* moved his things off the floor to chairs and table tops. There had been high water before, but no one had seen the river like they were seeing it now.

There was no let up. Some rain fell every day. The river burst over its boundaries, flooding a good portion of the village. A few homes were swept away. The *chefe do posto* slogged through the water in his house, piling his things on chairs which were now placed atop tables. Then the rain stopped. For some time, however, the water stayed high.

"Guess what?" said a man to Ayrin. As he spoke it seemed he might either laugh or cry. "This morning inside my house I fished as I lay in my hammock."

Steering a canoe from house to house had taken the place of walking. More serious than damage and inconvenience in the village was the effect of the flood on fields. Men and women alike went over the sides of canoes, diving down to dig cassava roots. They would surface with a root or two, throw it into the canoe, take in a breath of air and dive down again. By the time they got to some of their plantings, it was too late. The cassava had rotted. The task of rebuilding fields would be enormous, and some might better be abandoned.

Tamokrana was among the many who lost fields. On two of his fields crops spoiled and the soil was swept away, as was a house the chief's family used on their down river work trips.

Only one person escaped unscathed: Forosha. Not by Providential favoritism, but by his own foresight and willingness to do what many others were not willing to do. Forosha had chosen a site on high ground for his fields. His neighbors considered that a prudent decision, but they could not understand why after an hour's canoe trip he wanted to walk another hour, mostly uphill, to start his day's labor, and then down that long trail at day's end, toting on his back and the back of his wife heavy owchies filled with their produce.

That year's flood changed their outlooks.

"We were lazy," said old Wisho. "We settled for the easy places to cut for fields. The high water has waked us up."

Like others, Wisho was now searching out high ground, farther away from the river, for fields to replace those lost in the flood. Everyone, it seemed, was eager to do it Forosha's way.

Even during the flood, preparation for the conference pushed ahead. Much of the cassava dug so precariously went into the accumulating food supply for this coming event. Women baked bread and stashed it away, made starch drink and stored it, roasted the longer-lasting farina. As soon as they were able, the men entered the higher lands of the forest to get meat, which they dried by day-long roasting. It was like Christmas, only this time there would be many more people to feed. The umana would be turned over to the guests for sleeping; still, the men had to build a lot of temporary huts to house the expected overflow.

"Our fathers had parties and invited many people to dance and share strong drink," Forosha explained to one who asked what they intended to do. "We don't want a gathering like that. We want to have a good time together, but we want to help one another walk closer to God."

What they had planned was patterned on the successful conferences of the Trio believers. A large group of Trio was turned back by high water on the trail. Five men made it through, riding the swift current of the Trombetas to Porteira where, with the help of Wai Wai men and motors sent to rescue them, began to fight their way up the Mapuera. They appreciated the prayer meetings that had been held for them, also the feast on their arrival. For six days they had been without food.

Four of the Trio leaders managed to fly in by MAF plane. The 134 Hishkaryena who came walked over higher ground between their village and the Mapuera. A flotilla of canoes met them at the trail's end, and the arrival at Howler Monkey Rocks was a gala event, even by the standards of a Wai Wai welcome. A fifty-member choir stood above the port to sing their greeting. It was indicative of the care and hard work that had gone into the planning of this inter-tribal gathering.

Leaders of the Trio and Hishkaryena churches brought messages, as did Wai Wai elders and Bahm, who had come on one of his teaching and translation visits.

Mere anticipation of deep and serious study of God's Paper had had its effect on many of the Wai Wai. They'd prayed that pride, rebellious spirits, unforgiving attitudes, priorities—all would be dealt with. Before the conference began, there was resolution that the drift ensnaring their village had to end. The murky fog of weak leadership must be dispelled. A meeting in the church was called, following a regular Sunday morning service. Everyone was free to speak.

"Is Forosha the one we want to be our chief?" the chairman finally asked.

"Yes, yes," chorused the reply.

"Is he a bit young?" came a timid query, and that faint uncertainty was all the opposition to Forosha's election. Except for Tamokrana.

Throughout the session he said he did not want his son to succeed him. "Anyone but my son," he said, when he finally faced reality and acknowledged the people no longer wanted him. "I don't think God's Paper allows my son to switch from church leader to civil leader," he argued, putting forth one last straw. "Give me a verse that says it does."

No one did. But the point came at which he bowed to their will. Publicly he declared Forosha the new chief.

Forosha and Kuhku had gone home after the morning worship, the buzz of the people's excitement burning in their ears. With just the two of them sitting in their house together, she withdrew her rejection of the people's draft of her husband. She said perhaps she had been wrong. The elders, Kirifaka, so many had tried to get her to change her mind. She was stubborn, selfish, some of them charged; she refused to share her husband, even though the people had need of him.

"Dear," she said on this morning that the others were meeting, "maybe I was wrong. I didn't want you to be so busy. I know we've been happy with you as a leader of the church. But I guess God wants you to be chief. I'll not stand in your way any longer. Maybe it will be best if you do what they ask."

Forosha knew his father could not continue. Someone had to be chief. If God was speaking through the people, he did not want to be disobedient.

He said there were two conditions under which he would accept. First, he would keep up his work in the church. Second, he did not consider the appointment to be for life. When someone qualified came along, he would hand over the responsibility to him.

Tamokrana passed his duties to Forosha. In church he called his son to the front to sit on the chief's own bench. On a later Sunday after church, there was a discussion among the leadership about a work project. Forosha listened to the points of view, then gave his answer. His father said it wasn't to be that way.

"*Ahfah,* I am chief," Forosha reminded him.

"No, you're not, you're my assistant." But that did not go over with the people. He retired once again, this time for good.

25

Mawasha journeyed over the high mountains from Guyana and down the Mapuera to Howler Monkey Rocks for the second inter-tribal gathering to study God's Paper. He arrived, however, a month after the conference ended.

An epidemic of whooping cough had aborted this latest gathering, held a year after the first in-depth study by the Mapuera folk. For their good friend—this tall, quite unassuming leader of the Wai Wai who chose to remain in Guyana when most of the people moved to Brazil—the elders reconvened the conference. For him they gladly picked up the study again.

Few of the Wai Wai had seen Mawasha since pulling away from the banks of the Essequibo. Now they found his teaching a pleasure to hear. His people in Guyana had benefited from fellowship with the Wapishana Indians, and year by year had sent some of their young men out to the Guyanese savanna for training in church leadership. Others had learned radio communications, simple medicine, and school teaching. If the mass move of the Wai Wai over the mountains to Brazil established the presence of God's family in the vast rain forest north of the Amazon, the remaining remnant in Guyana certainly buttressed the steadfastness of the Lord and His people. Mawasha's son had become a government official for the area. The entire village was now looked on as a model for Indian settlements—not the showplace for tourists that some authorities had once proposed, but home to a hundred or so peaceful and industrious people.

On his journey downstream, Mawasha had not encountered any forest tribes. Lately, neither had the Wai Wai from either the Mapuera or the Jatapuzinho. But the search for them went on. Once in a while the sighting of evidence that people had recently passed through an area stirred excitement, and if the report gained credence, parties were organized to go out looking. Fawtaw swept in a wide arc from the Jatapuzinho to the Guyana border. From the Mapuera, Kuruyeme journeyed toward Surinam. Neither team found people.

The whereabouts of the Atrowari were, of course, known first-hand. But reaching them for Christ seemed just as impossible today as discovering elusive people hiding under the endless canopy of trees. The wall erected to keep out any Christian witness was, if anything, even stronger now. Joe and Tamara Hill had served two years as government-sponsored linguists among the Atrowari, teaching the people to read and write their own language, but their request for another term was denied. Shikin learned just how hostile toward the things of God the Atrowari and their mentors had become. He visited his people, and except for his brother Prara, found them to be filled with loathing for his identification with the Wai Wai and their God.

Viana had chosen the largesse of the builders of the hydro-electric dam and the tin-mine operators over friendship with the Wai Wai. His decision had rewarded him handsomely. The chief now lived in a commodious brick house with a metal roof. A truck stood ready to carry him at any time up or down the road bisecting the Atrowari forest. He had clothes in his closet, frozen chickens in his refrigerator, tins of guava jam and lady-finger cookies on his shelves. His wife dazzled everyone with a velveteen skirt, and in their house a prize rug decorated the floor. On a lesser scale, a few other leaders enjoyed such gifts, but for the ordinary people there was little to trickle down, mainly occasional distributions like the truckload once of three hundred pairs of boots, and commonly shared tools like chain saws to substitute for workmen's axes.

The Atrowari were calmer today than in the years of contact with the Wai Wai. The killing had had to stop—or no more handouts. The Waymiri, now living farther from the road, did not share equally in the bounty, so these close kin of the Atrowari were less inclined to pacification. But even Viana was not satisfied. They were currently in a time when the Brazilians, for some reason, were upset with the Atrowari and consequently had cut the food supply. Because many families no longer tended their fields and, indeed, young people were growing up not knowing how to raise their own food, some were becoming hungry.

Viana threatened to topple trees along the road and block traffic. Surely, on the halted vehicles they'd uncover food and perhaps other items the Atrowari wanted. Neither young nor old had lost the ability to pillage.

If the Atrowari had carried a grudge, a murderous grudge against the Brazilians for actual or supposed atrocities against them, their anger had been adroitly deflected onto the Wai Wai. Perhaps not to the white heat of murder, but to persecution whenever it lay within their power.

The Brazilians were the source of the things that made life pleasant, preached Viana, who certainly had collected sufficient things to make him happy (if things made anyone happy). The Wai Wai, on the other hand, stood for the surrender of personal prurience and greed. The Wai Wai were not true Indians, some officials dinned into the Atrowari; to protect the old ways of drink, dance, promiscuity, and crushing their enemies by any method, they should shun these fanatics. Prara, who left the Wai Wai to live among his own people, was too much of a reminder that God said all people harbored the seeds of badness and needed their badness washed away.

Prara had married a young Atrowari woman. Viana, her brother-in-law, could not make her give him up. She stood by him when others ridiculed and tormented him, and by her even temper helped him endure their caustic barbs and spiteful behavior. He possessed a Wai Wai New Testament and hymnal. One day while he bathed in the river, someone threw his hymnal into the fire. Habitually, he spoke of his faith to people. The *chefe do posto* warned him, "Be quiet! Don't spread this talk." But Prara would not be silenced. Even when his life and his wife's were threatened.

So greatly did some authorities fear that "religion" would set the Indians to thinking about serious issues that any means necessary to stop the inroad of the gospel became an acceptable practice. For Viana, the fear was not that his people might be enlightened on the issues, but that the source of his pride and power would erode if his benefactors weren't in control.

Shikin had gone with his wife to visit the Atrowari partly because the *chefe do posto* there had sent for him. He was no longer the shy orphan boy but a strong, tall, broad-shouldered, likable young man. His Wai Wai wife stood firmly with him; well that they had each other—this present stay with his tribe would force them to call on resources from above.

"You're an Atrowari," the government man reminded him, a little surprised but pleased that the young man had obeyed his call. "Enough of this nonsense—you living among the Wai Wai. You stay here where you belong. Don't go back among the Wai Wai anymore."

They talked at the government post on the highway some time after Shikin arrived to visit his relatives.

"Why are you different, my young friend?" asked the *chefe*. "Why do you insist on living with the Wai Wai? It is so much harder for you there. It's harder to get things. You don't have much food, no sugar cane."

"We have food," replied Shikin. "And we have something you do not have here."

"What is that?" Jorge could not believe that in possessions any tribe could surpass his Indians.

"We have God's Paper."

"Hah! Who is there to protect your interests? Is there a *chefe* to meet your needs?"

"I've learned to look to men for a little bit of my needs and to God for a lot of them."

"So, you have completely changed. You say God is your chief. Your head has been completely turned around. You and your brother Prara are a lot alike. You both answer the same way. You are different from all the other Atrowari."

"We are different because we are God's children."

"You talk like a pastor. Are you a pastor?"

"Well, if you want to call me that, I guess you can." Back on the Jatapuzinho he probably would not have said that. But if it helped this Brazilian to understand . . .

"I have Jesus, God's Son, in the pit of my stomach. I know something of God's Paper."

During the next several days Shikin gathered a few people from time to time in the shade of the main house of the village where he stayed. One day Jorge came by.

"Why do you talk to people about God?" the official asked him.

"Because God can protect them. He is our great protector. You government people can't protect us. You're people just like we are."

"Well, if you're God's servant, we here must be Satan's servants." The *chefe do posto* smiled with a bit of personal pride. "I've been successful in teaching Viana and Maryo that it is Satan they should be serving. It is Satan whom I serve."

"Seetin is not all-powerful," Shikin argued. "God is."

"No, Satan is stronger than God."

"No, he's not."

A few days after that Shikin was with his brother when Viana joined them.

"*Ahfah*," he asked the chief, "does the *chefe* really teach you Seetin is stronger than God?"

"Yes," Viana replied. "He teaches that Seetin is the all-powerful one and that we should be his servants."

"You are headed for destruction." Had he dared say that to this powerful, impulsive chief? Viana had once meant to kill him and Prara and only the protective mantle of Comprido had saved them. Now Comprido was dead and Viana decided who lived or died. On his last visit Shikin was warned not to return. But he had come, his faith intact. He had shared it with several people, and stood here now challenging this arch-enemy of all he believed.

Viana was in an argumentative mood, however, one of many moods he easily slipped into.

"Not destruction," he said. "All is fine with us. This life is all there is. When we die—that is all. Don't be concerned about another life. There isn't one."

Shikin turned from Viana to his brother. "Don't pay attention to what he says. Don't sit down and listen to such talk. What they say is wrong."

"Look," Viana said, ignoring the fraternal advice, "a long time ago people said Jesus is coming. He hasn't come. He's not coming."

"He came," said Shikin. "He came to the earth and died, to take our place by dying for our badness. One time in the old days God and Seetin had a big disagreement. God threw him out of heaven. You are following the one who has some power, but is not all-powerful."

"Why did you catch hold of Jesus?"

"Jesus protects me. That is why I am not afraid of you."

"Me, I think all you're telling me about Jesus is a lie."

"God is here. He hears us when we talk to each other. He hears us when we talk to Him."

Other people had gathered around, and one now spoke up: "No, you don't know what you're talking about."

"*Ahfah*, God loves you," Shikin said. "If you'd talk to Him, God would still take you to be His child."

"No."

Shikin wanted to talk to Gilberto, to encourage him to stand by the teaching he'd received. But this third Atrowari youth who had lived for some time among the Wai Wai had given in to the pressure of his tribesmen. His chief ordered him to give up his Wai Wai wife and he did. He also renounced whatever knowledge of God's Paper he had acquired. He became a strident voice against all that Prara had tried to tell the people, and shouted for all to hear that Seetin was the only god of the Atrowari. He now refused to speak to Shikin. He sent word he did not even want to see his one-time friend. The messenger was instructed to say also that there was no truth in the Big Fire, and, furthermore, that contrary to what some people thought, Gilberto had not caught hold of Jesus and become His companion.

Gilberto did come around, but only to disrupt Shikin's impromptu meetings with willing villagers and to dispute all he had to say.

After Shikin's return to the Jatapuzinho, Yakuta and Kurunaw journeyed to the Alalau. They were not well received. Viana angrily rejected their overtures of friendship.

"You've only come to teach us what God says. It has no value. We don't want you here."

The Atrowari one day would be won to God, the Wai Wai firmly believed. Just when or how, they did not know. For twenty-five years they had prayed for the Atrowari, sometimes setting everything aside to spend whole days in prayer for these mercurial warriors. Over and over they had risked their lives in personal contact, had tried living with them, getting them to live in Wai Wai villages, hoping to show them, as they had shown other forest people, the peace and happiness that came from God dwelling in their midst. They had attempted to learn their language so some day God's Paper could be read and understood in the Atrowari's own language. But they'd been shut out, excluded by sources even more powerful than the Atrowari themselves.

What over these twenty-five years did they have to show for all their endeavor? Two young boys who were now men, one living among the Wai Wai and one among his own people, but both firm in their faith. There were others who had shown interest in what God had to say—the eleven who began showing response to Fawtaw's message before it was cut off; a couple of families related to Prara; a young woman and her husband who asked Shikin to teach them about Jesus, in spite of her father's bitter disapproval. But the thread was a thin one. Yet, if He chose to, couldn't God dangle the world on a spider's web?

Perhaps by his consistent life and witness Prara would win his relatives to Jesus. But Viana's threats to kill him because he would not recant had to be taken seriously. For this reason Prara, Maiko, and Tamoshi and their families had recently moved away from the main settlements to a tiny creek of the Alalau. There was talk of cutting a trail between where they now lived and the Jatapuzinho. A larger group of Atrowari had drifted to the south, almost to the River Negro; being effectively out of the reach of Viana, it was rumored, they wished to hear the news about God. At his home in Boa Vista, Joe Hill worked steadily on the language, laying a foundation for translating the Scriptures into Atrowari, so key to all evangelism efforts.

And there was Shikin. This bright, energetic young man, now a husband and father, expressed hope that God would use him to teach the Atrowari about Jesus. He was trying to keep fluent in the language of his people, though Wai Wai came easier to him these days. He and his wife sought to hold themselves ready for the day they could return to the Alalau and once again tell the people how they might become companions of Jesus. And not often out of their minds or prayers, the Atrowari had fixed themselves on the consciousness of the believers at the Mapuera as well as the Jatapuzinho and in Guyana, and were the intercessory concern of Ayrin and Achi and Bahm and Ferochi and Kron and his wife and M.A. Mijnders in far-off Holland and countless others in Brazil and the United States and around the world.

Like Elka before him, Forosha, getting along now as chief at the Mapuera, was called to settle a dispute at Kassawa, the Hishkaryena village. The people asked him to be their chief.

"Be chief in both places. We'll choose a village headman, but you be the chief."

"No, I don't know your land. I don't know the good places to cut fields."

There were many things a chief had to know and could learn only as he lived among his people. Hardly did he think of taking on the Hishkaryena. Even leading the Wai Wai at the Mapuera might not be for life; the day someone showed himself fit to be chief, he would willingly step aside. There was his family to raise—seven children and Kuhku was still a rather young wife. There were the duties of the church, which had not diminished. Being chief meant continually carrying an owchi overloaded with heavy burdens.

"If the Gojodoa had been better shots," he joked one day, "I'd not be chief today."

Some days it was tempting to think perhaps an arrow in the back was to be preferred to the scars of office he already bore. Others, however, believed he led them by God's appointment. The problems he had to deal with steadily mounted, partly because the village had grown so large. The cry of a newborn often mingled with the nightly howl of village dogs. At times there were stillbirths. Other births were normal, quick, and easy, the offspring robust and eager to begin life. During the night hours of the twenty-fifth of July 1991, three boys were born. The latest of this trio to appear boosted the population of Howler Monkey Rocks to exactly one thousand.

How far the Wai Wai had come! The day Bahm and his brother Mistokin first set foot in a Wai Wai village in British Guiana, this branch of the tribe numbered forty-seven. Many other groups, their size ranging from a half-dozen to seventy and more, had joined them in the years since, but the sixteen hundred Indians in five locations going under the banner of the Wai Wai today nevertheless reflected a population explosion. There had always been many babies, but once so few of them lived. Old Tochi, now a doddering old granny at the Jatapuzinho, was said to have killed nine of her newborn in a row.

The Wai Wai were first seen by the Hawkins brothers as not only baby clubbers, but killers by witchcraft of anyone who may have spoiled their day. Lazy, begging, thieving, striving to drown their fear and misery in strong drink and riotous nights, they were a dying people, seemingly soon to become extinct like neighboring tribes which before them had slipped unnoticed from the human family. In the beginning they mocked the God whom Bahm explained was their creator. They laughed when he said Chisusu—Jesus—had come to the earth to die for their badness. Then one by one they began to get ears, first Elka, then Kirifaka and Yakuta and Yoshwi, and in a few years all but a handful professed to have caught hold of this same Chisusu. Baby killing stopped, witchcraft vanished, disease was brought under control, fear gave way to confident faith. The Wai Wai not only lived—they thrived, bloomed, flourished.

Now they had a new problem. Too many of them lived close together and off the same land. For one, Kirifaka's son-in-law said so many people in one place unnerved him. He shocked his neighbors when he said he was thinking of moving back to Kashmi, abandoned and burnt Kashmi, on the Novo River. A Katwena man mentioned several times that he hoped to take a group a couple of days upriver and there at the big rapids on the equator start a new village.

In Guyana there had been seven small villages under one chief. They were spread far enough apart to allow for ample fields and hunting preserves, but near enough to each other for all to meet at Kanashen for church and feasts and to visit Achi's clinic to be stuck by her shiny thorn. In those days to assemble a village work force was no problem. Elka or the local head-man picked up his ax and headed for a field to be cut; his neighbors then picked up theirs and fell in behind him. With little need for consciously organized effort, the work got done. Today, with a couple of hundred fields to be cut or planted, always canoes to carve and houses to build, and two hundred or more men and teenage boys perhaps not knowing which projects merited priority, the chief and his work captains had to constantly hone a system to keep it working.

Work assignments were announced in church on Sunday and Wednesday mornings. This was often done by Charamcha. This savvy, old right-hand helper of chiefs and work captains would read off the names of the men needed to clear a patch of forest. Then he would throw in a little lecture for the benefit of those who were not always cooperative with village schedules.

"You know who you are," he'd say. "You sneak off to get palm fruit then come to me and say because you have drink ready for the work crew your field must be cut today. What about the one who spoke to me three weeks ago and asked for this day? Now he has to wait, or we must divide the crew into groups too small to accomplish anything.

"Or you think your field can be cut in one day, but it can't. So you keep working on it instead of working with others on another field. Soon we'll have lots of tiny groups trying to do projects all over the place. You want to build a house during field-planting time, and you know that can't be done."

Charamcha had learned from Elka not to berate people—to chastise them when necessary, but never to call a man lazy. He might get carried away in his rhetoric in church, but on the job Charamcha proved that a small, wizened old man could put out as much work as anybody.

"We'll meet when the roosters crow," he'd say to his men the night before. In the stillness before dawn, the clap of paddles against the sides of canoes would be heard, gradually fading into silence as the work party pushed to the bend in the river and beyond it, well on the way to the start of another day.

Men were chosen to be work captains because they were diligent workers. Setting the example, they could not shrink from duty, and seldom did one try. One of them retired to his hammock one night with a bad headache. "Head," his wife heard him say, "you can't hurt. You've got to work tomorrow."

A man might get assigned to a work crew two days or so a week—never on Friday since that day was reserved for hunting. A job could last for a week, or half a day. While his wife worked long hours over food gathering and preparation and care of the house and children, he found time to fish, make arrows or create artifacts to be sold in the town markets. A good many men helped their wives. Some, especially the young, complained of their hard life. Among the complainers, down-river fever became an epidemic.

Boredom thrust many young men from the villages on the Mapuera and the Jatapuzinho and the Essequibo in Guyana. From the Mapuera they went to the tiny town of Cachoeira do Porteira or further downstream to the larger Oriximina, even more a land of liberty. A fellow might have paddled for two days to get to Porteira to sell the artifacts—baskets, stools, flutes, fans—which he and his family or perhaps neighbors had made. Once having sold them, the temptation then was to remain in town, spend a few cruzeiros on drink and a party and a blouse for the young woman who'd been so friendly and accommodating. His money thus gone, he was ashamed to return home empty-handed and disappoint and perhaps anger those who were expecting payment for their work. So he quite likely stayed on for a while, grubbing food where he could, sleeping where he dropped.

Many Wai Wai youth discovered it was possible to work for a man and be paid in Brazilian currency. Usually they labored long hours in a field, as they would at home, or did simple construction. But wasn't it worth it to be paid at the end of the week and be able to browse among the fascinating shops? How satisfying to empty out the week's pay envelope into the waiting hands of a merchant in exchange for a wristwatch or radio or a pair of long trousers or a colorful shirt! But after playing his radio or admiring his watch or strutting up the street in his new clothes, a man eventually did get hungry. And here in town, so different from home, he had to pay out money—or the watch or radio—for food.

"I don't see God here," one youth said to his companions, suggesting that unlike the village with its church, prayer meetings, and the watchful eyes of his elders, Porteira was a place where anyone could do anything he wished. For some, desire ran the gamut of all a frontier town had to offer—cigarettes, alcohol, and prostitution the main attractions. Falling into debt was easier than staying out of it.

Having to pay to eat and getting sick—these were the two miseries for a young man living among strangers and doing things the strangers' way.

A nineteen-year-old Wai Wai presumed to adapt well to Porteira, meaning to drink strong drink as the Brazilians drank it—in large quantities. He had not known the taste of fermentation back in the village, but found he liked it. Strong drink, however, did not like him. From the time he began feeding his thirst, he was often sick. One day he came down with malaria. A drink to cool his sweating head! In a very short time he was dead.

The news of his quick death spread through the town and down the river to other towns. Some stayed, but many frightened young Wai Wai quit their jobs and scrambled back home. For all, the specter of their own deaths dulled the luster of life outside.

Adversity—never being able to climb above the lowest rung on civilization's ladder—and homesickness drove others to return. Some came home resplendent in fancy clothes, some brought gifts for a mother or a certain girl, and if the returnee was married and had a family, a few colorful but flimsy toys for the children. Not all youths who went to town stayed out long or got swept up in sinful living. A month or two were enough to satisfy their curiosity and to convince them their future lay in the land of their people.

Fear of what might happen to them kept most of the young women in the village. Remaining home when their men went out did not, however, always mean contentment.

Forosha was much concerned with this restlessness of youth. There was much that could be done to improve life in the village—if the young people could only be taught the needed skills. He had fine teachers and health workers. Wanaferu, his youthful assistant, was quite good at administration. Their houses could be better, safe wells were needed around the village, dead motors ought to be brought back to life, fruit and nut trees could be cultivated to an economic advantage, worn-out soils caused all Indians to ever encroach on the forest, driving away the source of their meat. He knew that outside the jungle young people learned helpful crafts. He prayed that someday God would send to the Wai Wai those men and women who could equip their younger generation for a productive life in their own culture.

The church leaders—sometimes tugged, sometimes pushed by Forosha—often displayed ineptness but meant well, and it appeared God blessed them and the people on the basis of divine generosity. Though there were misunderstandings and quarrels arising in every part of the village, the people did care about each other. Whenever a man got sick and could not go to his field, other men pitched in and did his work, and the women the same for a wife who fell ill or was to have a baby. Deacons went from door to door to collect food for those who thus could not provide for themselves.

Interest in the church meetings was picking up, especially among young people. At the first inter-tribal gathering of Christian Indians called by the Trio in Surinam, Wai Wai delegates heard a new brand of music there. Since then, the singing in the Mapuera church had greatly improved. Hand-clapping accompanied animated songs, and the new choir presented trios, duets, and even solos. Guitars and tambourines added to the sound, the skill of the string musicians developing from a single chord through every song to

advanced techniques of harmony. The more spirited atmosphere prompted the young people to start a "sing-time" on
Sunday afternoons.

The clinic was going well. Fanahruwi had moved from
the vacated village of Kashmi to the Mapuera and with him
came unusual ability to treat ills and accidents. A young man
mangled the fingers of his right hand while hunting;
Fanahruwi stitched and dressed them and saved the victim
from disablement. The school also functioned well. Ayrin's
front room became an evening extension of the children's
day school. Adults, too, crowded into the room. True, they
were lured by the light bulb energized by a solar panel, but
they dropped in for ten minutes or a whole evening also
because in Ayrin they had a ready and sympathetic listener,
and the children's books and puzzles were not beneath their
attention.

The government did not permit gold hunting on Indian
reservations, but that did not mean it wasn't done. Forosha,
however, was determined to keep the *garimpeiros* out of the
Wai Wai land along the Mapuera. What the prospectors
brought into the jungle—strong drink and careless conduct,
the worship of the little nuggets and what they could obtain,
a fiery greed that pitted one man against all others—these
his people did not need. The elders agreed; everyone in the
village was obligated to uphold the government's ban on
gold mining, neither aiding outsiders in their quest nor getting caught up in the fever themselves.

A miner's camp had been spotted from the air, however,
though possibly it lay north beyond Wai Wai territory. Now
and then signs appeared that travelers had passed through
the area, though they steered clear of the village. A few families at Howler Monkey Rocks disagreed with the hands-off
policy. They saw the *garimpeiros* as a source for trade—
shells for their guns, radios, watches, tape recorders and
tapes of the white man's strange music, and maybe gold for
themselves as well. Outspoken in this dissent were the sons
of Yarka, the pair of rascally youth who sold Kashmi's

electric generator when it was not theirs to sell and who on leaving that village destroyed its fields and burned every building to the ground.

Along with their parents, they had migrated to the Mapuera. They frequently went down river and made friends with Porteira's odd assortment of frontier characters. Returning from one of their trips, their passage upstream was greatly aided by an outboard motor.

"A gift from a friend in town," the youths said as people trooped to the river to admire this expensive acquisition.

"You will have to work for him many months," one of the curious reasoned.

"Oh, no," denied Esura. "He gave it to us because he likes us."

"I know the man you speak of," said one of the village leaders. "He is a *garimpeiro*. Many times our chief has prevented him from entering our land. What does he want?"

Esura looked at Sakaraya, his brother.

"A little *weeyu*," answered Sakaraya. He spoke of a tree sap that burned for a long time and was used as a candle. It seemed this *garimpeiro* had a variety of business interests.

In a few days Yarka approached Ayrin to withdraw his younger children from school. He said the whole family would travel north together.

"You said you wouldn't take the children out," Ayrin reminded him. "Why are you now doing this?"

"My sons returned from down river, and they want to go upstream. *Okwe,* what can I do?"

"You could tell them 'No.'"

"*Hnnnnn . . .*" That this father could not do.

Before the family left, Yarka had occasion to stop in at Ayrin's house.

She asked him directly: "Are you going to look for gold?"

Yarka turned a shocked face toward the missionary. How could she ask such a question?

"I am not going with that in mind," he managed to say.

"What will you tell them if your sons say, 'Let's look for gold?' "

"I want to tell them no."

"I didn't ask what you want to say. What will you say?"

He looked at the slats in the floor without answering.

Esura's canoe left with an extremely heavy load, odd sizes and shapes poking up here and there under cover of palm leaves, owchies, and all sorts of cooking utensils, boots, axes, guns, and personal belongings. Three other families shoved off upstream a day, a couple of days, after Yarka's left. The casualness with which they got underway made their going appear a coincidence. But when Takatutu joined this strange emigration, a few of the more suspicious—astute—villagers began to add together the fragments of the last few days and concluded that each departing family was part of a planned foray into the forbidden gold fields.

A few days later this was confirmed. Forosha returned from meeting with government officials. As he passed through Porteira he heard reports that prior to his arriving there Esura and Sakaraya had left the town with two Brazilian *garimpeiros* in their canoe.

"We did not see them here," someone informed the arriving chief at an impromptu council at the port.

"It's plain what Yarka's sons did," another volunteered. "You can believe they pulled in some place downstream and let the gold hunters out."

"True," agreed still another. "They told them how to find their way by land to some spot on the river upstream."

"You can be sure Esura and Sakaraya will pick them up again there."

Over time, the various families drifted back one by one to Howler Monkey Rocks, none of them saying much about the events of the last few months, except that when questioned Yarka swore neither he nor his sons had harbored any gold miners. A letter from Porteira came for Yarka one day and eventually fell into Forosha's hands. It was from the benefactor of his sons, though in less than charitable language he asked for payment for his outboard motor. Forosha let this letter pass. Then came a second, more demanding in its tone. A third letter arrived, warning that if payment was not immediately made the Brazilian police would be dispatched to the Mapuera. At this point, the chief escorted Yarka and his sons to Porteira.

The police confiscated the motor off the brothers' canoe, but would not give it to its claimed owner. In a showdown at headquarters, Yarka demanded payment from the man.

"What payment?" the Brazilian entrepreneur asked.

"For the two men I fed for five days while hiding them in my house."

Forosha was stunned. Yarka had lied to him outright. He had sworn his sons had brought no miners into the village. He had said he himself had had nothing to do with the *garimpeiros*. A Wai Wai sometimes shaded the truth to protect his interests and felt guilty for doing it, but this man whose principal weakness seemed to be an inability to control his rebellious sons had for a year lived among the people with a blatant lie clotted to his tongue.

"You've lied not just to me, but to the church, to all your neighbors," Forosha said in private to Yarka. He spoke with as much disappointment as chastening. "You leave me little for speaking strongly in your behalf."

Forosha was equally frank with the Brazilian.

"How many times have we met and I've told you not to send gold hunters our way? You are one who is not to be trusted."

The chief volunteered to take Yarka and his sons back to the village in the community-owned motor-driven canoe. Yarka, still in a peevish mood, refused his offer.

Getting their father off to one side, the sons tried reasoning with him.

"*Ahfah*," said Esura, "Forosha is not angry. We should let him take us. If we don't, there's all that distance against the current to paddle."

With the intent of making his old opponent sick, Takatutu placed a curse on Elka, or so went the talk at both the Mapuera, where Takatutu lived, and on the Jatapuzinho, Elka's present home. Indeed, Takatutu had motive for revenge against the former chief, not only because Elka had named him as the slayer of the old man found among the rocks downstream in the Mapuera, but also because Elka accused him of deliberately sinking the chief's canoe and outboard motor. And because of his friendship with Shayukuma, who never denied dabbling in the spirit world, it would not be surprising for Takatutu to employ sorcery to settle his grievances with Elka.

Elka was very ill. His back pained him extremely. On the rare occasions he left his hammock, he used two canes for walking, and then often fell. His sight was poor. His grandchildren read God's Paper to him. His flesh puffed to an unflattering look. On some days his mind lost its sharpness. It was easy for people to say he suffered from Takatutu's malediction.

One day Yakuta asked his brother if he thought he was sick from a curse.

"I've heard the talk," Elka replied. "But I believe it is God who is the Strong One. He has kept me. No, I am not sick because of evil spirits."

Still, the talk persisted and word was circulated far outside the jungle that Elka believed he was cursed by Takatutu. There had been a day when Elka assented to another's charge that Takatutu had made him sick. At the Mapuera Takatutu once brought drink to Elka, which Takatutu had prepared, and after consuming it Elka suffered severe cramping and nausea. At the outset he failed to connect his discomfort with the drink.

"It was Takatutu who made you sick," someone told him.

"Oh, it was Takatutu who made me sick?" Elka asked. "Oh, he's why I feel so bad!"

This exchange was circulated around the village, and now, a long time later, it picked up currency again, though probably unconsciously switched from the physical to the spiritual realm. Suspicions heightened when the Jatapuzinho failed to send Elka's daughter to a health attendant training session at Howler Monkey Rocks. While mission leaders in Boa Vista wondered why Racu did not show up to claim her reserved seat on the flight to the Mapuera, one of Elka's sons surfaced in the town and said their father would not permit his sister to attend.

"He believes someone at the Mapuera has blown a curse on him, so he forbids her to go," the son said. The next day he clamored to be appointed in his sister's place. He had no training in clinical work but a known desire to get to the Mapuera, so the mission turned him down, and the Jatapuzinho went without representation at the workshop, and the talk—*ha tu*—increased.

Racu had a logical answer for her absence. As time for the training approached, it became necessary that she escort her father to the town nearest their village for medical treatment. She chose her father's desperate need over nurse's training.

The controversy seemed less over whether Takatutu had called down evil, which few doubted he was capable of doing, and more as to Elka's believing in a curse's power. Whatever the bias toward believing the worst about this old warrior against witchcraft, it was strengthened even more when Takatutu journeyed all the way to the Jatapuzinho, reportedly repentant of his action and eager to remove his spell.

"I will place my hand on him and take away the curse," people quoted Takatutu as having said. He called at Elka's house. Seeing who it was, Racu refused to let him in.

Forosha was unfamiliar with the sorcery the older generation had known. There was the chance that a naive and susceptible youth would pick up knowledge of witchcraft from one who did not abhor it or from visiting anthropologists who wanted to test their academic knowledge against the reality of the forest. The elders felt it better to starve the topic by denying it their attention. Wherever it popped up, they chose to deal with it on a case-by-case basis.

Kuruyeme worried about the likelihood that the ugly head of witchcraft would rear again. If the Wai Wai had a happy saint, it was Kuruyeme. Why should the "smiling one," as he was called, be so concerned about a relapse into the world of evil spirits? For whatever reason, he was—not worried about others falling back into sorcery, but that he himself might.

Not really a Wai Wai but a Shedeu, or perhaps more accurately a Katwena, he was the child of a beautiful, talented woman, for whom men had killed—perhaps as many as nine times. Because his mother became the victory prize in a war between the tribes, he was raised among her captors, the Shedeu, in the northern forests of Brazil. Kuruyeme was the first in the Shedeu villages to hear of the Creator and His love for His creatures. It was he who urged the nine Shedeu villages to go en masse across the mountains to the Wai Wai settlements along the Essequibo in Guyana, and there to get ears about Jesus. He went back to search the forest for stragglers who needed this message of a reconciling God, and he'd been going on missionary journeys ever since. The latest was just a month ago. His party found no people, but the trip left him quite disturbed.

In his youth, Kuruyeme had been a witchdoctor, just as his father had been before him. But the day he began the trek to Guyana was the day he renounced his charms, leaving them all behind. Little did he think of them in the years that followed. But on this last trip he had a dream that caused him to search the inner depths of his existence.

In his dream a large pack of wild pigs appeared to him in the forest. As a witchdoctor, the bush hogs had been his spiritual pets, just as they had been Elka's pets when he was a witchdoctor. Because of the association, he loathed the dream, but it recurred, even after he returned home on the Mapuera. Always, a fat pig separated itself from the bunch, and always Kuruyeme shot it. Each time this pig immediately lost weight, deflating to nothing.

One day returning from hunting, Kuruyeme came across a band of wild pigs. This was no fantasy. But just as in his dreams, the others in the party ran after the pigs and he was left with the owchies—and a single, fat pig. He shot it, and as he butchered it discovered several unusual layers of fat under the skin which, when removed, left a skinny runt.

Days later while weaving a basket outside his house, Kuruyeme pricked his finger. It was a small wound, but it festered, and soon a sore appeared on his foot and then another near an eye. He developed a fever. It was decided he should be flown out to Oriximina for treatment. Kaywere, the young husband of a daughter of Chief Forosha, was sent along to aid him.

At the hospital, Kuruyeme awoke from a sound sleep and asked Kaywere if he had bumped the bed. The young fellow had not touched the bed. Three other times Kuruyeme awoke and asked the same question. Finally, he said he had been dreaming, and that in every dream wild pigs had rushed toward him, brushed against him, and jolted his bed. He spoke of the dream he'd had while on the trip to the north and the recurring ones since.

"I was once a witchdoctor," he informed Kaywere, "and the pigs were my pets."

"*Hnnnnn . . .*" said Kaywere.

"The pigs are trying to get my attention."

"*Hnnnnn . . .*" said Kaywere again.

Another day Kuruyeme dreamed that the lone pig again appeared, but this time kept itself mostly hidden, only the tip of its nose visible. The pig told Kuruyeme that his illness was caused by his old spiritual pets. It said if he could find the nest of the tale-bearing wren and rub it on his sores, they would clear up. Another time it was the bark of a certain tree that would bring a cure. Kuruyeme was frightened to hear these things. It frightened Kaywere to hear Kuruyeme describe them. How different from what he'd heard this man preach in church.

The patient weakened. Doctors inserted an intravenous hose in his arm. Once he was freed of the tube so he could walk around. He went back to bed, his condition worse.

Kaywere heard the older man pray.

"Father in the Sky," began Kuruyeme. "This is your servant. I am very weak. Why am I sick? I really would like you to take away my sickness so I can continue to work for you. Many of my fellow tribesmen do not walk close to you and I want to continue teaching them. But if you want to take me to live with you I am ready. That is all I am saying now, *Ahfah*."

Though suffering much pain, Kuruyeme sang a lot. His unsuppressible joy marked him throughout the hospital as an unusual man—especially for an Indian. Some days he felt better, others worse. Back and forth, but no longer did he speak of the pigs appearing in his dreams.

He did not forget them, however. Their tug was strong, supernaturally strong. He said to Kaywere that if he lived, Seetin would not rest until he had pulled him back into witchcraft.

"I don't want to serve the evil spirits again," he said. "I've asked God to take my life if that's what is needed to keep me from falling back into witchcraft. Let me die first. I'm ready. God, I know, can use others to complete the work He's started among my family and friends."

Two days before Christmas, he awoke to ask Kaywere when they were going home.

"We'll have to hurry or we'll miss the Christmas festivities."

"Uncle, you're too sick to travel. We'll spend Christmas together here at the hospital. I don't mind not being home, really."

"You're wrong, Little Body. I've had another dream. We are to go by river boat to Porteira and from there by the motor canoe. Before reaching the rapids at home, we'll stop the motor, paddle through the darkness to a place upstream, and there meet the men who have been hunting the Christmas meat. We'll come back with them."

In this latest dream all the people at Howler Monkey Rocks were surprised to see him. They peppered him with many questions. But he did not answer, going instead directly to his house. Kaywere, heading for the umana, could answer their questions.

Those instructions given, Kuruyeme turned to singing. He was a happy man.

On Christmas Eve morning the hunters returned with bulging owchies. In the afternoon students practiced the Christmas pageant in the umana. Whether children reciting lines or men roasting game on a spit or women sweetening the last pots of starch drink with crushed palm fruit, all dropped what they were doing when they heard a plane approach and ran to the airstrip.

Kuruyeme was coming home! The smiling one arriving for the celebration!

As the government plane pulled up to a stop, nearly all of the thousand-plus villagers surged around it. In good nature they elbowed past one another in order to be the first to look on their returning friend. Fathers lifted youngsters to their shoulders. Even taller ones stood on tiptoe. Men nearest the plane gave the order, "Stand back. Give room to open the door."

The pilot unlatched the door. A dozen arms reached out to swing it open. Just inside stood a coffin. A cry of disbelief swept over the crowd. Kuruyeme, the smiling one, had come home—but he was dead!

Laughter immediately turned to tears. A shocked group of men lifted out the plain box and bore it directly to Kuruyeme's house. Kaywere went to the umana. There he described the days in Oriximina's hospital.

In returning home, they'd used an airplane—one provided at Kaywere's request by the town's mayor. But just as Kuruyeme had said it would be, arriving in the village he went straight to his house and Kaywere to the umana. He was silent; Kaywere answered all their questions.

What else of his dreams had they seen unfold?

Had God taken this happy servant because He would not let the evil spirits reclaim him?

26

With God's command deep in his heart, Chief Forosha's encouraging words fresh in his mind, and his wife's assistance always close at hand, Bob Hawkins pushed forward in his translation of the Old Testament. He continued to visit the Wai Wai to teach as well as check his text. The people respected his teaching and his visits stimulated the elders to do their jobs better. On one trip he made the difficult journey to the Jatapuzinho. Elka had written a warm invitation to come see him. They met on another occasion in Boa Vista. Bahm was saddened for Elka's devastated health, realizing that medically all had been done for him that could be done, but it was a glad day when the misunderstandings between them began to evaporate.

Elka had confessed his sins to God. He was ready, as Kuruyeme had been ready, for God to take him whenever He chose. In his remaining time he would suffer ceaseless pain. After the tali tali sang yet a couple of times, he would be gone, not the first Wai Wai to reach heaven, but surely none had been more eagerly received.

While Bahm habitually met with the elders to encourage them and sometimes to help them work through hard problems, he realized that today he could only advise. The strings had been cut. The leaders had made errors, and they would make more errors, but they were learning from their mistakes. He could observe from a distance, but especially now that they had the New Testament and soon would have the Old alongside it, the development of the church of Jesus Christ in this Amazon jungle was largely a matter between the Wai Wai and God.

Not completely, of course. Ayrin still lived and worked among them. From time to time other missionaries, mostly Brazilian these days, came to assist. But it was Ayrin who was there day after day. How long had she been there day after day? As she tacked a 1992 calendar on the wall by her kitchen table, she did a simple calculation. Twenty-seven years. In three locations she had conducted schools for the Wai Wai, at times for adults as well as for the children.

Irene Benson might have had a career teaching a specialty in a sophisticated school system in the United States, with access to all kinds of books, films, tapes, computers, copiers, and limitless gadgets supposed to make learning better and teaching easier. In contrast, by devoting these years to the Wai Wai, she had made books, cut up magazines for pictures, used chalk until only powder on her fingers remained, and constantly hurried from first-graders to teenage classes and, in some subjects, all 280 students at the same time. She was both a front-line teacher and an administrator.

Her Portuguese was better than that of any of her Wai Wai teachers, so this subject required a lot of her time. But she felt it important for students in Brazil, even those far up an Amazon tributary, to learn the national language of their country. Just as important, she maintained, was for them to read and write their native tongue. Critics of assimilating Indians into the larger society decried the loss of hearth languages. One's language was the basis of one's culture. As long as she had a say at the Mapuera, degeneration of the Wai Wai language would not happen.

Ayrin had no medical training, but because the *chefe do*

posto usually had no source for medicines, she worked with the attendants to order the pills and inoculations and fluoride and bandages and splints that were in perpetual short supply for this growing population. Fanahruwi and his associates often came to her with an emergency case needing a flight to a city hospital. Some patients required a doctor's attention but were in no immediate danger, so she sent them off by canoe down river to Porteira. There the Indians were attended by a friendly Brazilian doctor. "Good Doctor Roberto" was cut of the same cloth as Brigadier Camarâo and one or two of the men who had served as *chefe do posto*. The Air Force continued to help; where once the flights delivered much-needed food, today they brought visiting doctors and medical supplies. Many politicians flew into the Mapuera and a few of the more daring and vigorous reached the Jatapuzinho, always to canvass for votes, sometimes to leave a community gift that made life a tiny bit easier for the people.

The Wai Wai accepted their voting responsibility as a serious obligation. Election time became a gala event. Most of the village on the Jatapuzinho moved by trail or river to the end of the road, camping there for two or three days. The people enjoyed the freedom from field and major kitchen work. It was fun to be visited by the rival candidates for various local offices. Some came laden with bananas or pineapples, some only with eloquent words extolling the praiseworthy Indian, but all with posters and cards featuring their pictures and graphic instructions on where the voter should place his X. On election morning a large open truck began ferrying the voters from the camp site at the river to the polls. That evening the owner of the campsite, who was a candidate, learned he had lost, and figuring "his" Indians hadn't helped him, let the Wai Wai know they were no longer welcome on his land.

Because of its size, Howler Monkey Village was becoming a community to be reckoned with. And precisely because it was growing so large and becoming engulfed in civilization, the impetus to divide it intensified. A Katwena man who advocated moving upstream to the rapids on the equator, or even to the Cafuini near the Surinam border, was challenged by the families he figured he needed to make the move a success. They pointed out the difficulty of slicing off a portion of the village and transporting it to another site.

"Who will teach the children?" some wanted to know. "What will we do when whooping cough strikes? Would we have good church leaders, men to organize our field work? We'd need a chief and they're hard to find."

Another group appeared more likely to actually break away. Kirifaka's son-in-law did not like to live so hemmed in by other people. Crowds irritated him. He said he had not wanted to leave Kashmi, but moved only because his old parents came to the Mapuera. He now wanted to return to the Novo, and several other families said they would join his.

He and his wife had accompanied Yarka's sons on the mysterious expedition to the north. From their lack of bounty it appeared that if they had sought gold they found none. Esura and Sakaraya now said they would also be moving to Kashmi, causing no little concern about the venture's prospects. Besides the irascibility of the pair, their father, also in on the move, was going away with rancor toward the chief.

"I'm not going to stick around here with people who don't care if I get my motor back or not," Yarka was heard to say.

Esura boasted he had killed people. His brother was said to be every bit as mean. Had it not been for the spiteful torches of these two, those intending to resettle Kashmi might have looked forward to overgrown but producing fields and at least the frames of buildings.

The party left, taking their belongings, even a pet green parrot perched on the stick that a woman rested on her shoulder. Some thirty individuals out of more than a thousand inhabitants made only a slight dent, but if they managed to start again on the Novo, others would likely join them. At the Jatapuzinho they stopped for a break. There

Yarka and his sons left their women and children and themselves pushed on to a Brazilian settlement. They decided to work for a while, then return to the Mapuera. Whoever in the world actually knew what they would do?

Back at Howler Monkey Rocks, Kirifaka thought a great deal about the aim of his daughter and son-in-law to restart Kashmi. Should he join them?

"Father in the Sky," he prayed. "The land there was given to the Wai Wai. Do you want someone to live on it? My son-in-law watched in sadness as thoughtless men chopped down the fruit trees and burned the houses before they abandoned the village. Now he wants to rebuild it, or to start a new village close to the old. Who will teach them and their children about you, *Ahfah?* Who will be their spiritual leader?"

Perhaps he should go. There would be all the hardships of starting anew, and at his age and with his physical weakness he lacked the resources to go through again what he had endured when younger. He had experienced trouble upon trouble on the Novo. Old Mud Hole. Old Place of the Mosquitoes. Old Place Where the Cassava Doesn't Grow Well. He'd had many descriptive names for the banes of Anaua, their first settlement on the Novo. Kashmi had been an improvement, but no paradise. Whatever else it was, it was The Place Where Lies My Beloved Fehya.

Yet another name he had given that region might still apply, he was sure. The Place Where God Is.

He sat on a low stool outside his house carving a canoe paddle. Rubbing his hand over his work, he looked up to say to no one in particular, or maybe to Jesus his companion:

"They'll need a teacher. I'll go."

Unconsciously, Kirifaka had slipped into the role of his late father-in-law. Old William used to go everywhere, do everything his family needed of him.

Communion consisted of cassava bread and starch drink, sometimes with palm fruit, sometimes not, and was served on the Sunday nearest the full moon. Elders once passed pots of the drink down each row. More recently, small glass cups took the place of the pots and sugar-cane juice substituted for the starch drink. A more fundamental change than these practices was instituted, and it lifted the embarrassment the sacrament had held for certain people.

Formerly as he distributed the elements, an elder might lean over a person and whisper loudly, "You're not to take communion today." That, suggested a young Brazilian missionary named Onesimo, brought only awkwardness and provoked gossip. While visiting the Mapuera for a week to give the people New Testament teaching, he advised the elders to confront an offender earlier, and if it was learned only Saturday night that a member should be denied communion, to call that person out before the Sunday service began and inform him privately.

They hadn't realized what they'd been doing. They readily took to Onesimo's advice.

There was much they could learn, and for the most part the Wai Wai were eager to learn—perhaps not surprisingly, the younger people more than the older folk. Here and there fine young men and women were beginning to take positions of leadership and responsibility. Most were the products of homes in which the parents had lived out the teachings of God's Paper and showed clearly they were companions of Jesus.

There was Kaywere, now a songleader who operated the church's loudspeaker equipment, tinkered with it, repaired it. And Fanahruwi, who for years looked to Kirifaka his father as his role model: music, medicine, languages—he excelled in all. Forosha's assistant, Wanaferu, was capable and dependable. Chiago had won Ayrin's confidence; in his eleventh year on the school staff she appointed him head teacher. He regarded his pupils as a responsibility from God.

"Some day Jesus will ask me all about them."

Kimi, Kwarakwara, Tamsho, Tamochi—these young wives, mothers, teachers, the Dorcases and Lydias of their time and place would, among others, go far in shaping the destiny of the Wai Wai.

Perhaps years ago when all but a handful of the Wai Wai claimed to be companions of Jesus, it appeared a pure Christian society was in the making. But it was not to be; the "leaven of the Pharisees" contaminated the apparent purity and continually threatened to leaven the whole lump. Isolation from the world mattered little; there was no immunity to Satan's attacks. Even far back under the thick canopy of the forest old Seetin sought to use the antipathy of the unbelievers and the vulnerability of the believers to thwart God's zeal for a church in the jungle. He battered the Wai Wai parish but was not able to break it. He tried to dilute it, trivialize it, sully it, discourage it, and at various times in varying degrees succeeded in gaining small victories. Yet for forty consecutive years the Wai Wai Christians had maintained their witness to the redeeming love of Jesus Christ.

What was difficult for the Wai Wai was difficult for everyone—keeping their lives in balance, managing the right tension among the forces that without letup pulled and pushed at them. There was a daily battle over the power of materialism, even deep in the jungle. Why paddle against the current if a motor could propel you? Why chop and scrape cassava roots on a board of tiny stones all day when a machine did it better in far less time? Why suffer the pain of thorns in the path when simple plastic thongs kept them from piercing feet and made walking easier? Why pull the knots from a shim-shim day by day until an anticipated date was reached, when calendars and watches were more precise and more likely to avoid misunderstandings?

"We like these things," said a young father who worked for the *chefe do posto*. "They make life easier. But if we have no gasoline, the women won't say they can't grate cassava. The men will get out their canoe paddles. We will hold on to our Indian ways, but situations will change. We'll use the conveniences we've adopted from outside the forest, but we'll back them up with the old ways, and hope we'll be content whatever state we're in.

"We young adults have learned the ways of God ever since we were children. Changes will come, but some things we will hold on to. We are not about to walk outside of God's path."

Convincing words spoken by a confident young man. Yet who among the Wai Wai felt capable of sticking to the trail Christ had cut through the jungle? Prayer would be needed, prayer by the Wai Wai and for the Wai Wai by people everywhere who learned of their story. Having God's Paper complete was vital, and no less so their becoming doers of the word and not just hearers. Daily submission to the will of God, humility, faithfulness, practice of the manifold fruit of the Spirit—these were all required for the Wai Wai witness to the world to continue.

Prayer was key. Prayer by the baptized believers as they met for a half-day's session each cycle of the moon, by parents looking on their sleeping children before climbing into their hammocks at night, by men and women in the trail or on the river or as they baked bread or hunted game in the forest. By fervent, in-season, out-of-season prayer the new challenges would be met.

Like it or not, the Wai Wai—like most Amazon tribes— were part way to the mainstream of civilization. There was no turning back. For some little while they might stay nearly where they were, neither in nor out, clinging to a low rung on mankind's ladder. They could die out, culturally if not physically.

And for the Wai Wai, cultural demise would come from losing their Christian distinctive. Merely resembling the dozens of other Amazon tribes would not set them apart as their Christian faith had set them apart. By coldness of spirit, by sliding down the slope of indifference, by exchanging their love of God for anything less would, by the experience of other people in other ages and places, slowly extinguish the light they held aloft in the dark world around them. The children of the first generation of Wai Wai believers had in large measure acquired their parents' faith as their own, but if the following generation grew up indifferent and took their heritage for granted, spiritual reversion would overtake them as surely as the jungle reclaimed an abandoned field.

On the other hand, through faithful prayer, a growing knowledge of God's Paper and obedience to the Father's leading, the Wai Wai could enjoy renewed strength and for generations to come blaze new trails in Christ's name, throughout the Amazon forest and beyond.

The challenge now facing these rain forest believers appeared less the rounding up of lost tribes and more the evangelizing of the lost souls living among them. Today's bidding consisted also of teaching and training their children in all the ways of the Lord, of witnessing to the Brazilians who visited them or whom they met in the towns and cities, of sharing the good news of their freedom from fear and bare-bones existence with any Indians they came across— whether Atrowari, Karafou, or others in the forest, in distant villages or in Indian hostels in the cities.

"We can no longer bring in people to live with us so they'll learn about God and His Son," said Forosha. "We'll not give up the search, though it seems there are few people in our forest we haven't reached. But those we find, we will go to them, live with them, and as missionaries ourselves win them as missionaries won us to God."

Even the Atrowari, some added. Surely, God in His providence hadn't overlooked these once hostile but now almost pitiable people.

Nourishing their witness, by both word and life, was God's Paper, and together in church and by families next to their night fires they had memorized key passages of it. That they would soon have it complete thrilled all who held it precious. But a controversy over the future printing erupted—a minor and mostly good-natured argument, but a difference in opinion nevertheless. Should the completed translation be published in one volume or two? The thickness of it spoke for two; travelers carrying it on the trail might find a huge book too bulky to take along. On the other hand, to separate the Old and the New Testaments would cause the Old to be slighted.

"Bahm and Ayrin and Achi all have God's message in a single book," various ones pointed out. "Why can't we?"

Whether one volume or two, unless the words lifted off the pages and dwelt within the believers, God's Paper would mean little to anyone. It had to be read, studied, obeyed. To help in the study of it and (it was hoped) to result in greater obedience, the Wai Wai church in Guyana called a conference for 1992. The tali tali locust sang once more and as the long dry season began, plans for going over the high mountains to the Essequibo were discussed at the Mapuera.

On the morning of departure, two large canoes drifted idly in the port, a few things partially filling up the bottoms. A couple of men skipped down the high bank and into the canoes and each started testing the motor that hung on the end of his craft. Other people came and deposited baskets and plastic containers, a shotgun, extra paddles. Slowly a crowd gathered, part of it on the sandy shore, part on the bluff above. About nine o'clock Forosha appeared. He stepped aboard one of the canoes and it lowered appreciably in the water. He sat on a strut in front of two big gas cans in the rear. The vessels' freight capacity seemed to have been reached, and men spread a cover of colorful plastic. Still, other assorted goods were brought for stowage. A woman handed in a large bundle.

The chief sat back, smiling, appearing relaxed. He wore yellow and white shorts, a tee shirt with a blue pattern and a blue cap. Two men sat in the other canoe eating a breakfast of water-soaked farina and fish. More women came, passed supplies to the men on the shore, then climbed the clay bank again. In the shallow water a father bathed his naked, year-old son, a mother her infant, a granny a third child. Another mother and father, having finished the bath, swung their little boy back and forth to shed the water and dry him.

Suddenly, preparations for departure seemed at a standstill, but no one appeared to be bothered. After a morning of rain, the sun emerged from the clouds. A woman brought a half-dozen canes of sugar. A man handed down another paddle, and a young man a guitar. Kaywere, a bandage covering the yaws on his leg, rushed to the brink and called down that he was going after all. He ran back along the path and disappeared into the village. In a few minutes he appeared again, in one hand a gun and in the other a canoe paddle. He stepped into Forosha's canoe and took a seat.

On the sandy shore stood a senior elder. He spoke softly to the men in the canoes, six in one, seven in the other. Then extending his arms toward the north, he prayed. The pilot in the chief's canoe started his motor and swung his vessel toward the middle of the river. Then the second motor started, and this craft followed in the wake of the first. Someone in the front of the second canoe shot off two big firecrackers. The boom pounded overhead, then whooshed across to the opposite shore and disappeared over the trees to the west. Babies cried, dogs barked, and chickens and children scrambled for cover.

The voyagers reached the bend in the river and two more firecrackers burst with a rocking sound. Again babies cried, dogs barked, and chickens and children scrambled for cover. Then all fell quiet, almost hushed. The canoes had passed from sight. Wakes were swallowed by the current. People at the water's edge retreated up the footholds in the clay bank and, falling in with the well-wishers on top, slowly made their way back to their homes and on to their fields to the day's undertakings.

Another chapter in the story of God's dealings with the Wai Wai was just beginning.